TABLE OF CONTENTS

DOWNLOAD YOUR FILES

Downloading your files is simple. To access your digital files, please go to the last page of this book and follow the instructions.

For technical assistance, please email: info@vaulteditions.com

Copyright

Bibliographical Note

This book is a new work created by Vault Editions Ltd.

ISBN: 978-1-922966-71-1

PANTHER HEAD

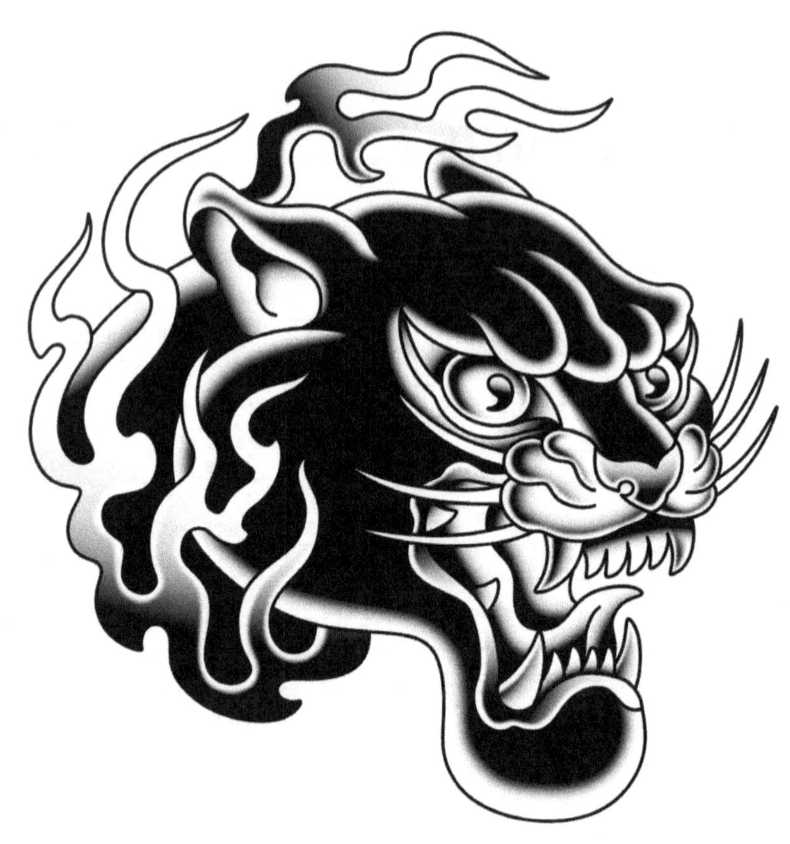

Pro tip: Use the centre line and curved guide to place the eyes and nose

Start by drawing a curved horizontal line through the head circle to establish the eye line. Position the eyes evenly along this curve, with one eye sitting just inside the left edge of the circle and the other closer to the right-hand edge, following the curve for a natural tilt. Place the nose on the centre line where it intersects the lower section of the circle. This gives the head a clear, balanced structure to build the panther's features on.

01

02

03

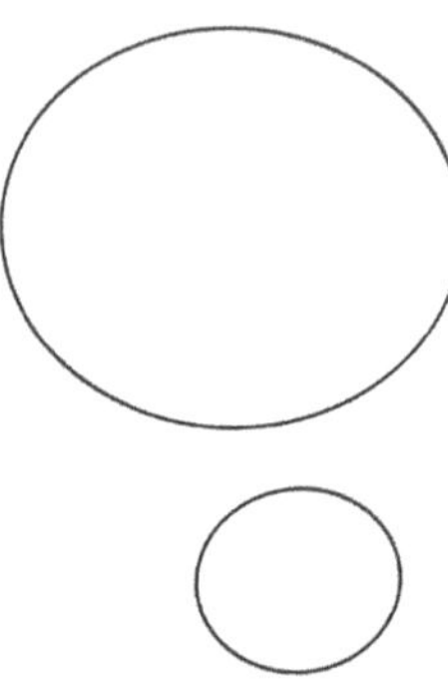

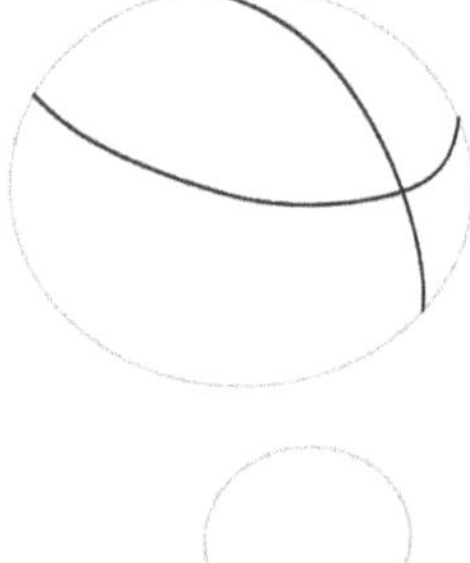

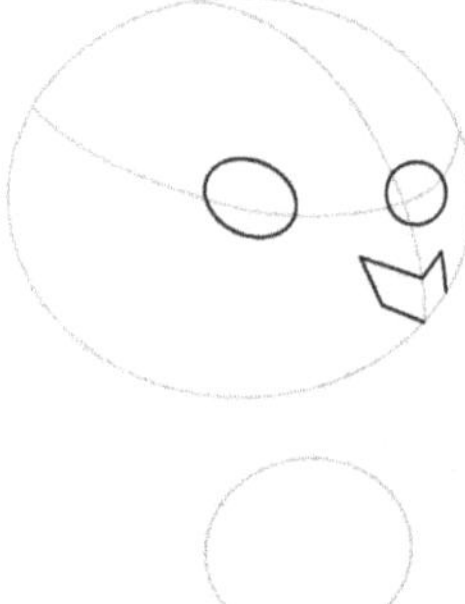

04

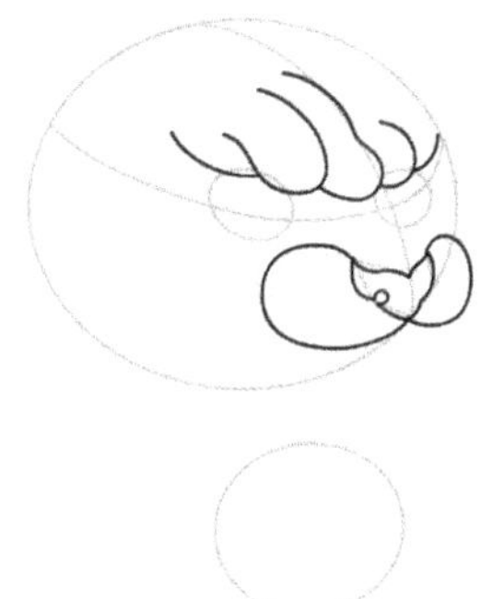

05

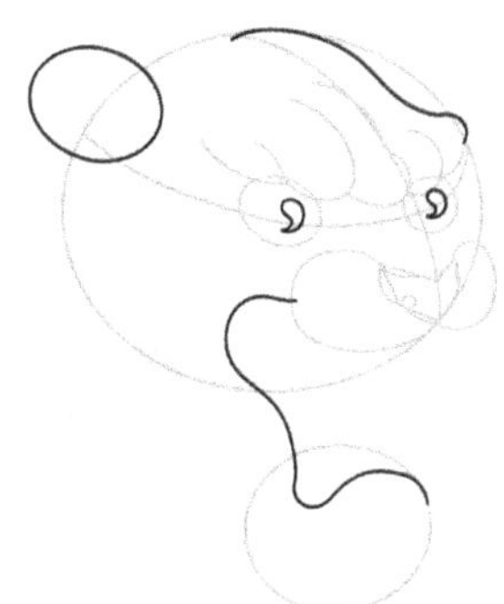

06

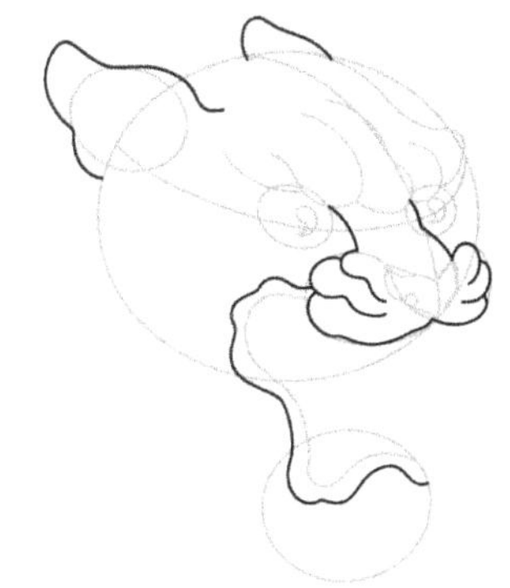

07

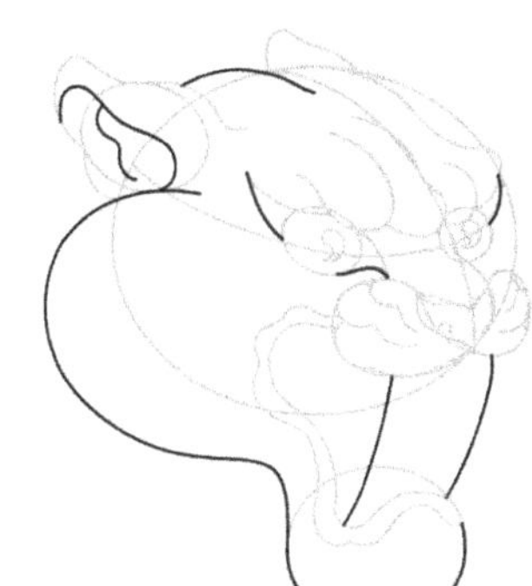

08

09

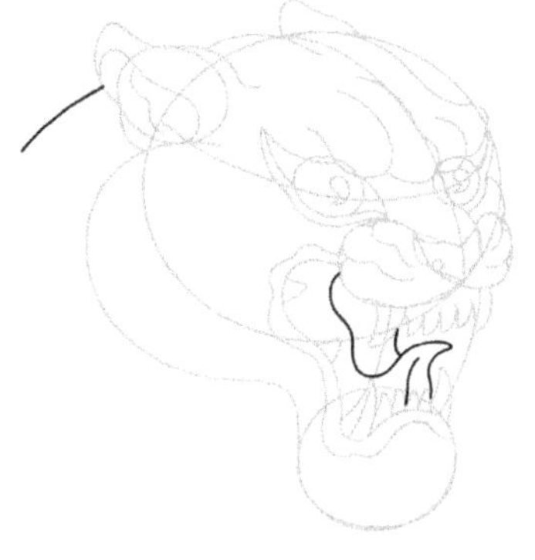

10

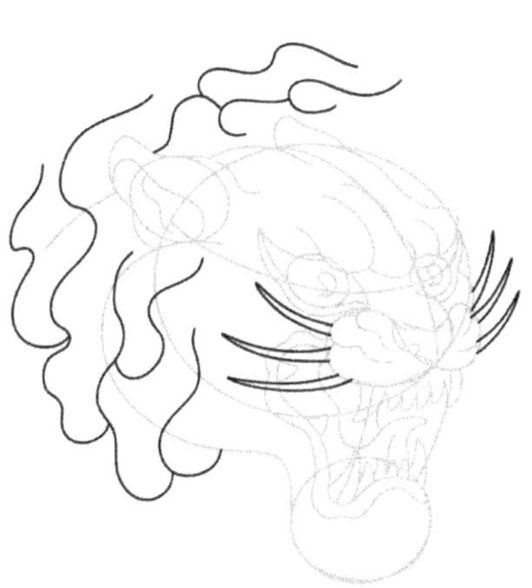

11

12

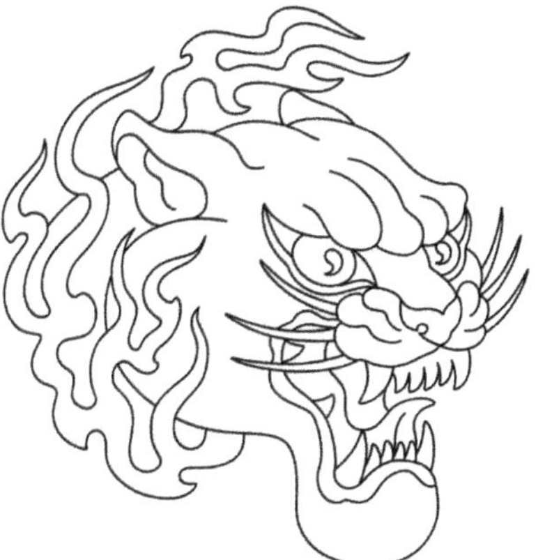

DEMON

Pro tip: Use the five-eye rule to set head width

To establish the correct width of the demon's head, draw five equal horizontal spaces across the face. The overall width should be roughly the equivalent of five eye widths. The second and fourth spaces mark the placement for the eyes, where you can draw clean oval shapes. This method keeps the features balanced and proportional, giving the head a strong, structured foundation before adding details.

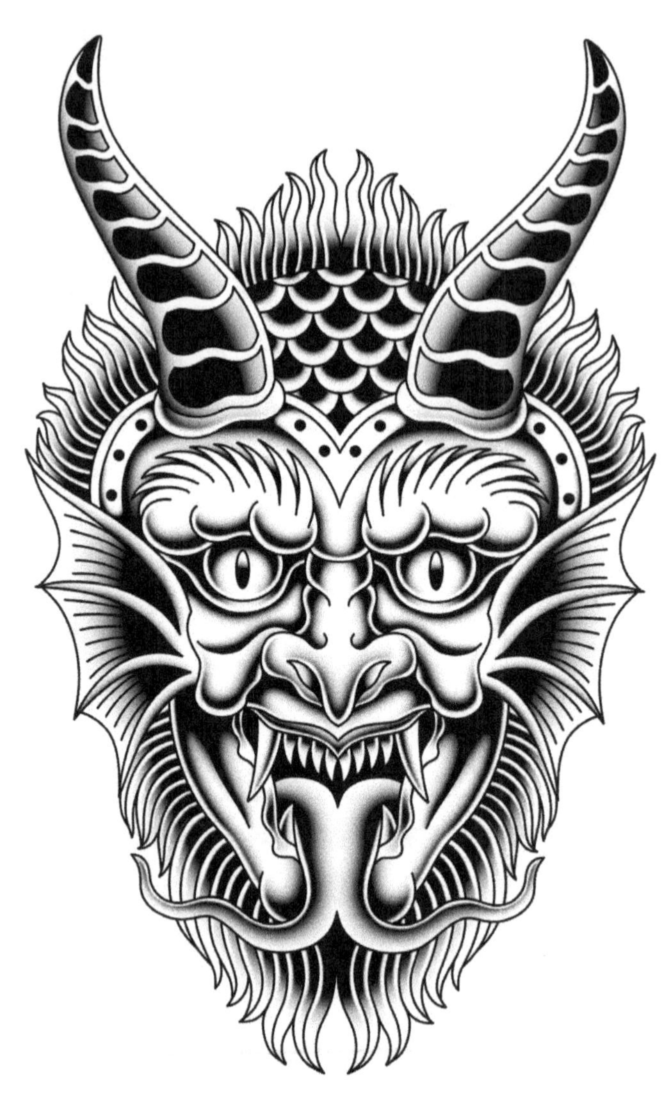

01

02

03

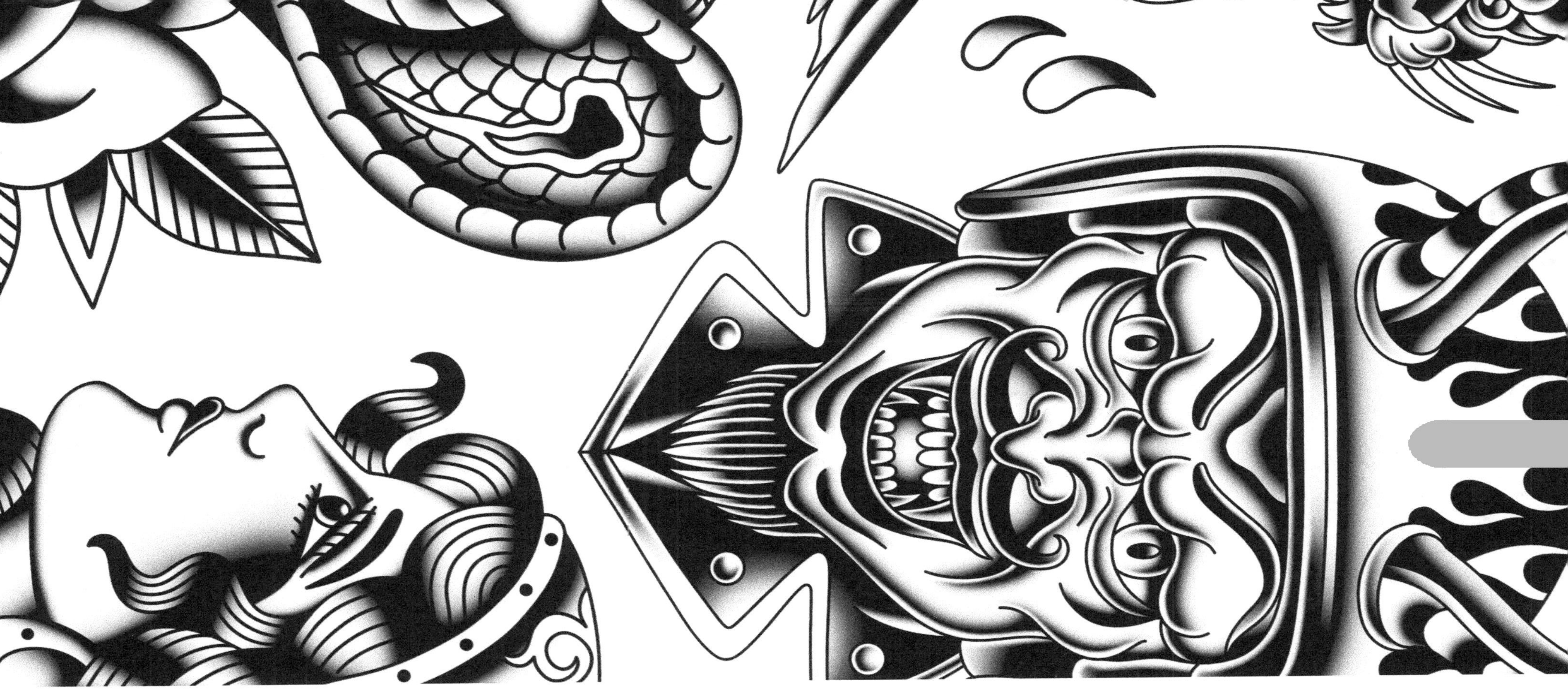
EDITIONS Vault

HAND DRAWN
UNIQUE 40 DESIGNS
BEST QUALITY

STEP BY STEP

A HELPFUL MANUAL FOR ARTISTS AND DESIGNERS

HOW TO DRAW
TRADITIONAL TATTOOS

THE VAULT EDITIONS GUIDE TO
MASTERING
THE ART OF
DRAWING

INTRODUCTION

For more than a century, traditional tattoo art has embodied courage, identity, and rebellion. Born from the hands of sailors, soldiers, and artists, its bold lines and timeless symbols have become a universal language of strength, love, and fate. *How to Draw Traditional Tattoos* is your complete step-by-step guide to mastering this iconic style through 40 classic designs.

Learn to draw legendary motifs like the panther head, gypsy woman, anchor, and swallow, alongside dynamic compositions such as the eagle and snake, skull and dagger, tiger and dragon, and handshake with the devil. You'll also find modern interpretations including racer ladies, plague doctors, and flip-face portraits that merge beauty with the macabre.

Each design is broken down using the Vault Editions 12-step drawing method, transforming complex artwork into clear, achievable stages. You'll develop an understanding of line hierarchy, shading, and flow while learning how to balance power and simplicity, the essence of traditional tattoo design.

Whether you're a tattoo apprentice, illustrator, or traditional art enthusiast, *How to Draw Traditional Tattoos* is both a practical guide and a creative companion. Master the craft, honour the tradition, and bring your own flash designs to life.

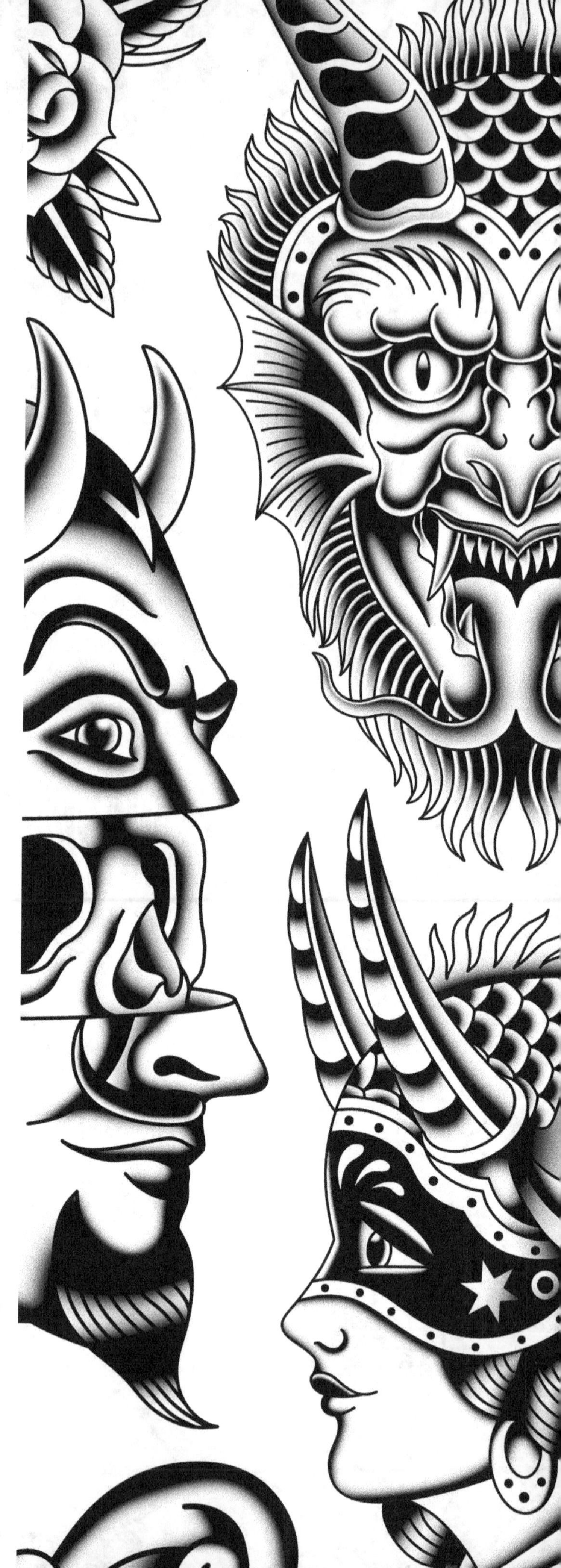

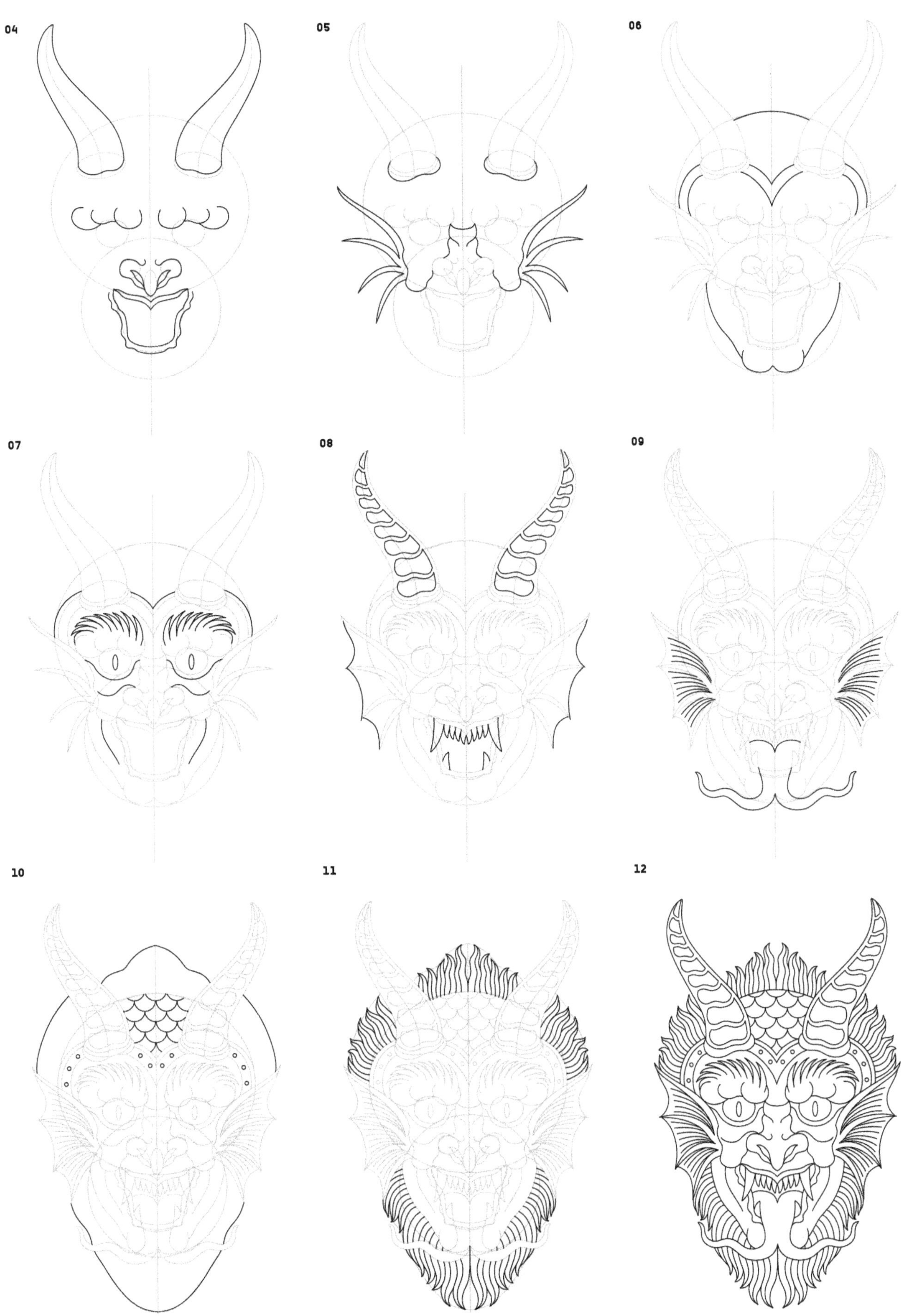
04
05
06
07
08
09
10
11
12
HOW TO DRAW TRADITIONAL TATTOOS

GYPSY HEAD

Pro tip: Use a 45-degree guide to position the eye

Draw a line on a 45-degree angle in the lower quarter of the circle. The top left point of this line marks where to place the top of the nose. Move a small distance in from this point, following the line downward, to position the eye accurately. This ensures the angle and placement look natural.

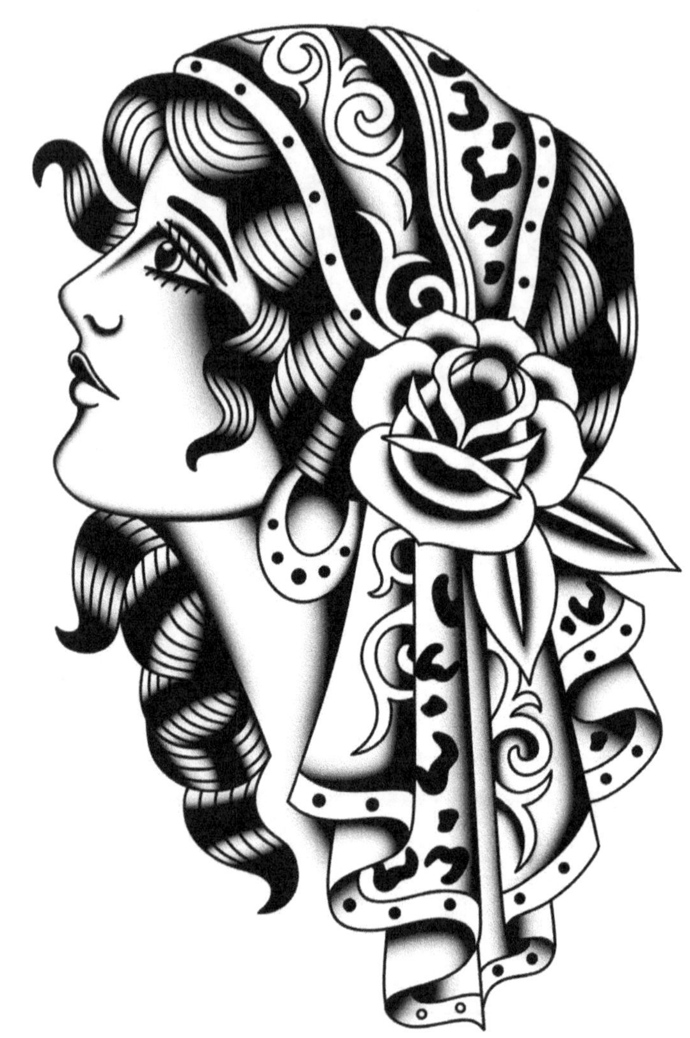

01

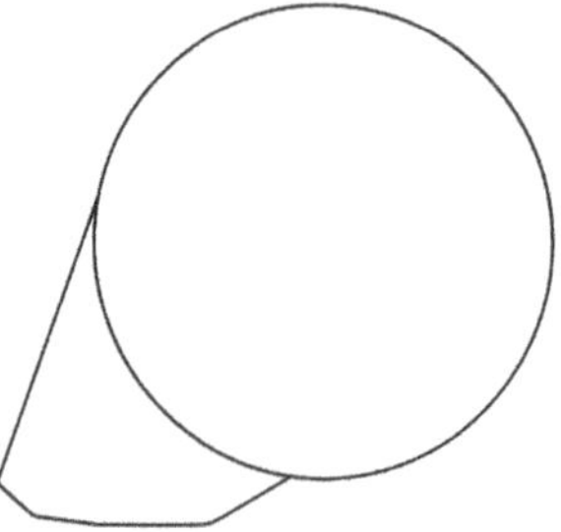

02

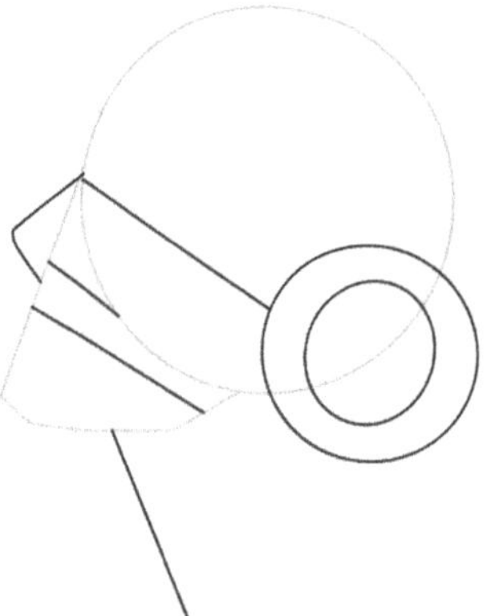

03

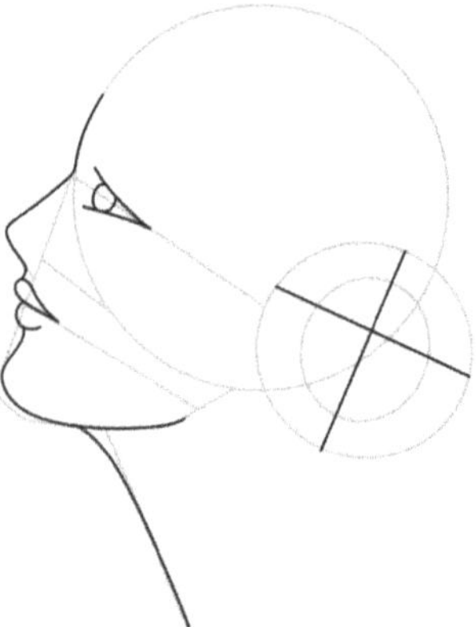

04

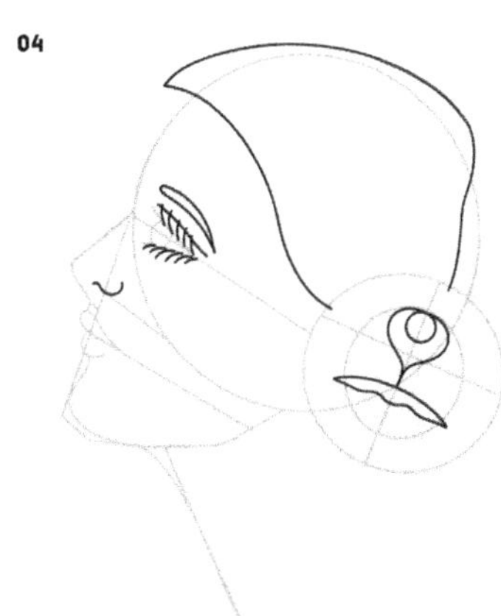

05

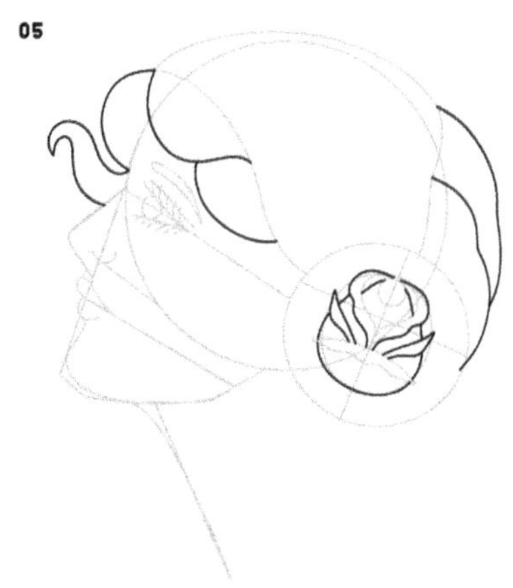

06

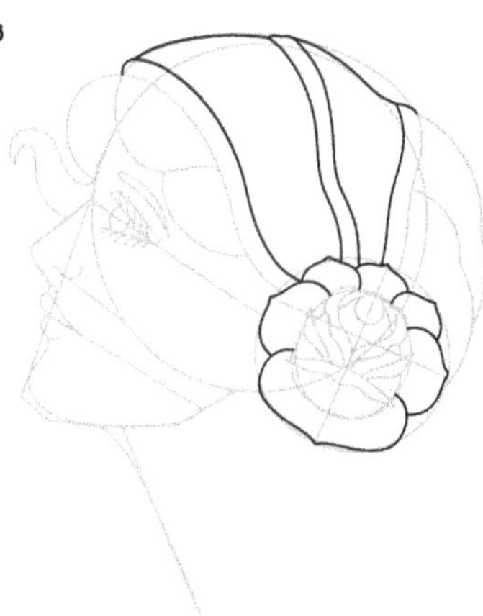

07

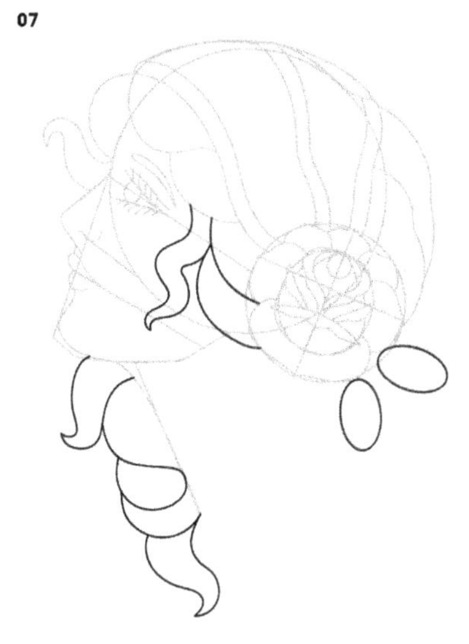

08

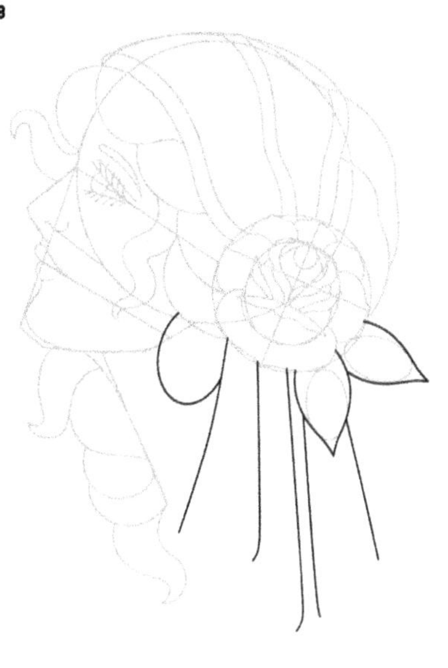

09

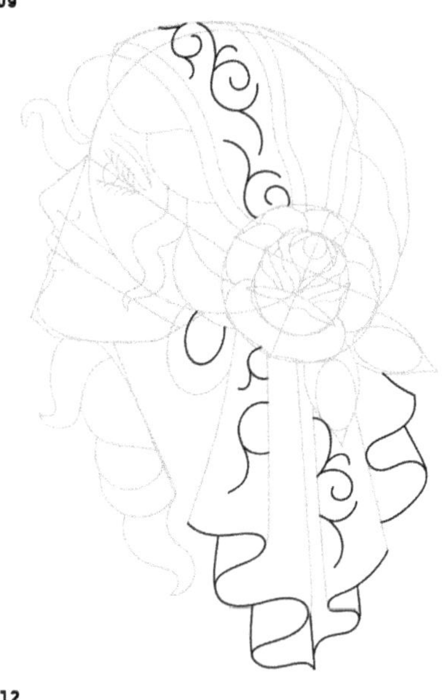

10

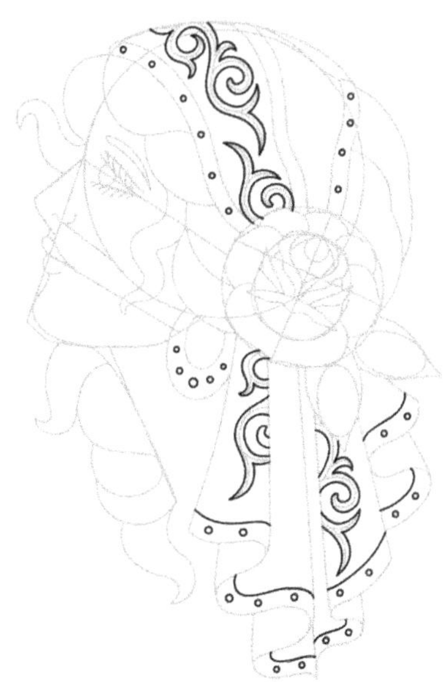

11

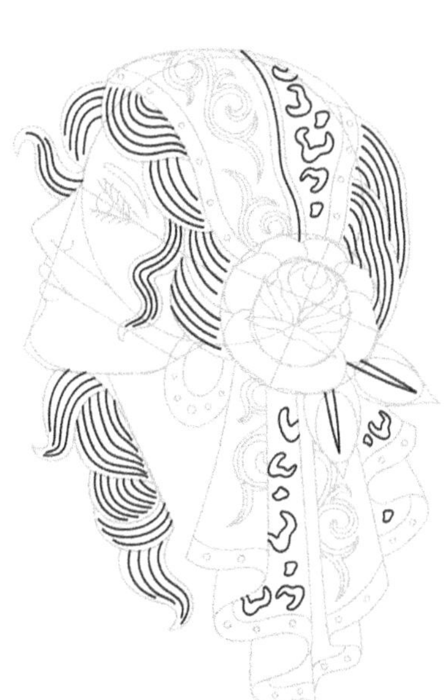

12

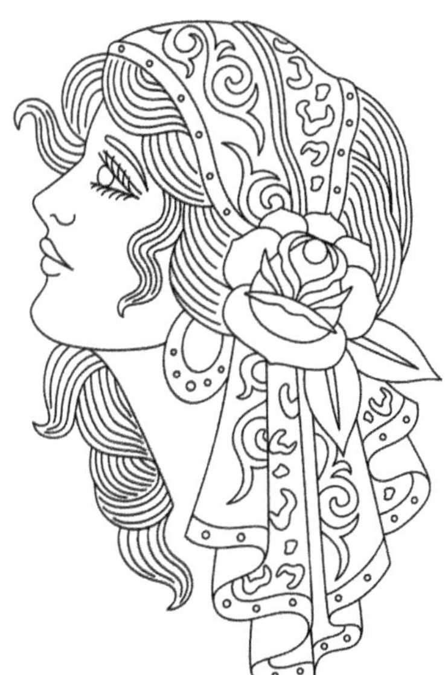

WOMAN & DEMON FLIP-FACE

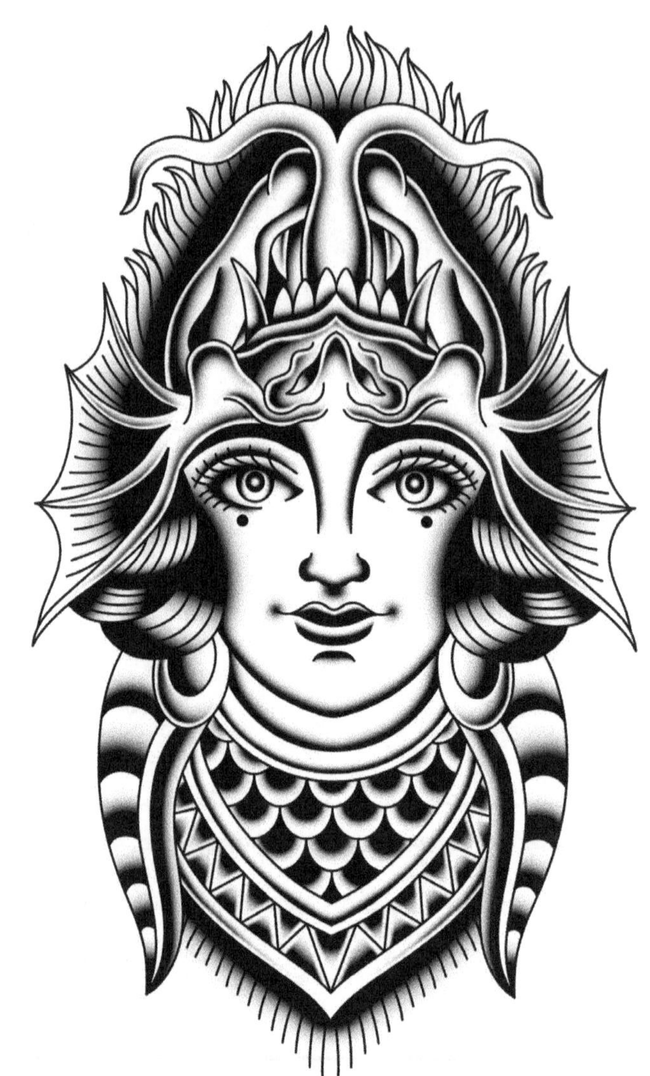

Pro tip: Establish a central axis for perfect symmetry

Start by drawing a clean, vertical centre line through the design. This axis serves as a reference point for mirroring elements on either side of the face. Regularly check your line work against this axis to keep features balanced and maintain the striking, mirrored quality that makes traditional flip face tattoos so visually powerful.

01   **02**   **03**

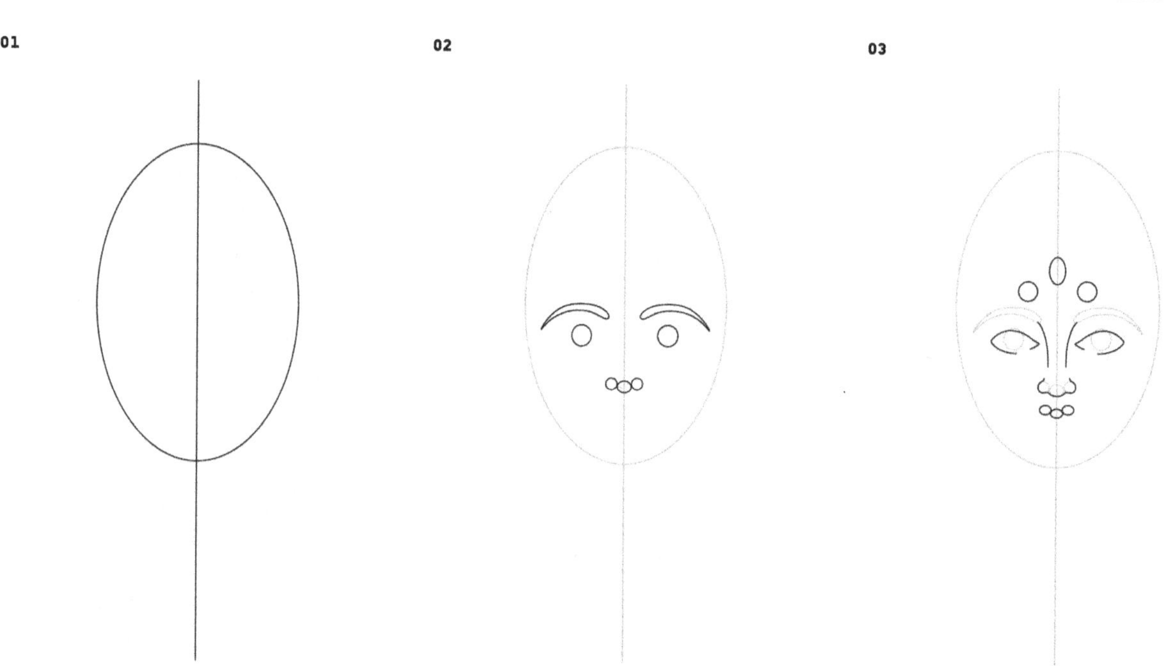

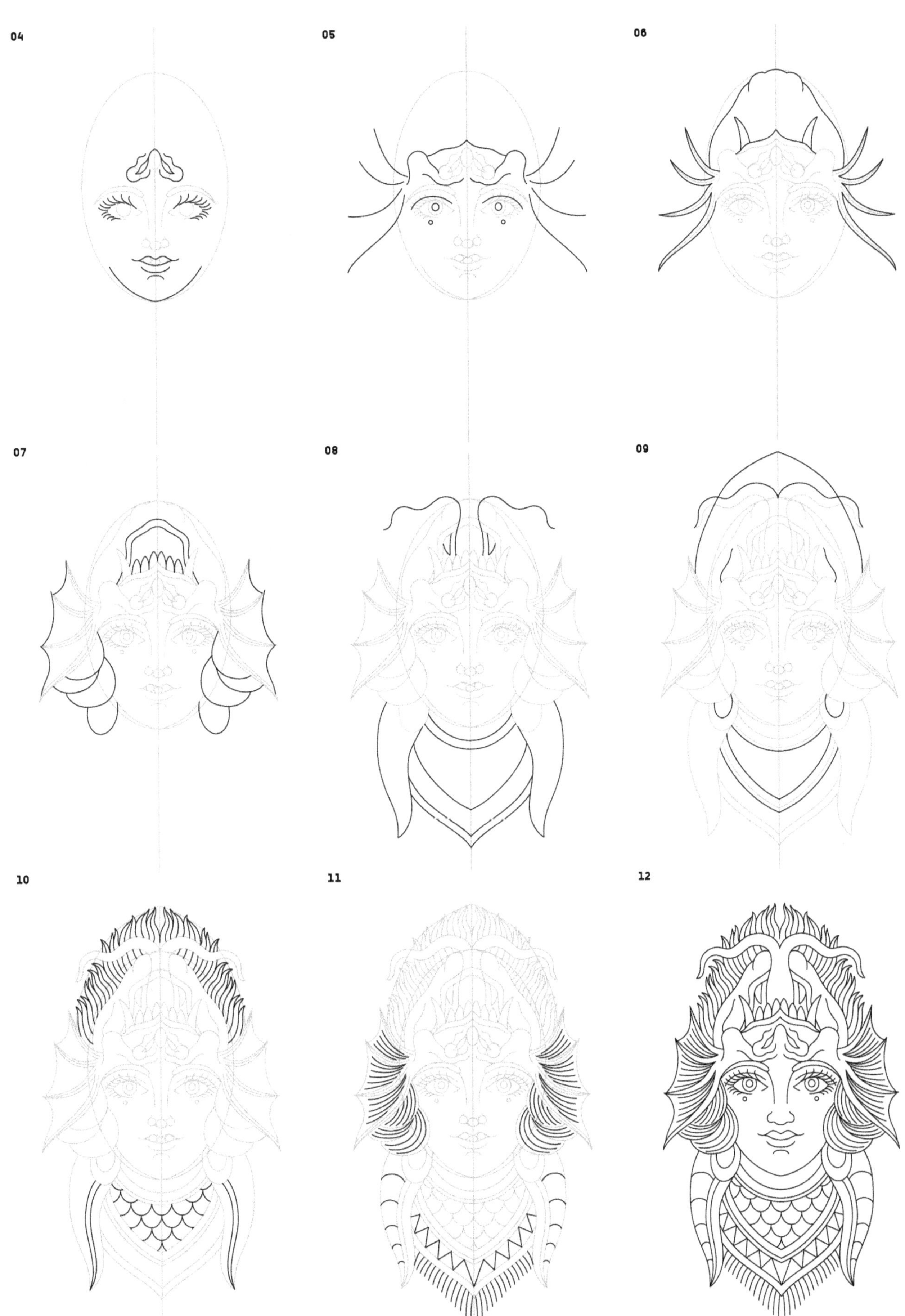

04
05
06
07
08
09
10
11
12
HOW TO DRAW TRADITIONAL TATTOOS

HANDSHAKE WITH THE DEVIL

Pro tip: Use the centre line and oval to position the top of the hand

Draw a vertical centre line to divide the composition in half, then place a horizontal oval across it. Position the top edge of the hand so that it sits diagonally across the oval, with the base of the small finger intersecting the centre line.

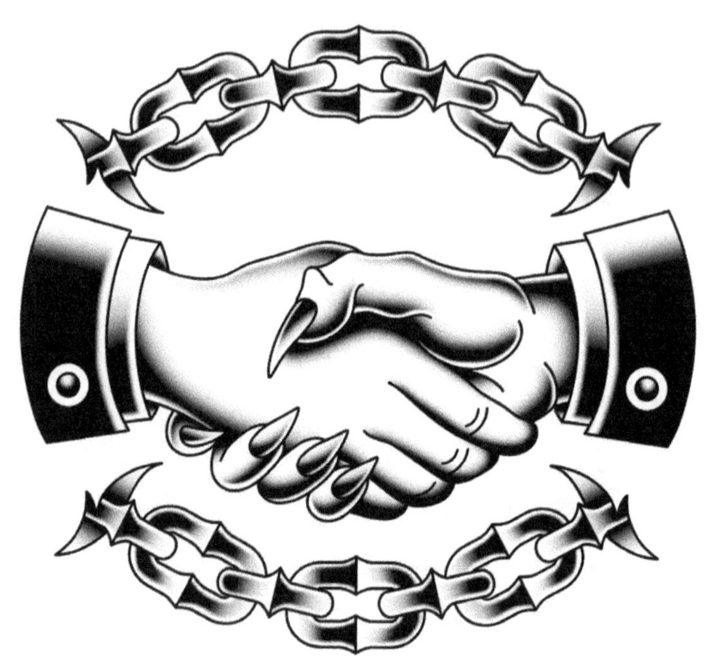

01   **02**   **03**

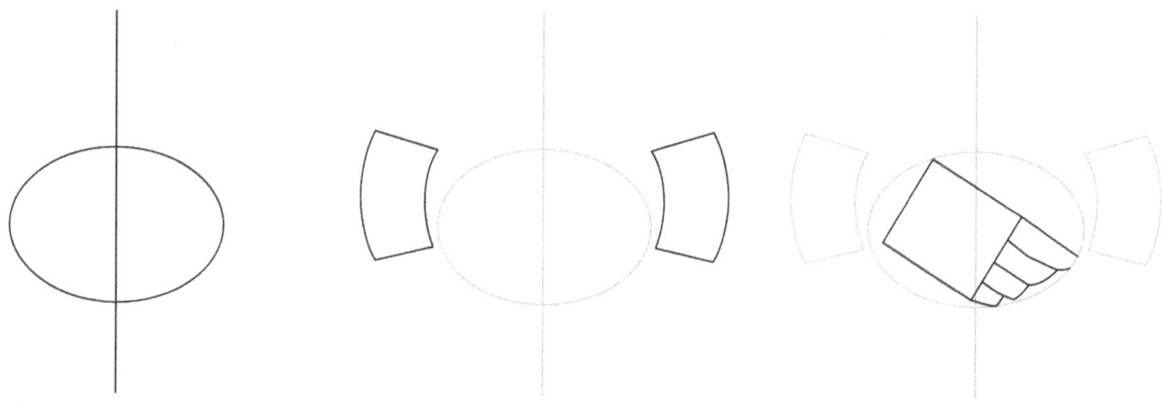

04

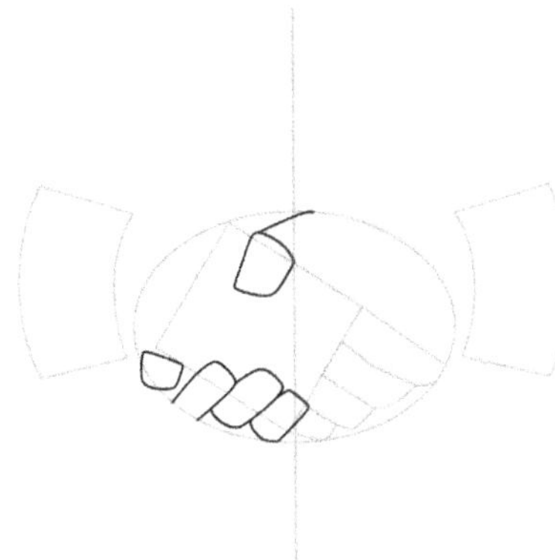

05

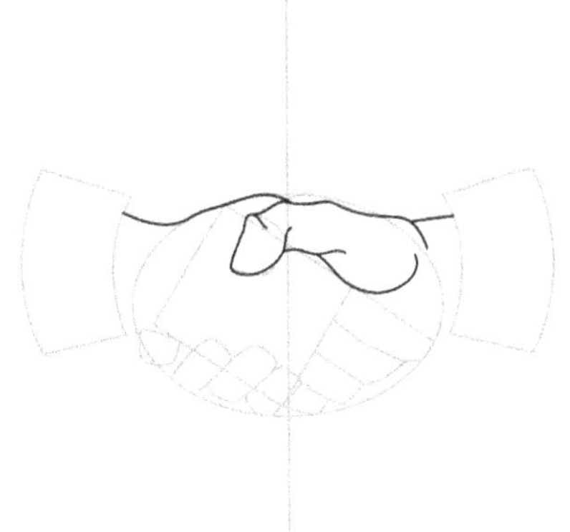

06

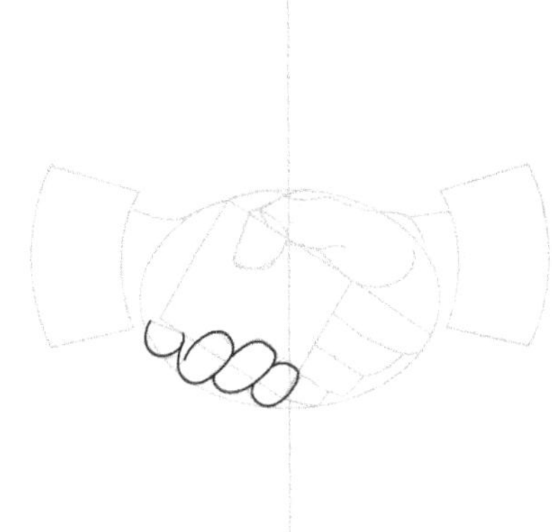

07

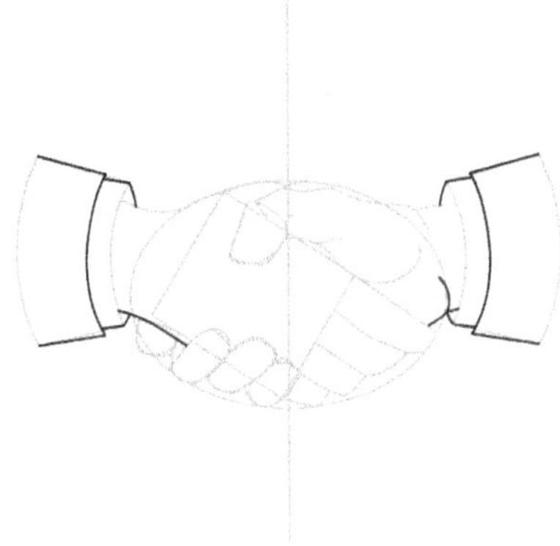

08

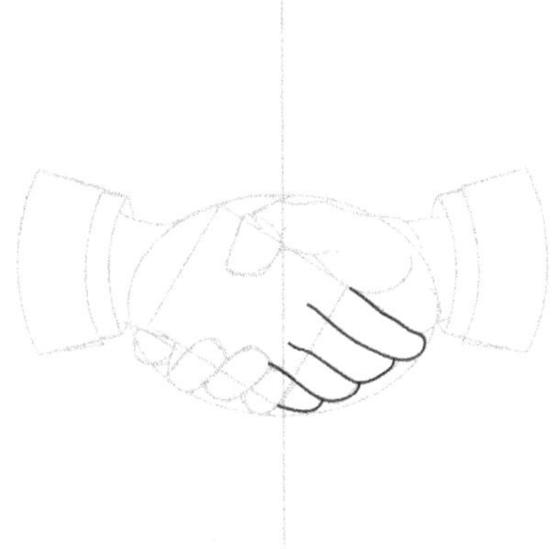

09

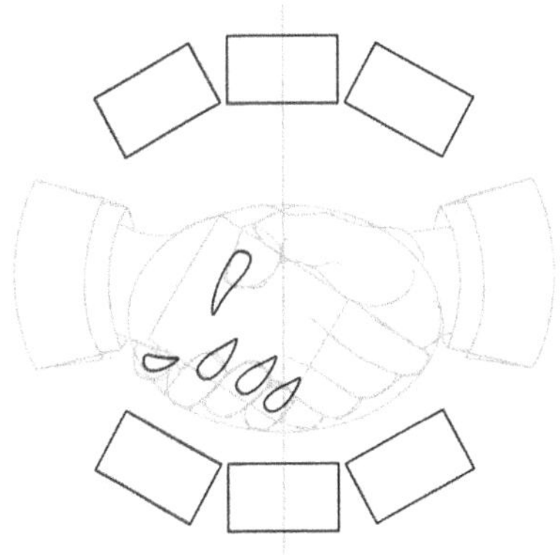

10

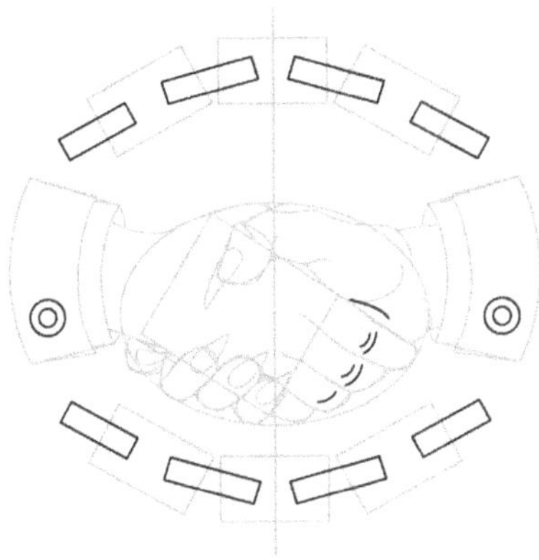

11

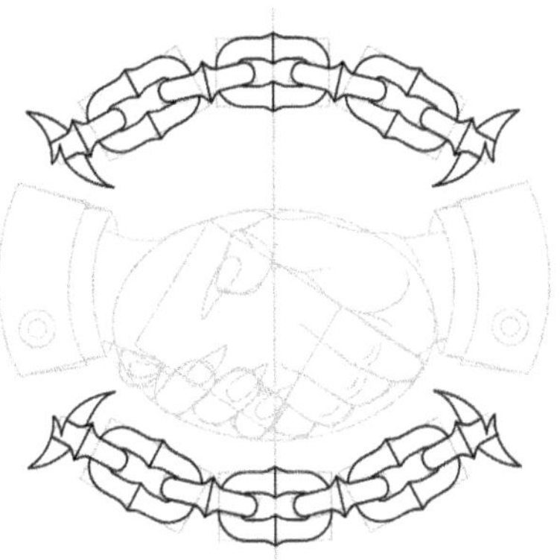

12

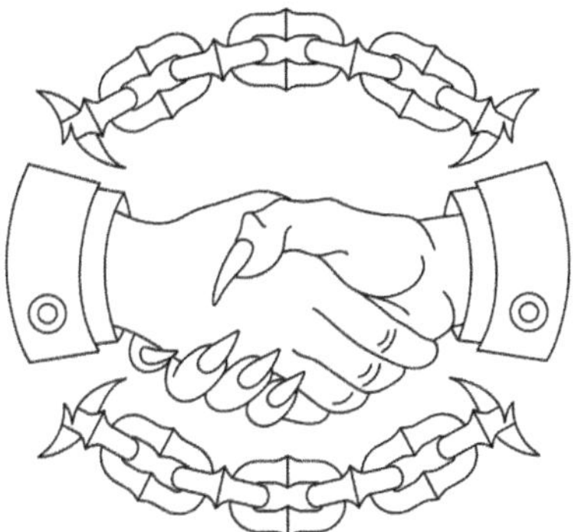

HOW TO DRAW TRADITIONAL TATTOOS

DAGGER & HEART

Pro tip: Use a cross to position the heart accurately

Draw a short diagonal cross over the centre of the blade where the handle meets the upper curve. The intersection of this cross marks the central anchor point for the heart. The vertical line helps you align the heart with the dagger's angle, while the horizontal line indicates the widest part of the heart, ensuring it sits symmetrically around the blade.

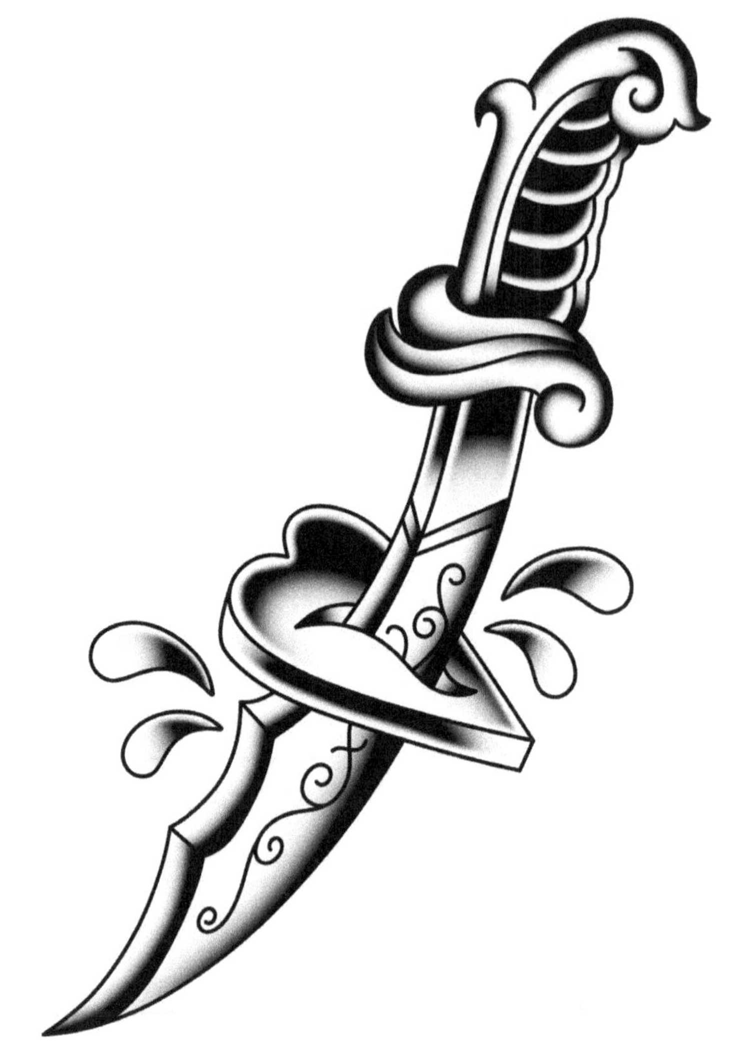

01

02

03

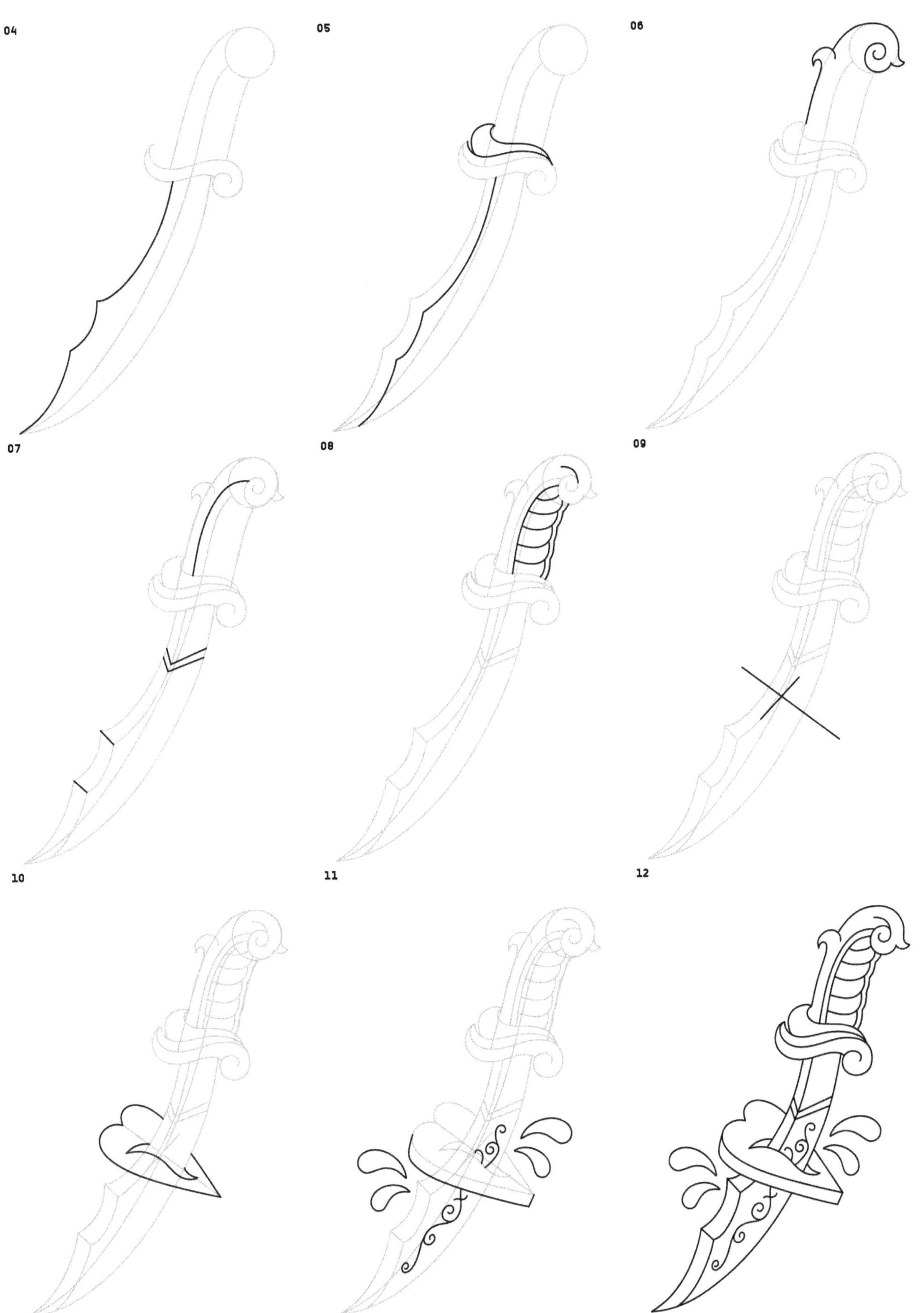

HOW TO DRAW TRADITIONAL TATTOOS

RACER LADY

Pro tip: Use a 45-degree guideline for nose and eye placement

Draw a 45-degree line across the lower quarter of the circle. The top left point of this line marks the exact position for the top of the nose. Place the eye slightly in from this point, following the line down. This creates a strong, consistent structure for positioning facial features in profile.

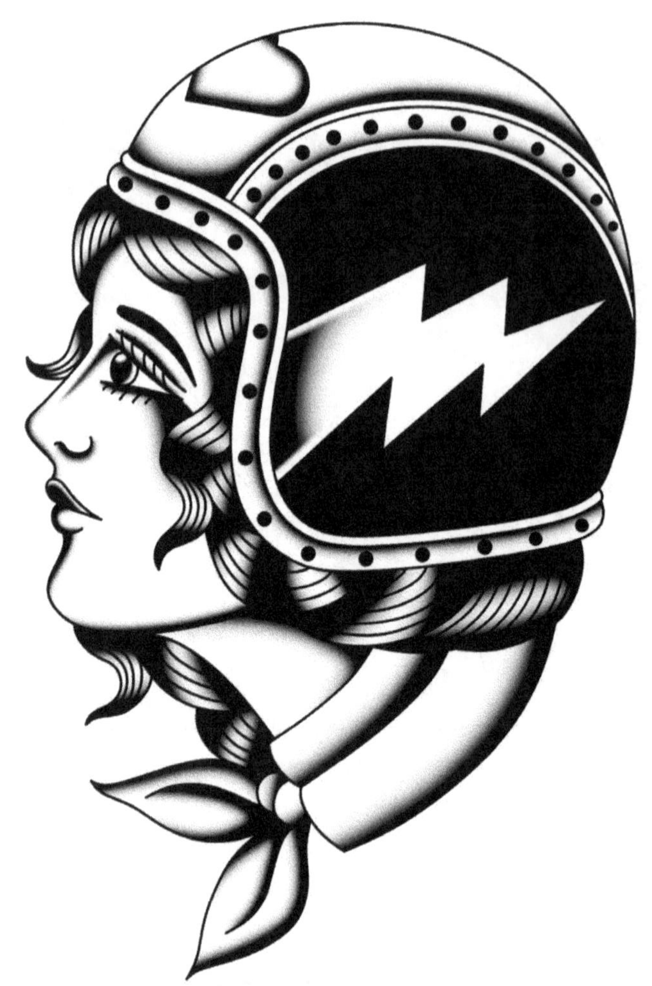

01

02

03

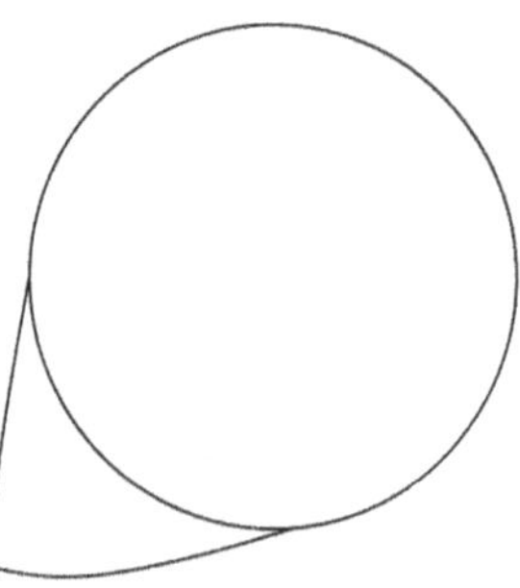

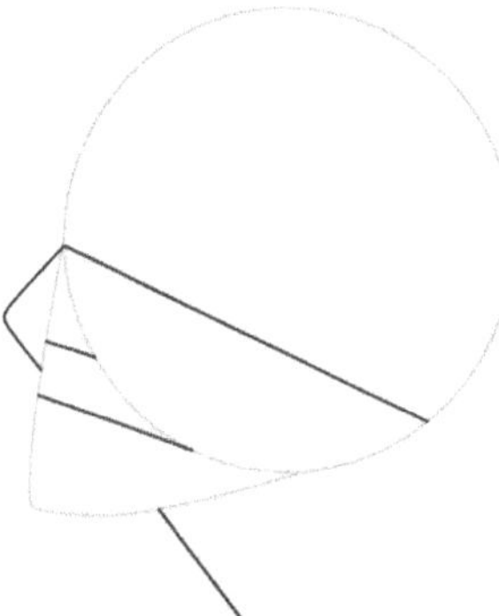

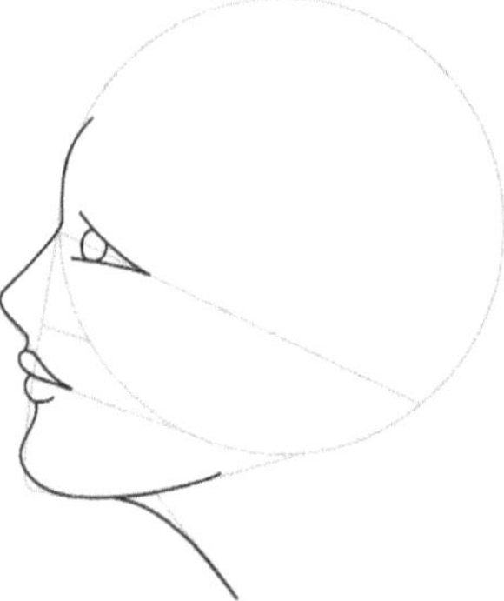

04

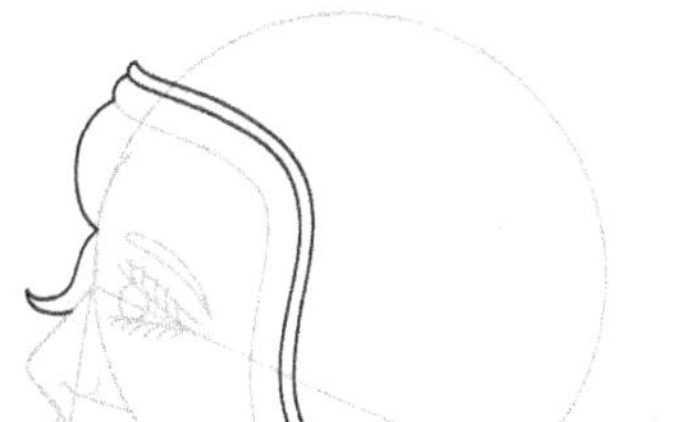

05

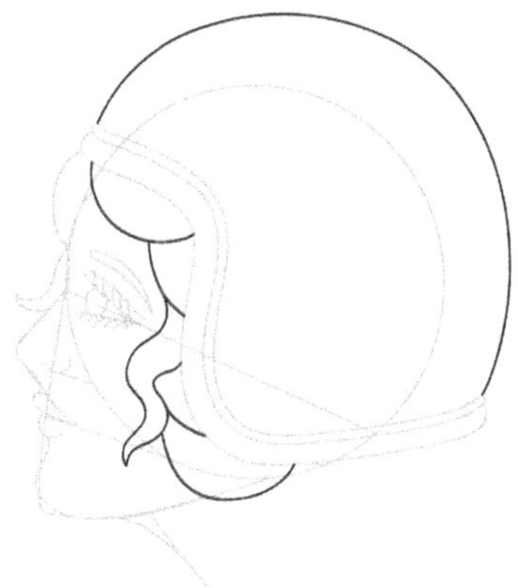

06

07

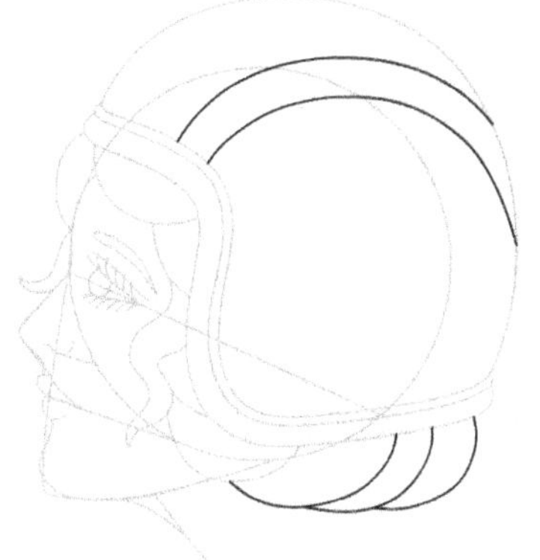

08

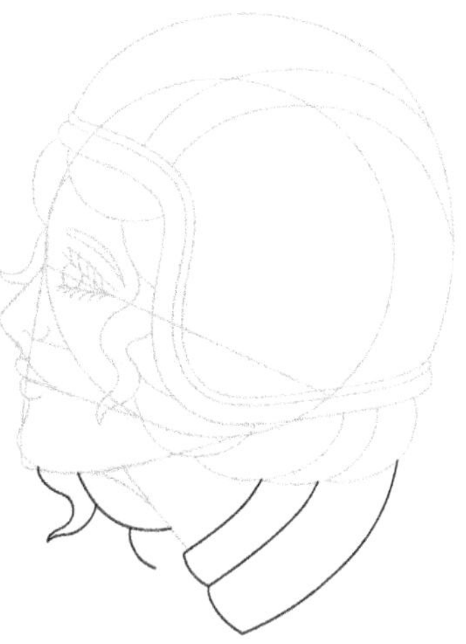

09

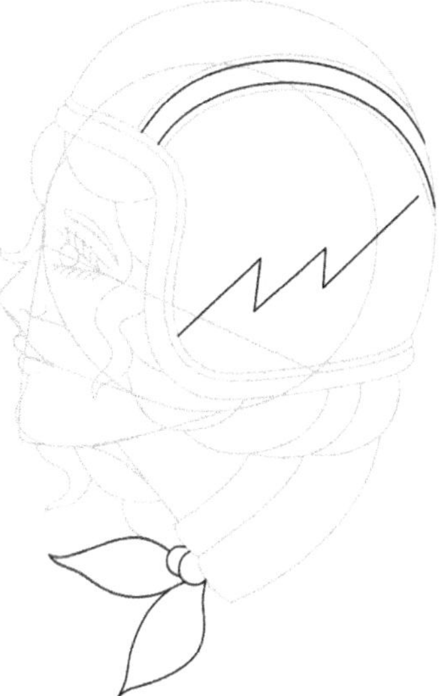

10

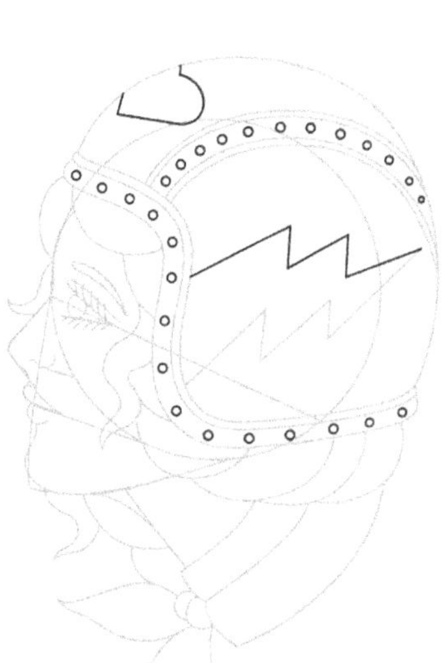

11

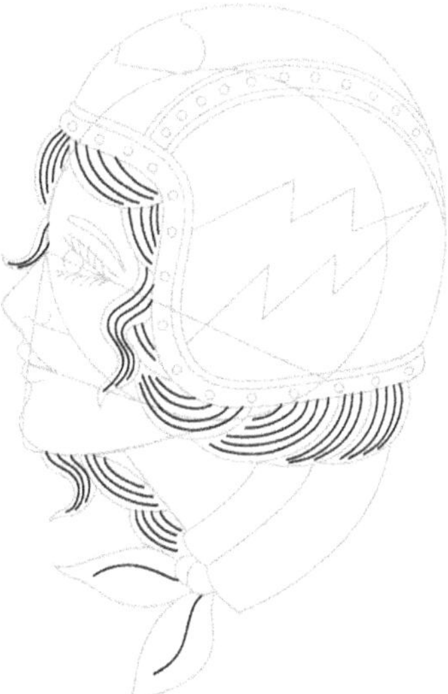

12

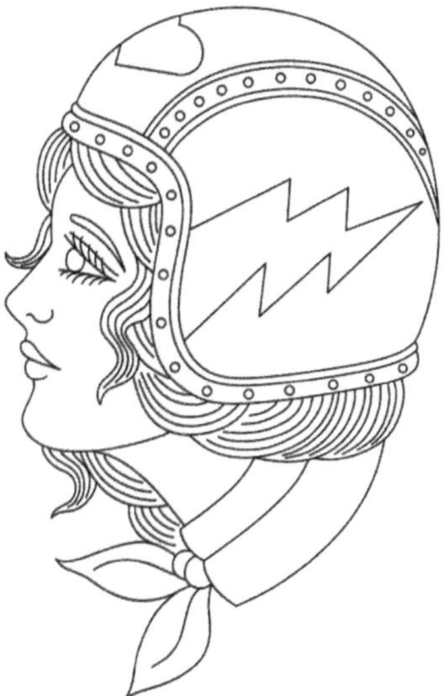

GENTLEMAN

Pro tip: Use the circle to plot the chin position

From the centre of the left-hand side of the circle, draw a line on a slight angle that extends roughly one third of the height of the circle below it. This will give you the position of the lower chin. Draw in the rest of the chin by sketching a line inclining back up to meet the base of the head just past the centre point.

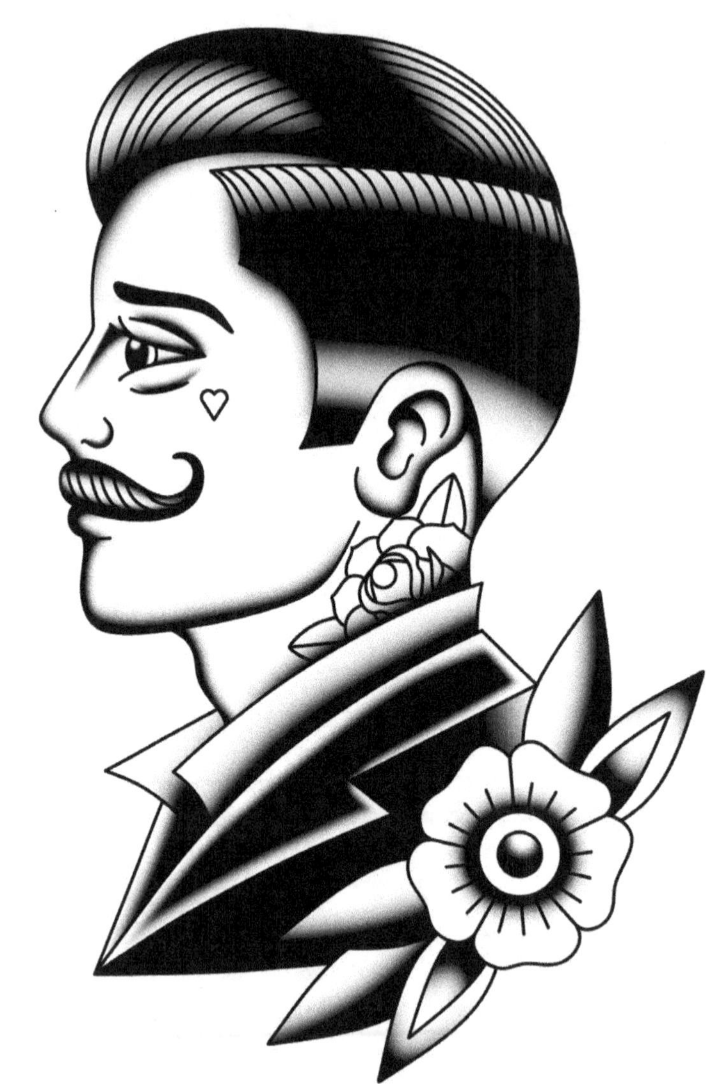

01

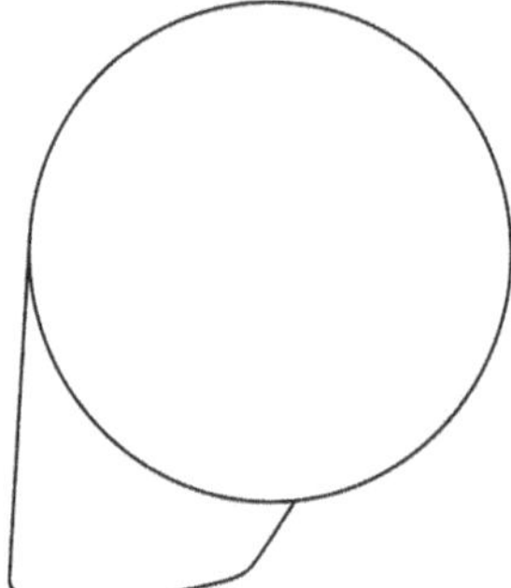

02

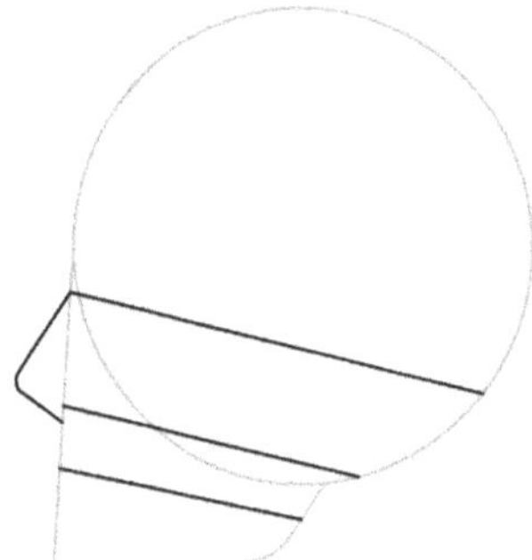

03

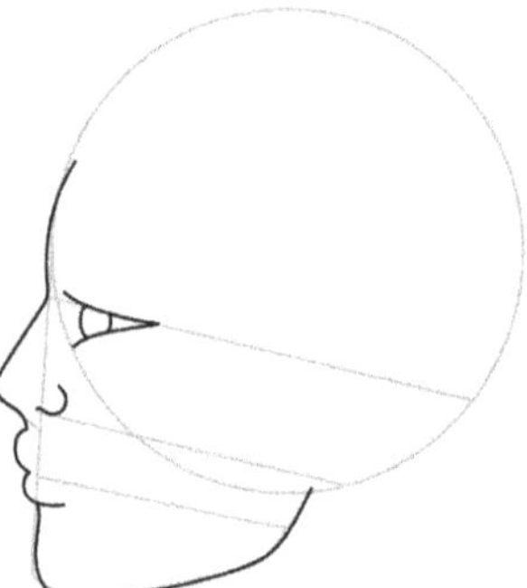

04

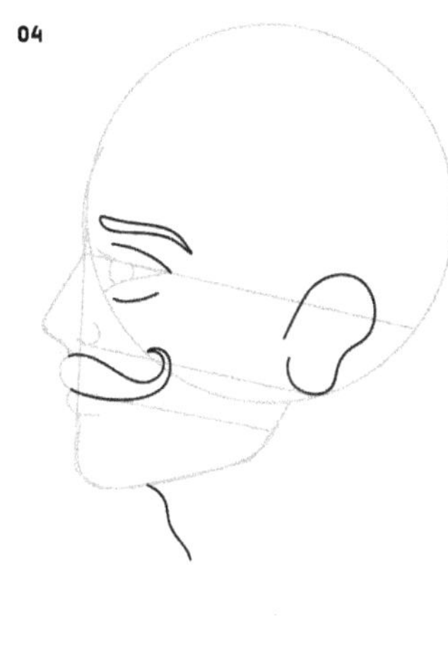

05

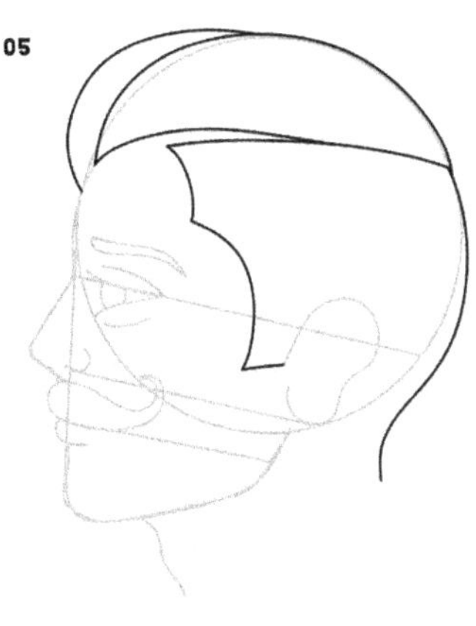

06

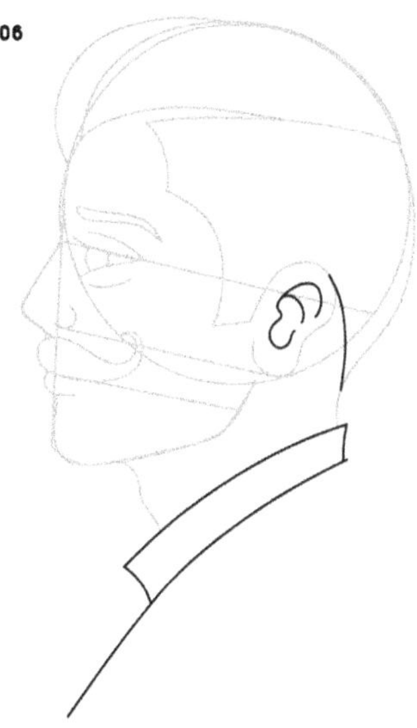

07

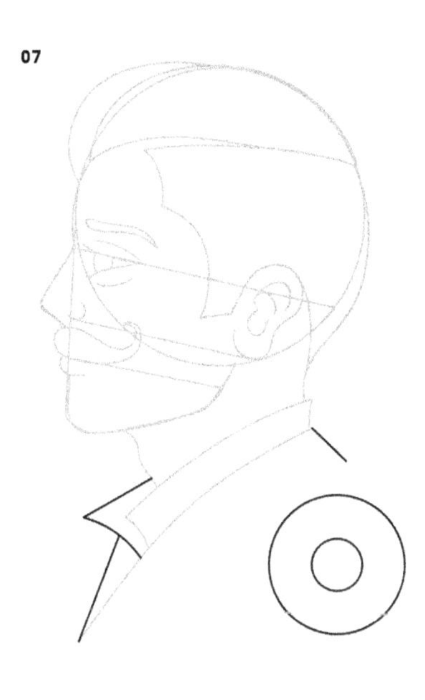

08

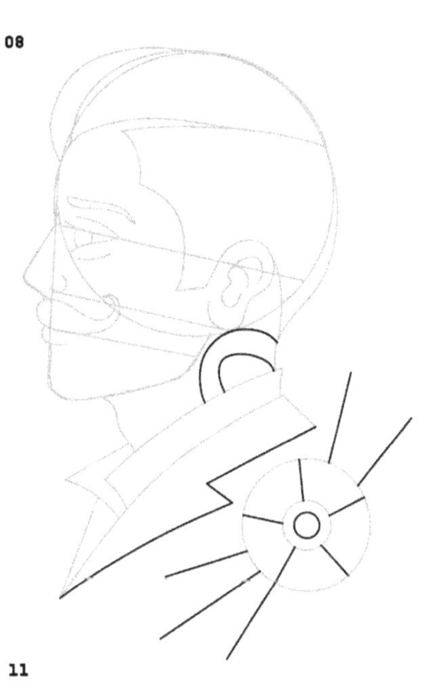

09

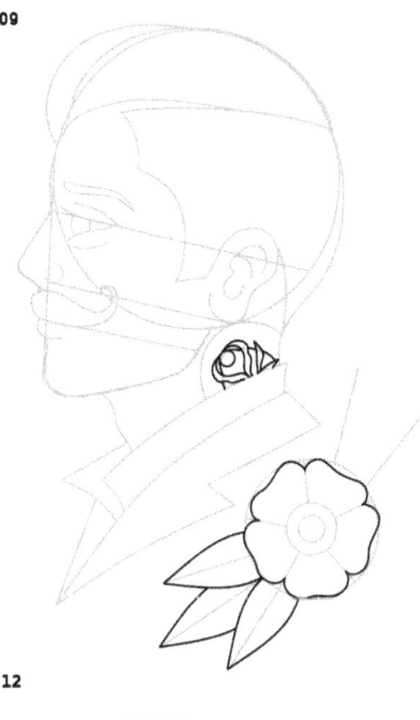

10

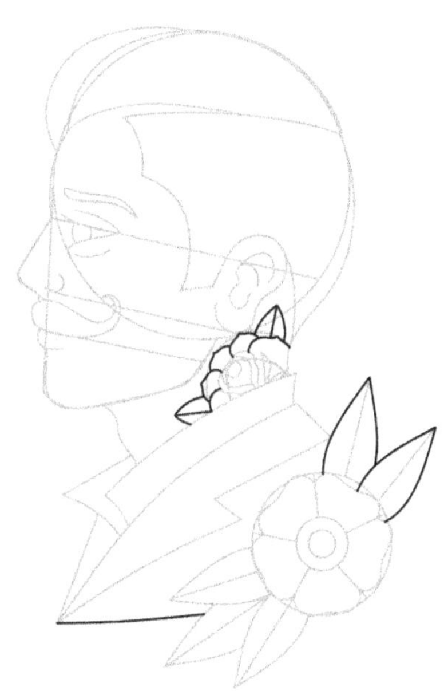

11

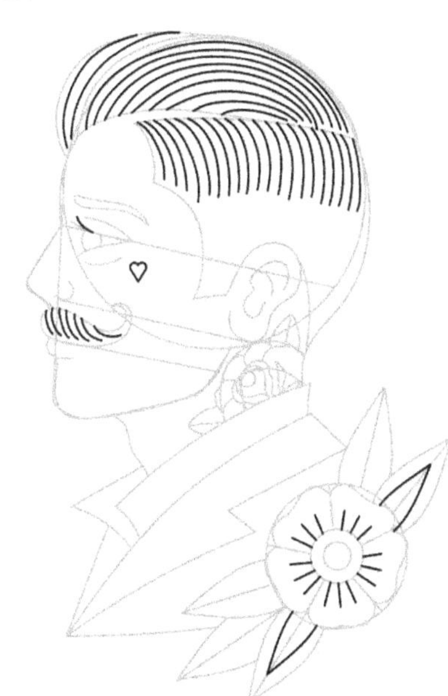

12

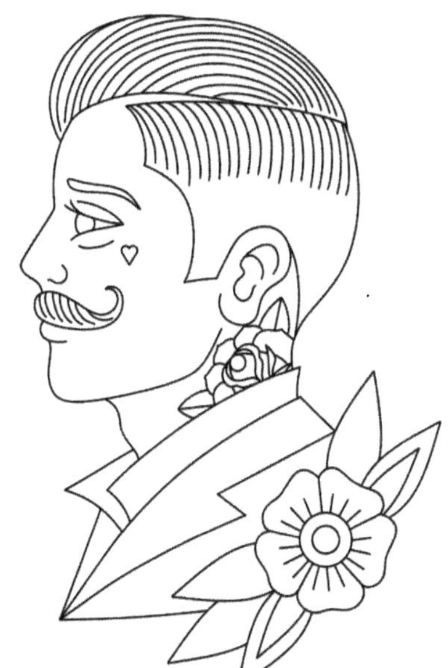

DEVIL RACER

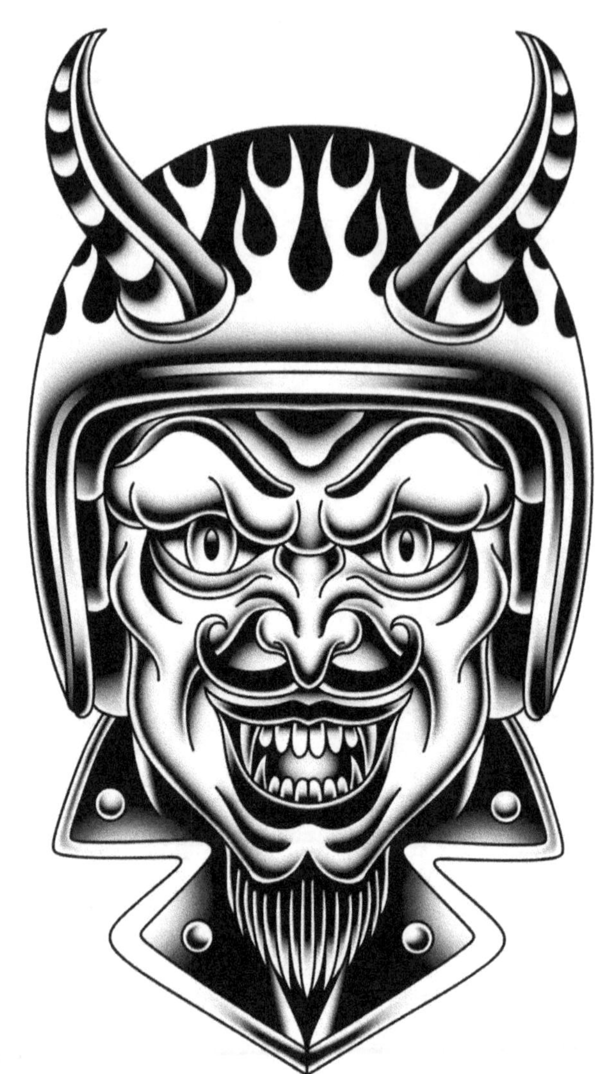

Pro tip: Use the circle's height to define the jaw length

To work out the jaw length accurately, start by drawing a vertical centre line through the head circle. Extend this line downwards by roughly half the height of the circle. This point marks the base of the chin. Drawing the jawline to meet this point ensures balanced proportions.

01

02

03

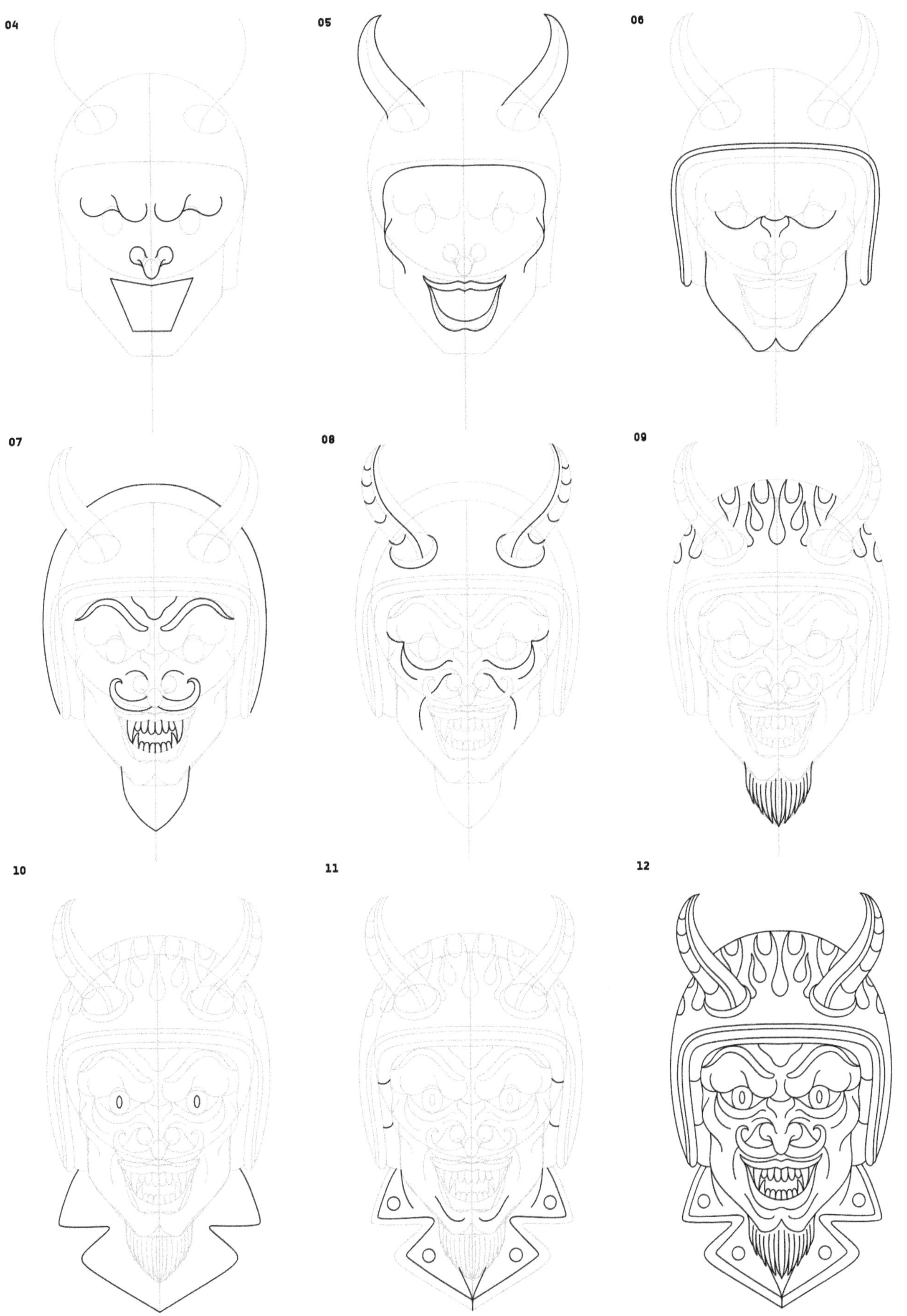

04
05
06
07
08
09
10
11
12
HOW TO DRAW TRADITIONAL TATTOOS

PLAGUE DOCTOR

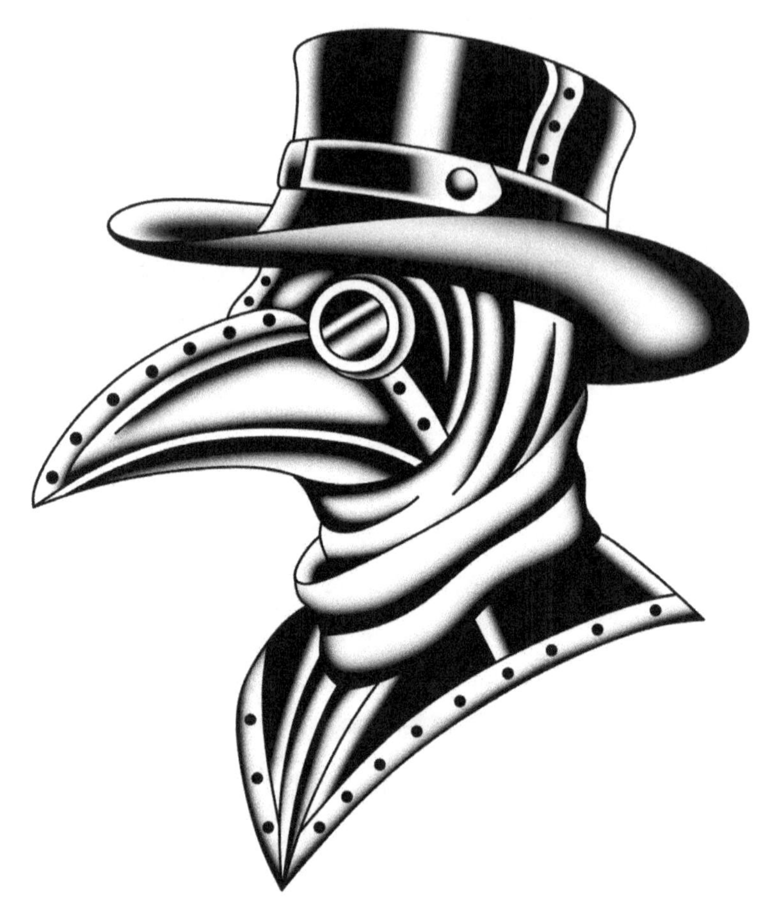

Pro tip: Use a 45-degree line to set the beak length

From the lower left edge of the circle, draw a line at a 45-degree angle extending outward roughly the same length as the circle's diameter. This gives you a reliable reference for positioning and sizing the beak so it integrates naturally with the head shape.

01

02

03

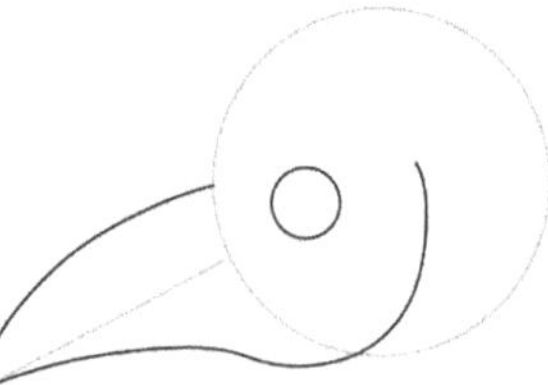

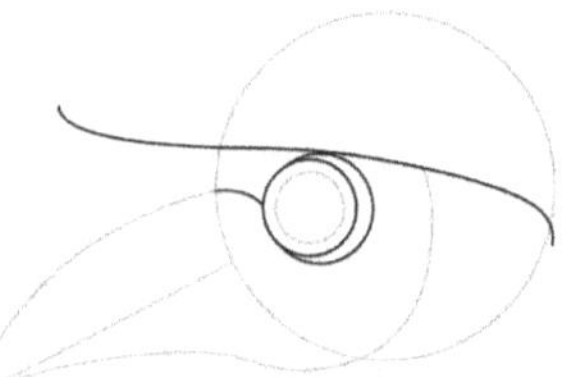

04

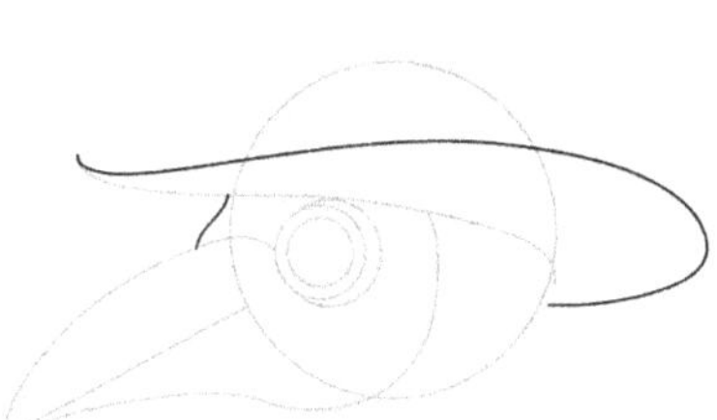

05

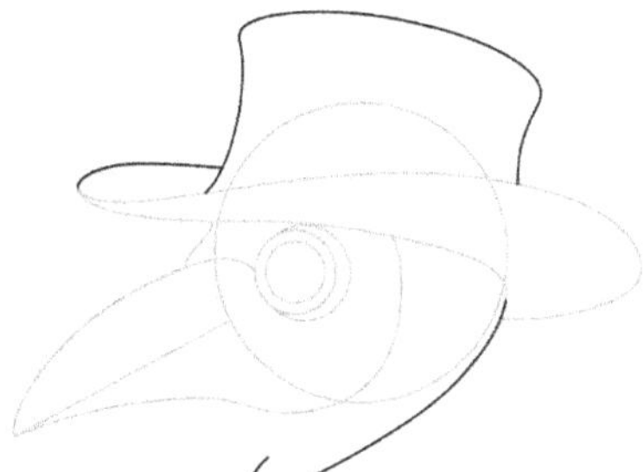

06

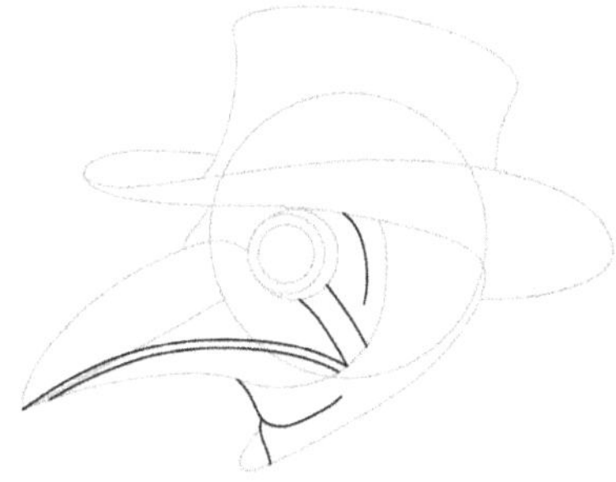

07

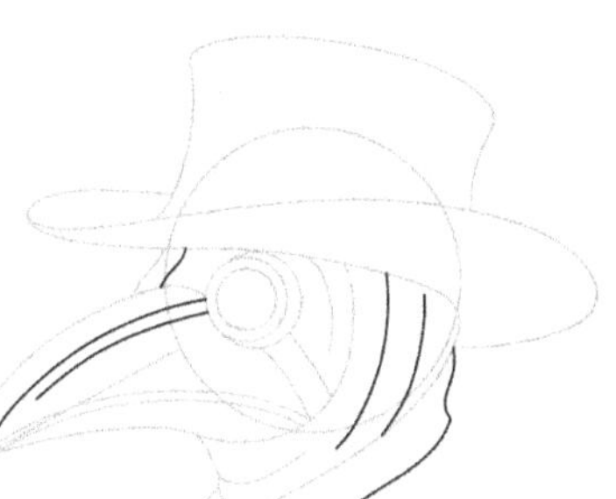

08

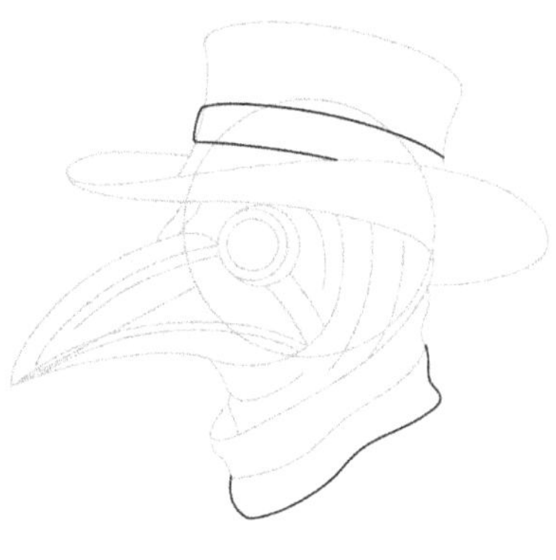

09

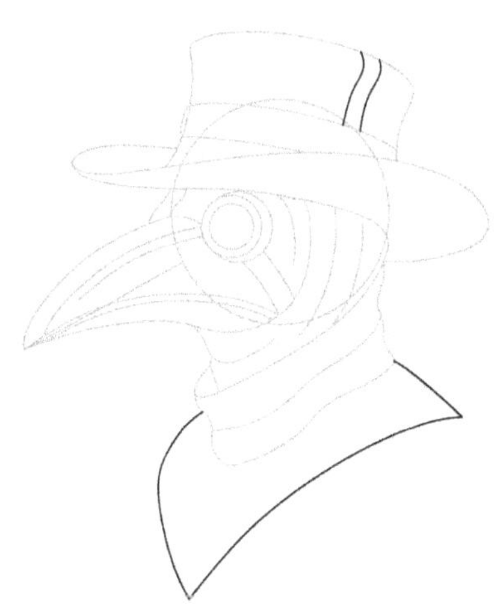

10

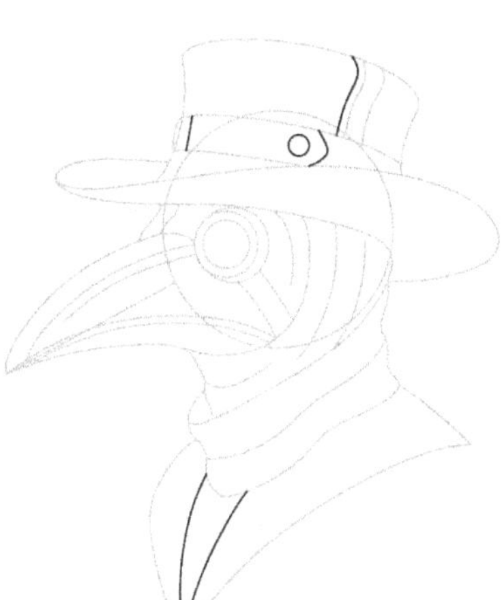

11

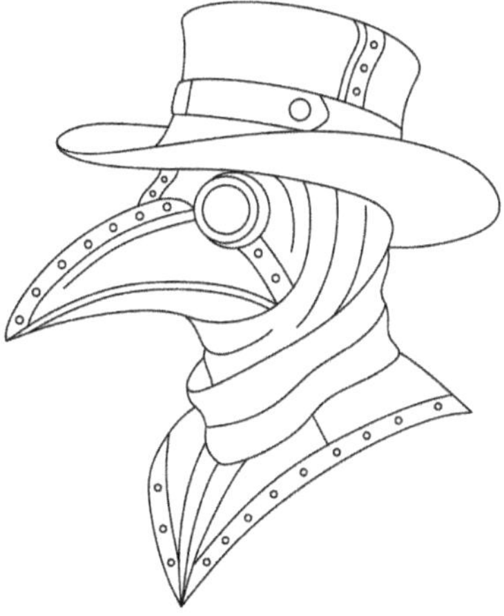

12

HOW TO DRAW TRADITIONAL TATTOOS

COBRA SNAKE & ROSE

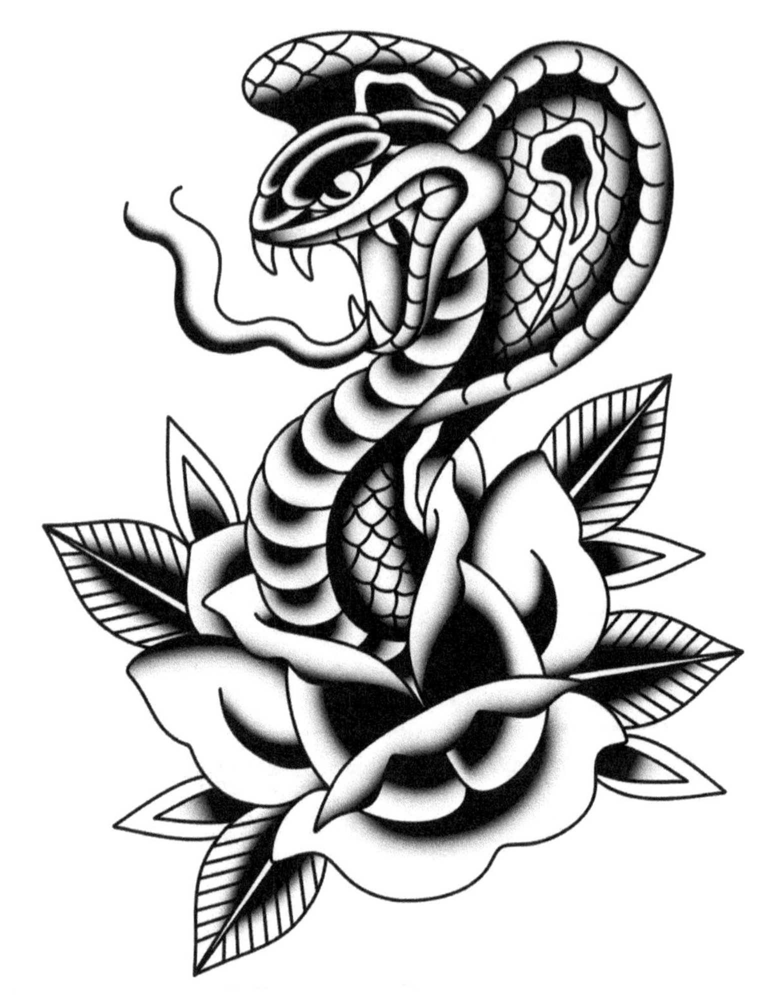

Pro tip: Use the head as a measuring unit for the hood

To work out the size of the hood, use the width of the head as your measuring guide. The hood should extend roughly one and a half to two head-widths out from either side, creating that characteristic flared shape. Position the base of the hood just behind the head to give a smooth, natural transition between the two forms. This proportional approach ensures the hood looks dramatic without overwhelming the rest of the design.

01

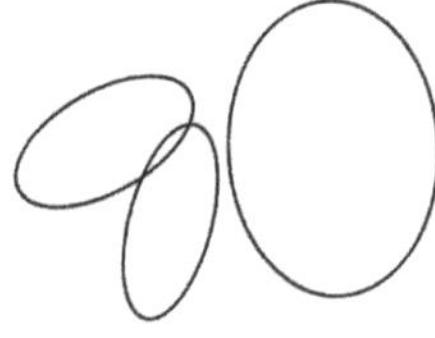

02

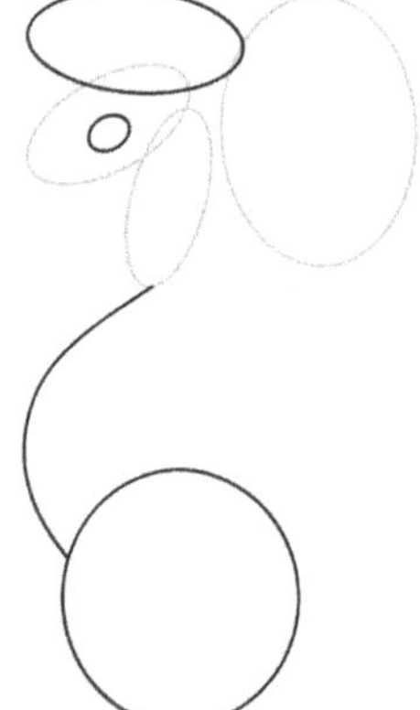

03

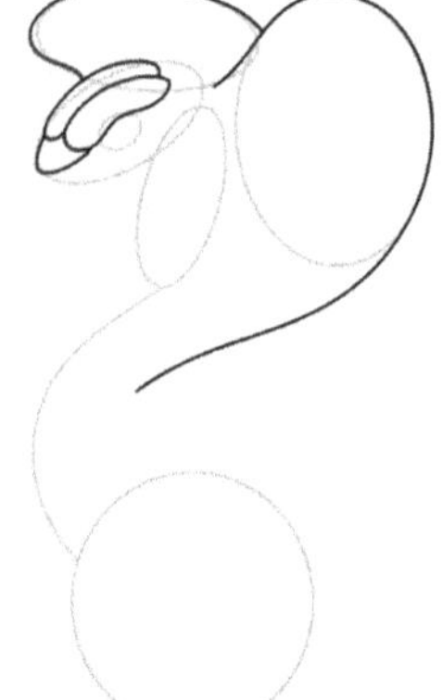

04

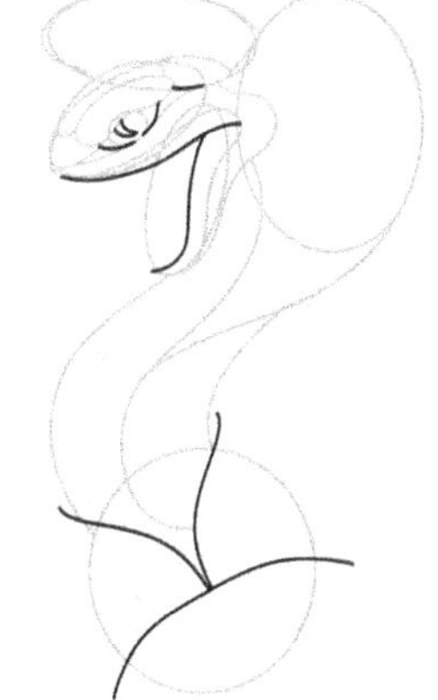

05

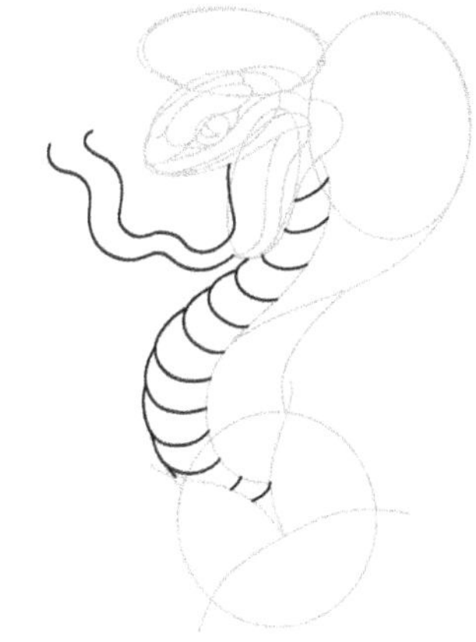

06

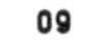

07

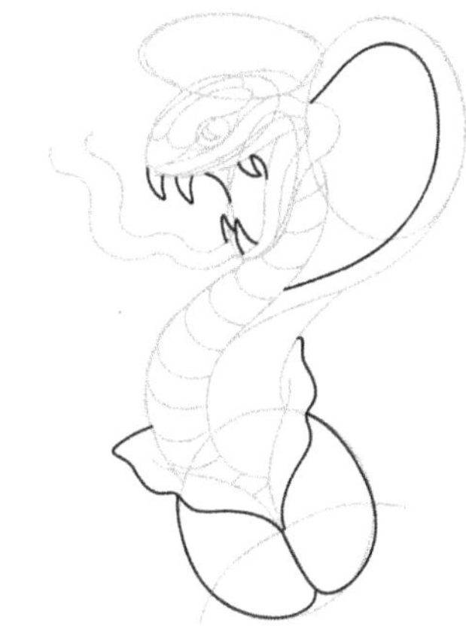

08

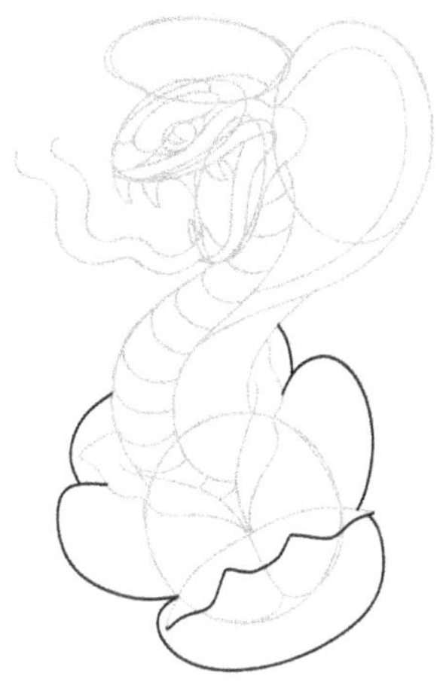

09

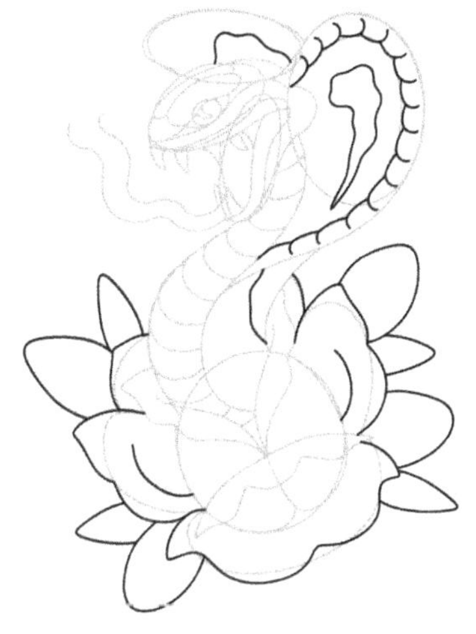

10

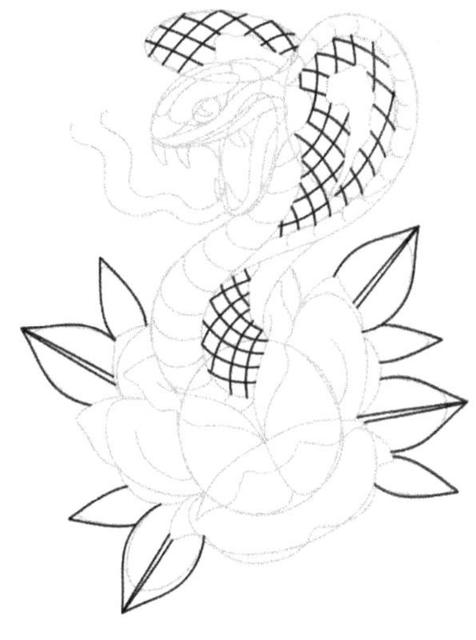

11

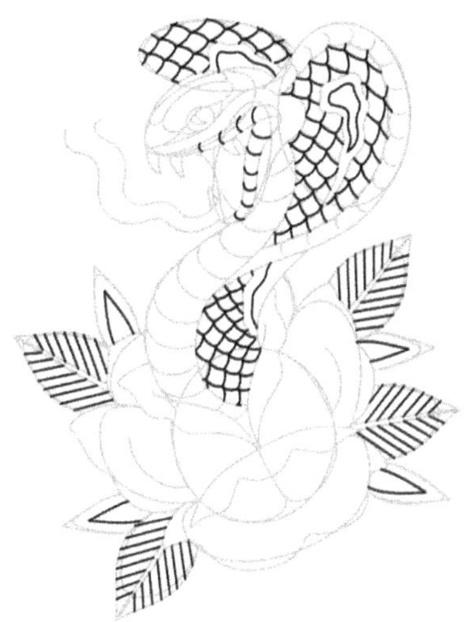

12

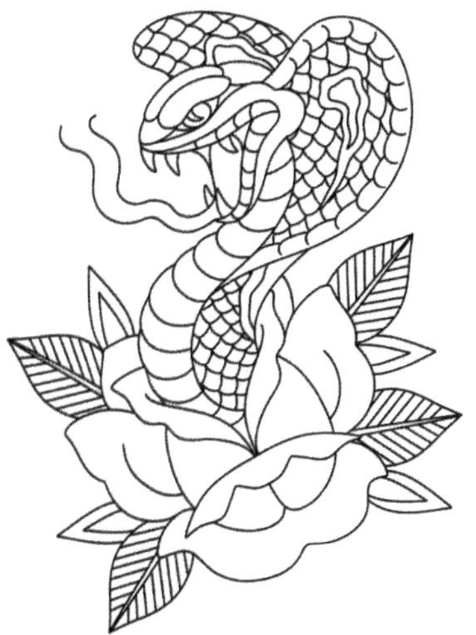

BUTTERFLY WOMAN

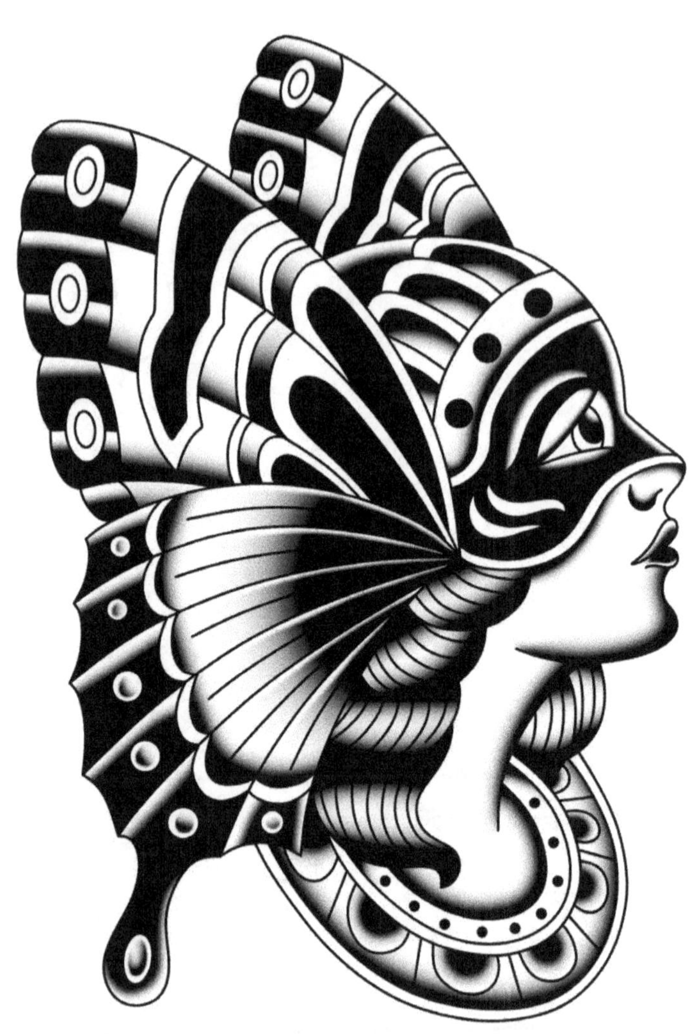

**Pro tip: Position the eye slit at a 45°
angle**

To create a strong foundation for the
butterfly woman's face, start by drawing
a guiding circle. Place a short slit on a
45-degree angle on the right side of
the circle where the eye will eventually
sit. Position it just above the horizontal
halfway line of the circle. This angled
placement helps establish the tilt and
orientation of the facial features, ensuring
the final design has a dynamic, upward-
lifting expression.

01

02

03

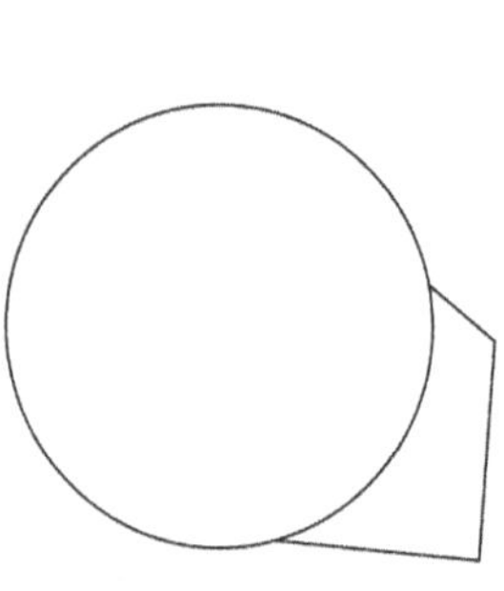

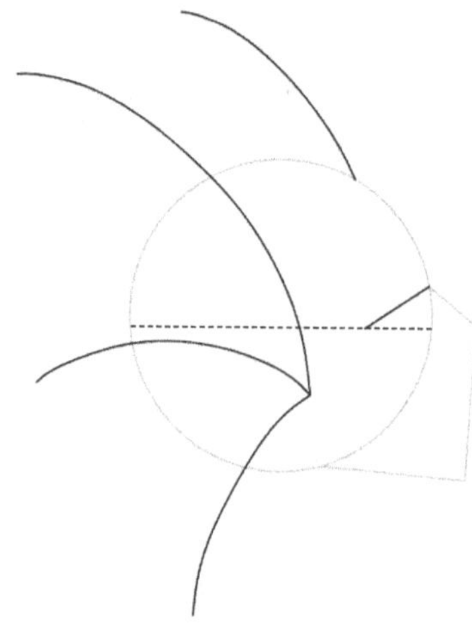

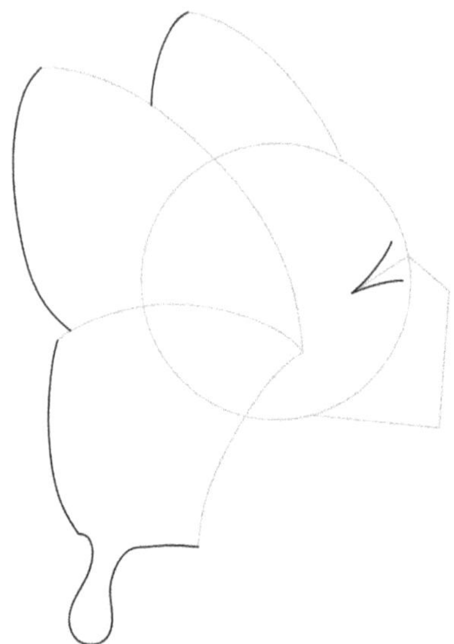

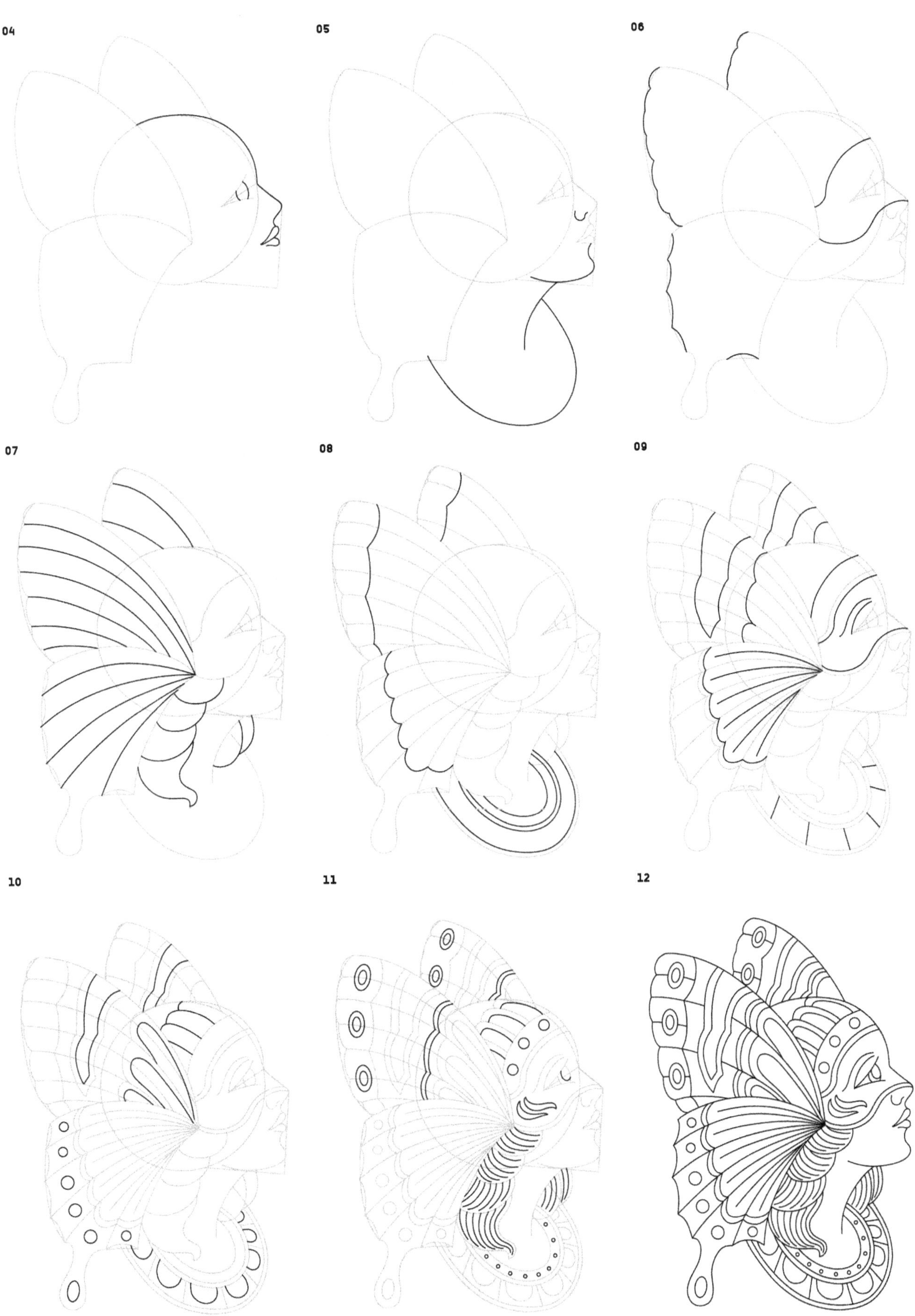

04
05
06
07
08
09
10
11
12
HOW TO DRAW TRADITIONAL TATTOOS

MASKED WOMAN

Pro tip: Use the circle to plot a compact jaw shape

From the centre point on the left-hand side of the circle, draw a line on a slight downward angle, extending roughly one third of the circle's height below it to mark the chin. From this point, draw lines inclining back up to meet the base of the circle at the centre line. This creates a shorter, more contained jaw shape that suits a softer head structure.

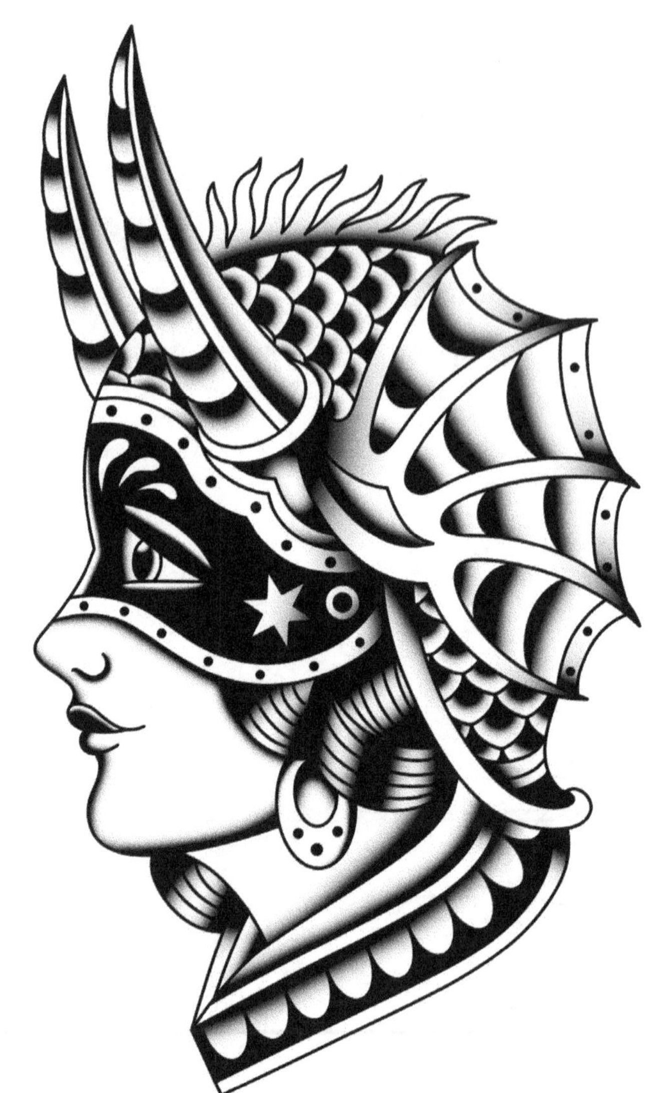

01

02

03

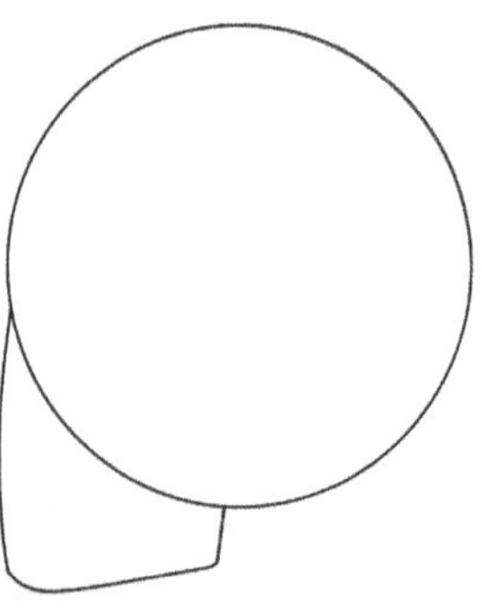

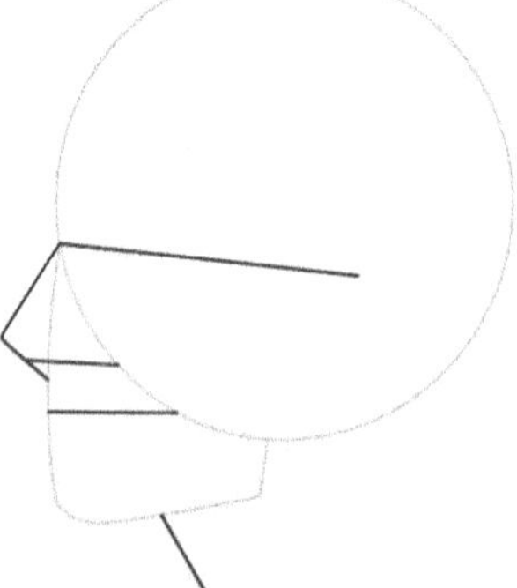

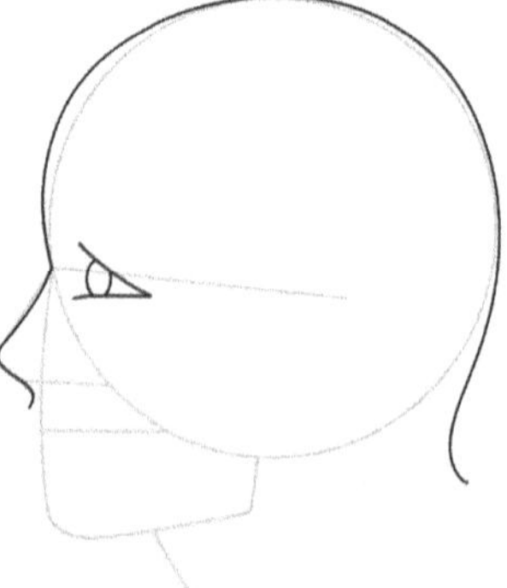

04

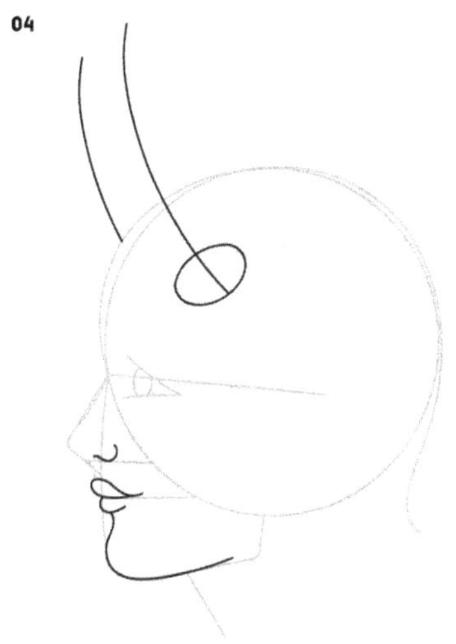

05

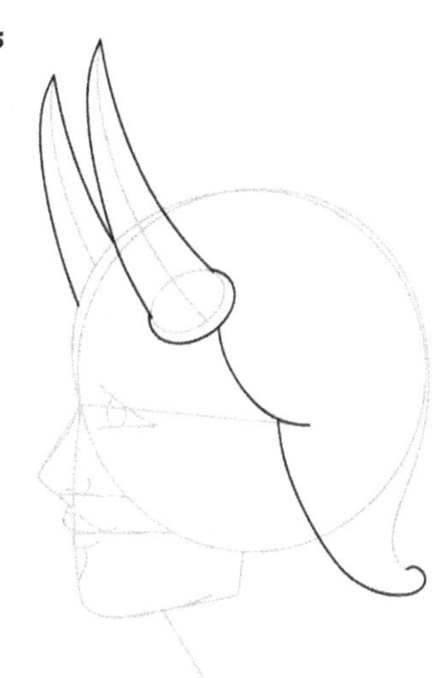

06

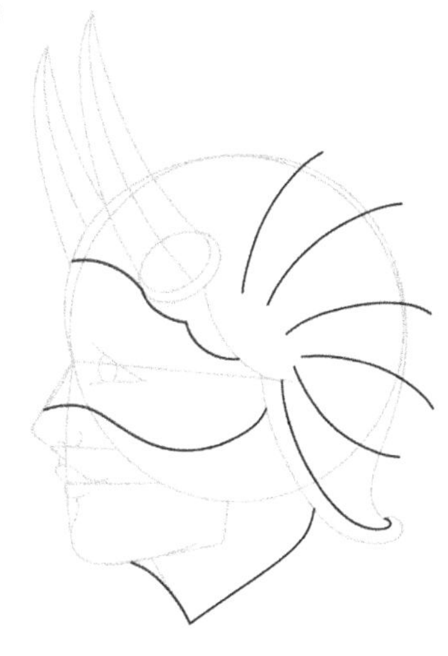

07

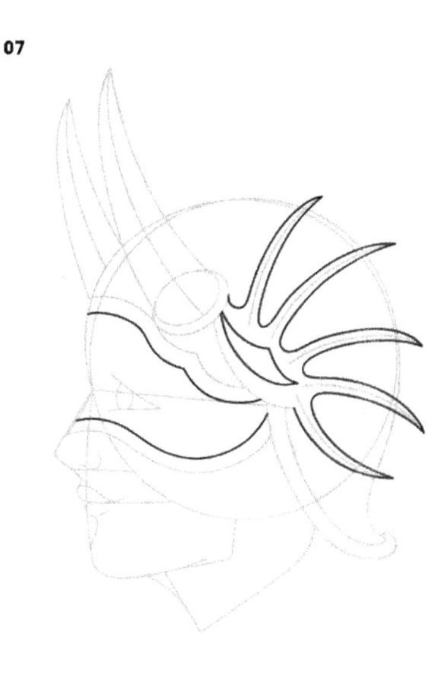

08

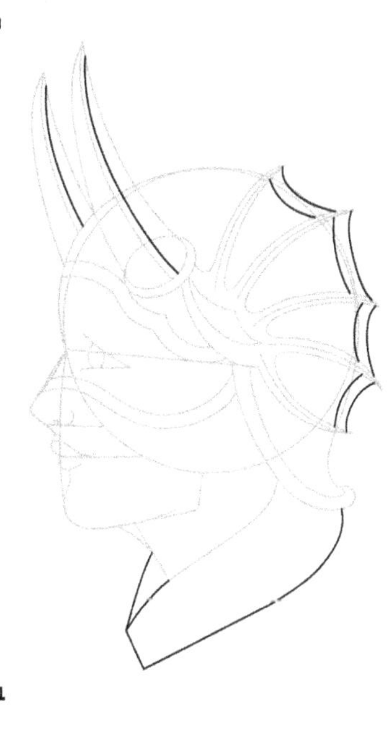

09

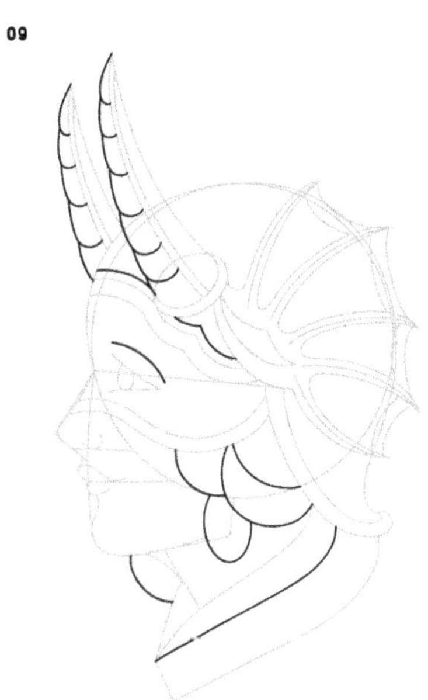

10

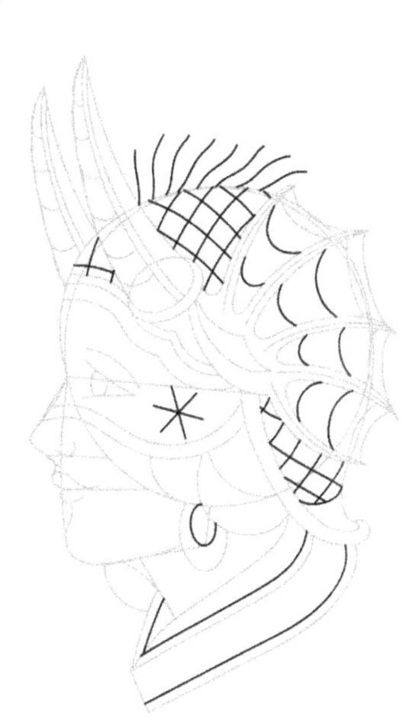

11

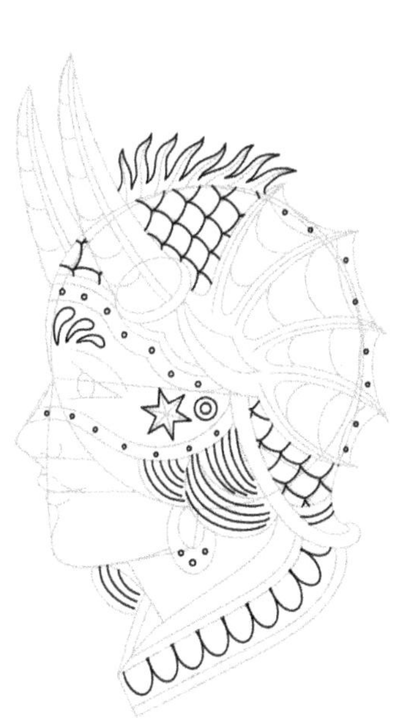

12

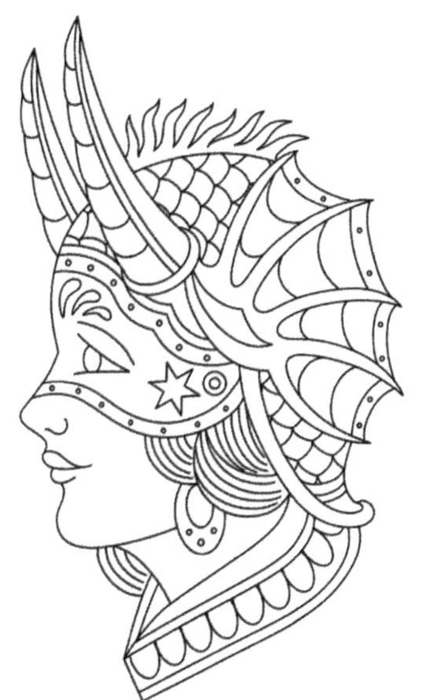

DEVIL LADY

Pro tip: Use the circle to measure the chin length

From the bottom of the circle, measure down a distance roughly equal to one third of the circle's height and mark this point. This will define the tip of the chin. Draw guiding lines from the sides of the circle down to this point to form the jaw, keeping both sides symmetrical for balanced proportions.

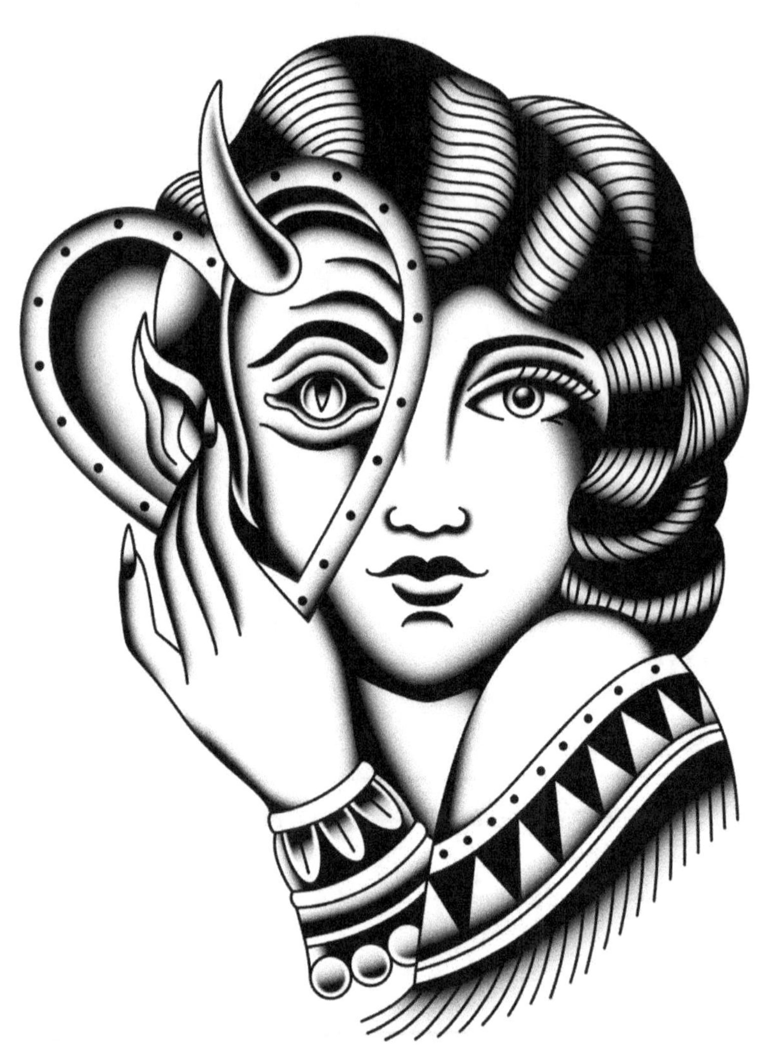

01

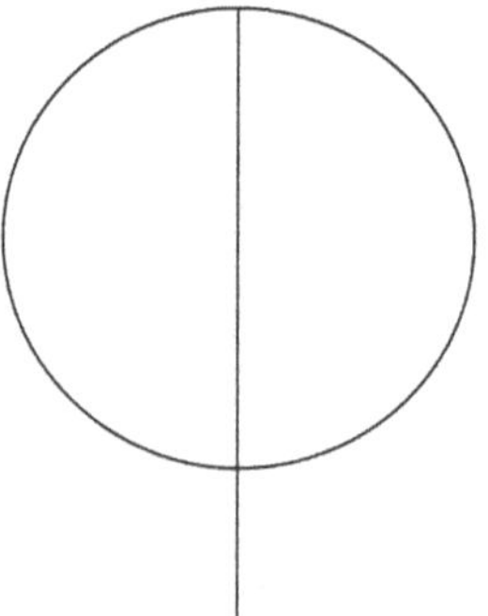

02

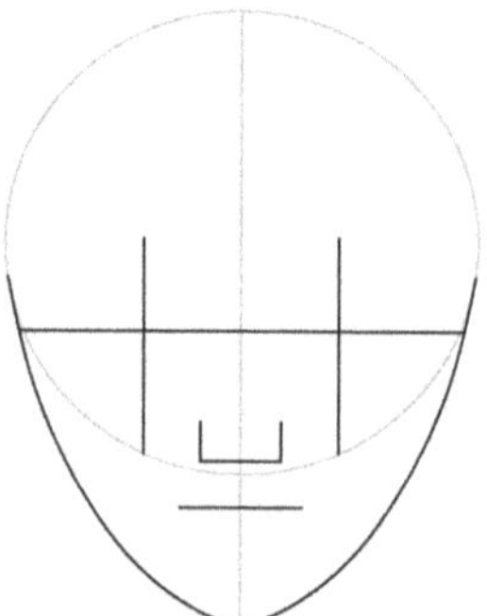

03

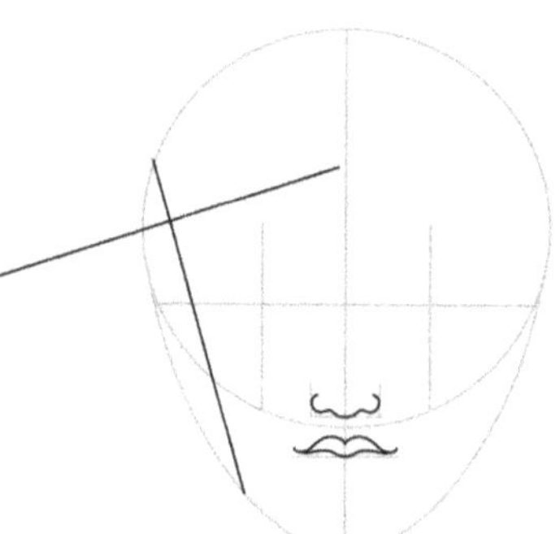

04

05

06

07

08

09

10

11

12

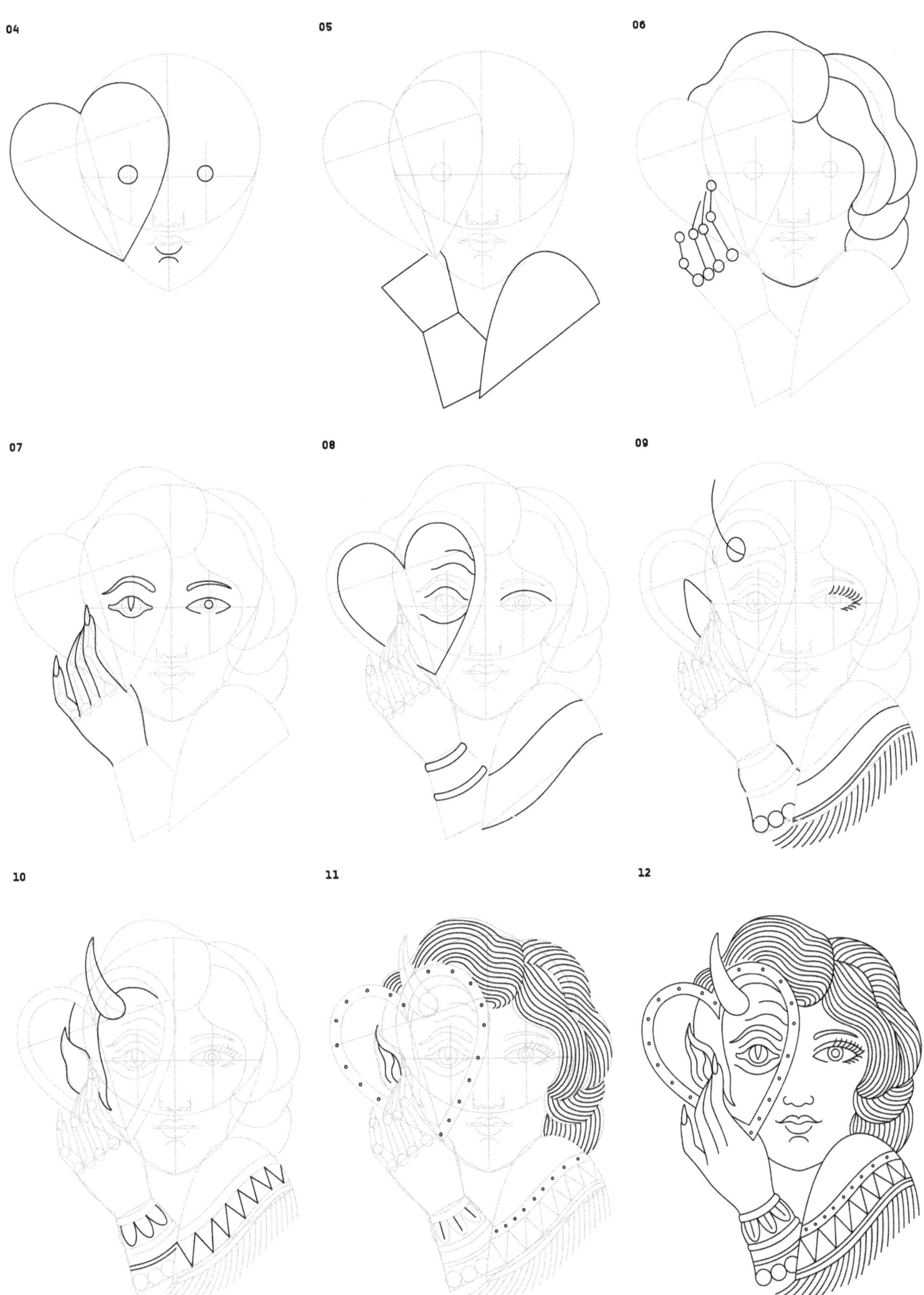

HOW TO DRAW TRADITIONAL TATTOOS

BOXING WOMAN

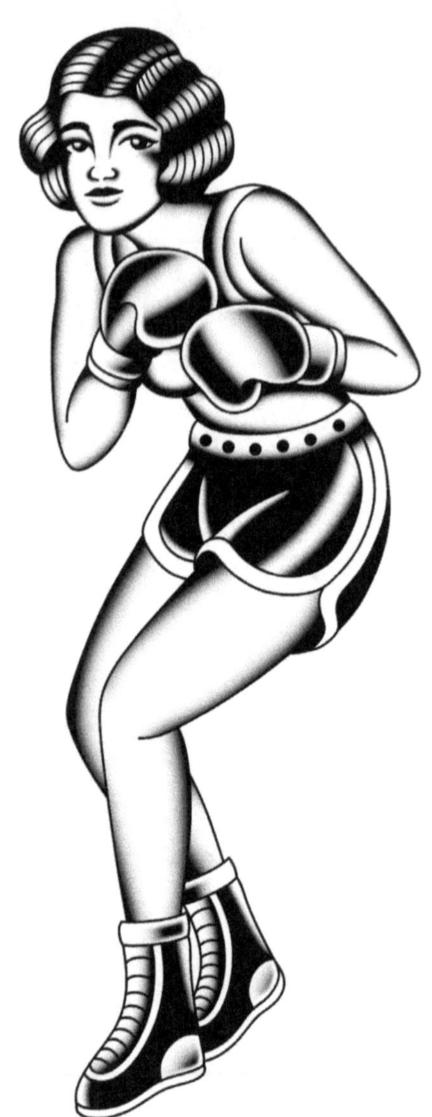

Pro tip: Tilt the upper torso for a convincing boxer's pose

Angle the upper torso forward so that the chest leans slightly over the hips. This tilt creates a sense of readiness and aggression, essential for a believable boxer's stance. The shoulders should angle downward toward the leading arm, helping to frame the head and give the figure a dynamic, forward-driven posture.

01

02

03

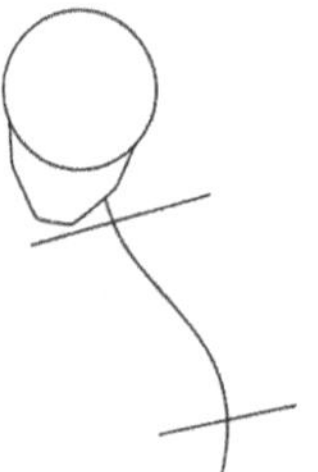

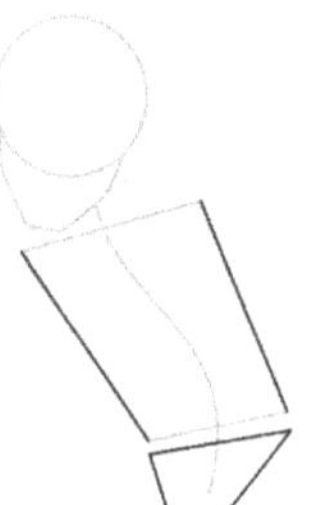

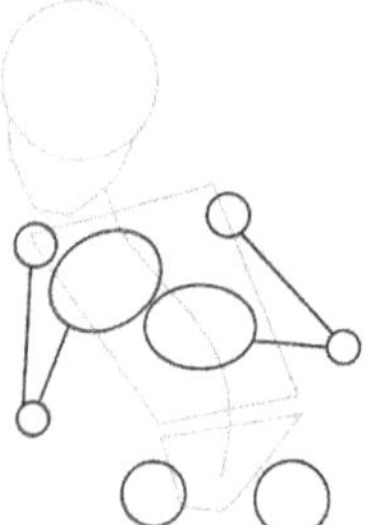

04

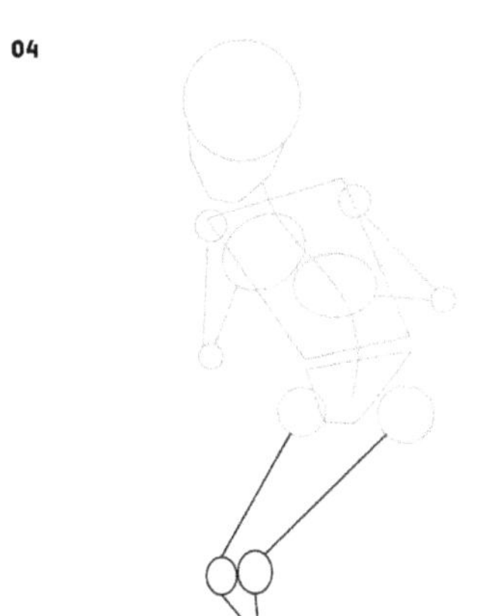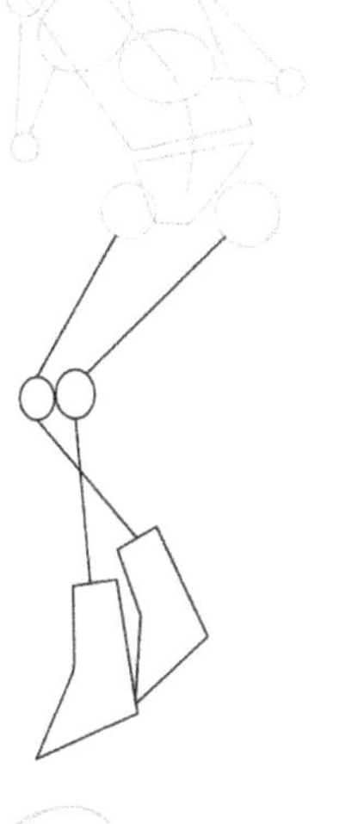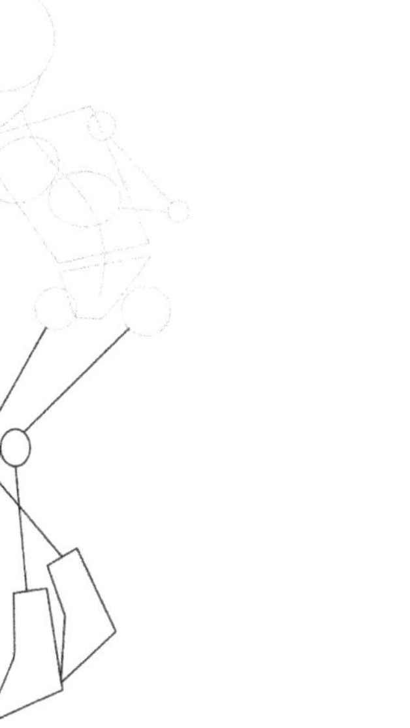

05

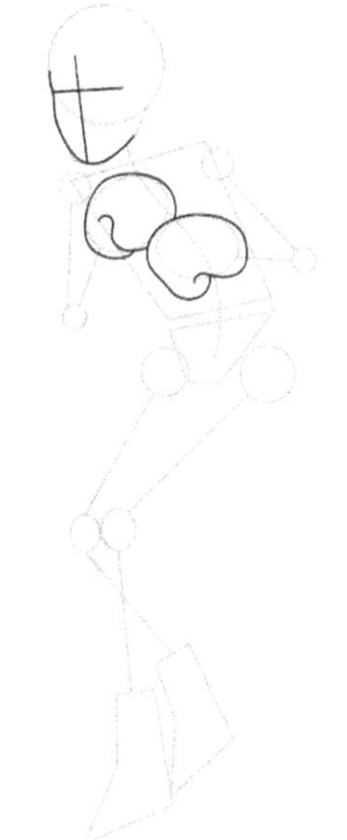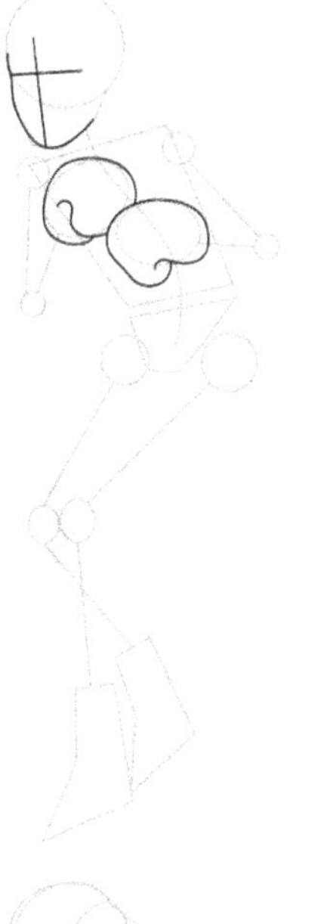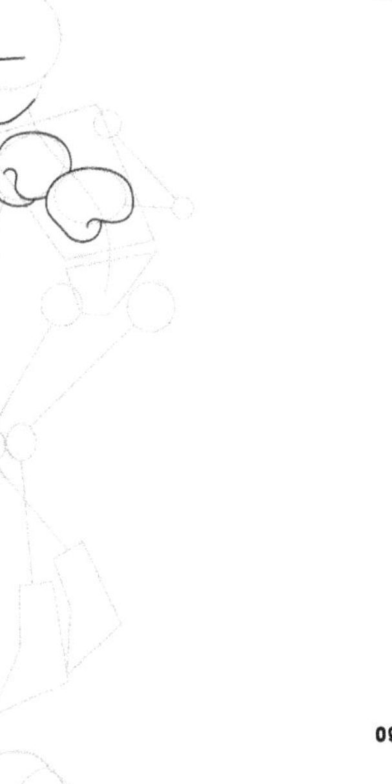

06

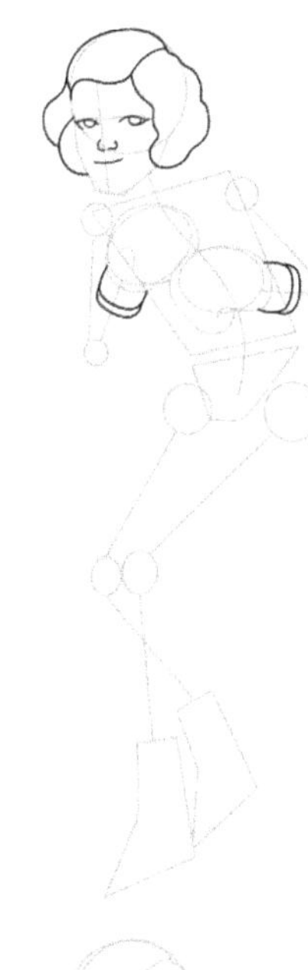

07

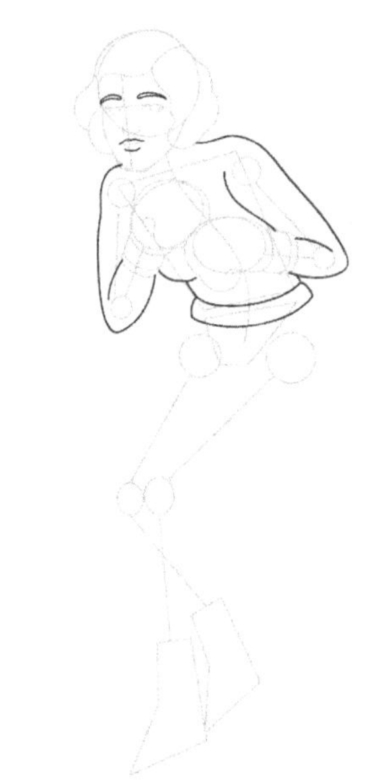

08

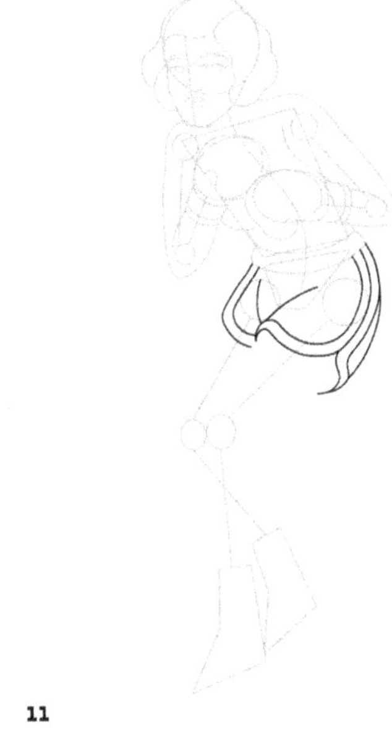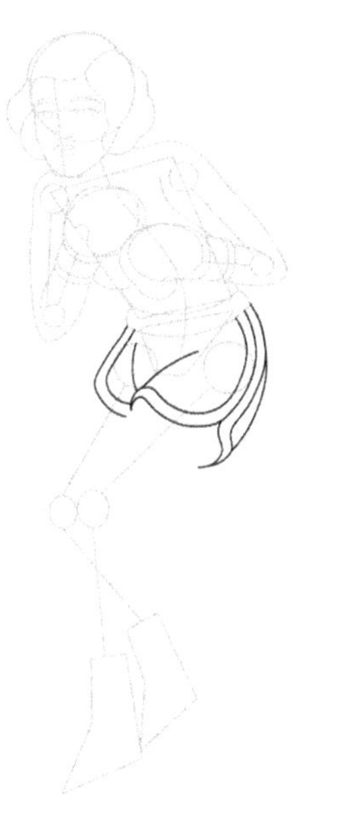

09

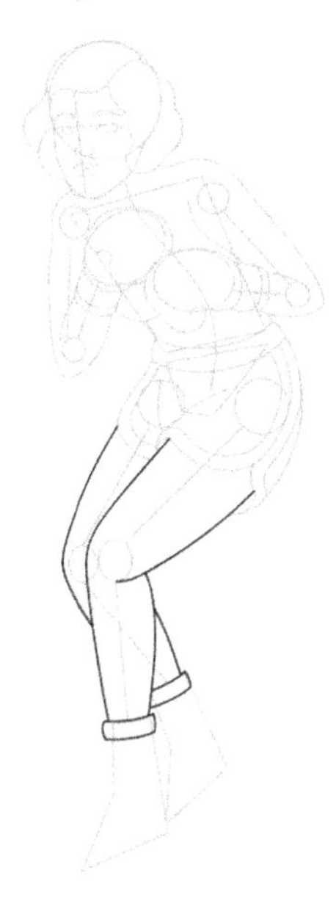

10

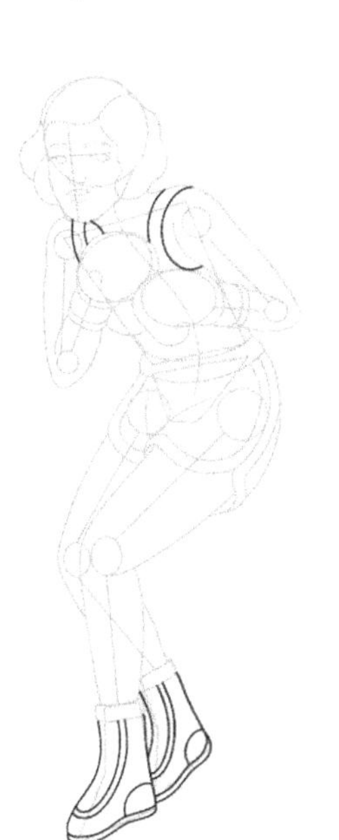

11

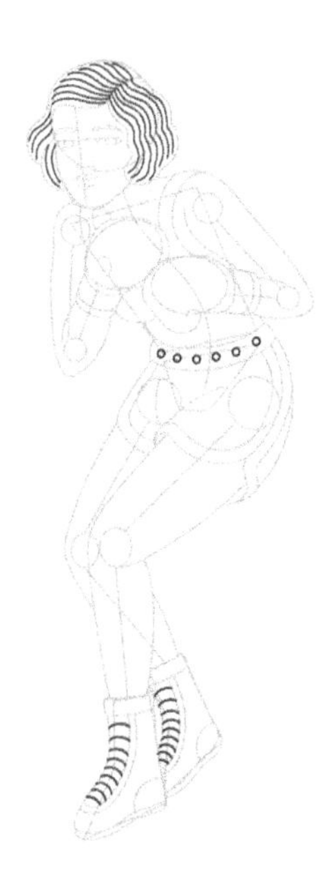

12

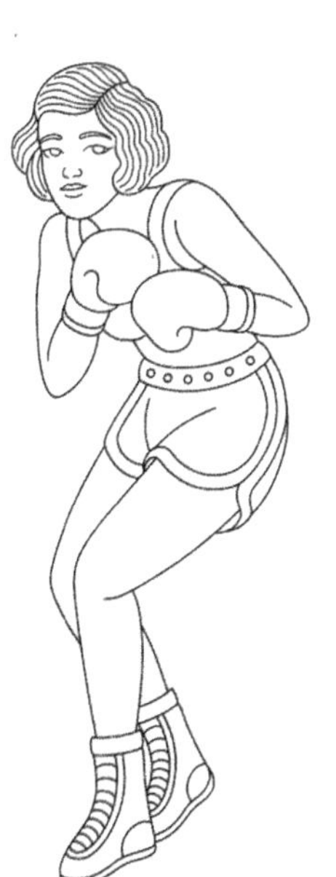

BOXING MAN

Pro tip: Offset the head for a dynamic duck and weave stance

Shift the head slightly off the central axis of the torso to create a more natural, defensive boxing posture. This subtle offset suggests movement and readiness, as if the figure is preparing to duck, slip or weave. It also helps break the stiffness of a perfectly centred pose, giving the stance more realism.

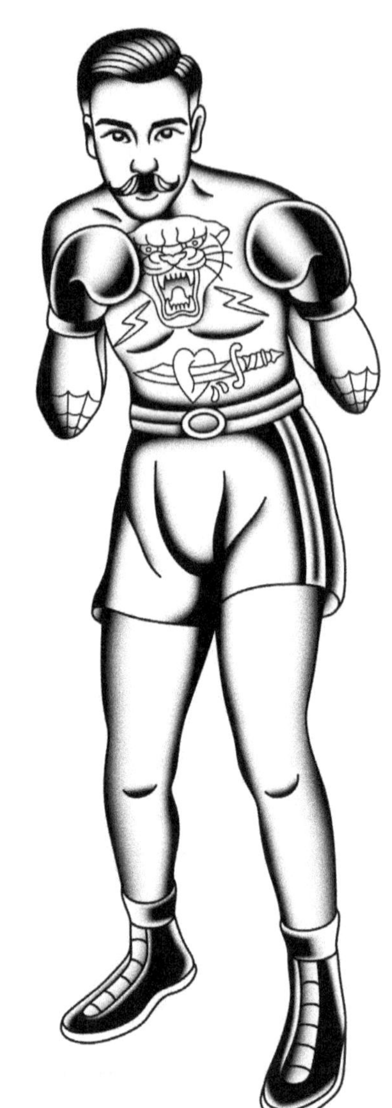

01

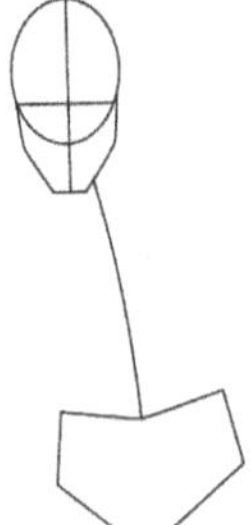

02

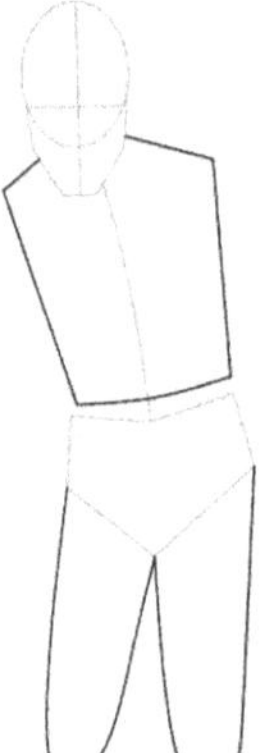

03

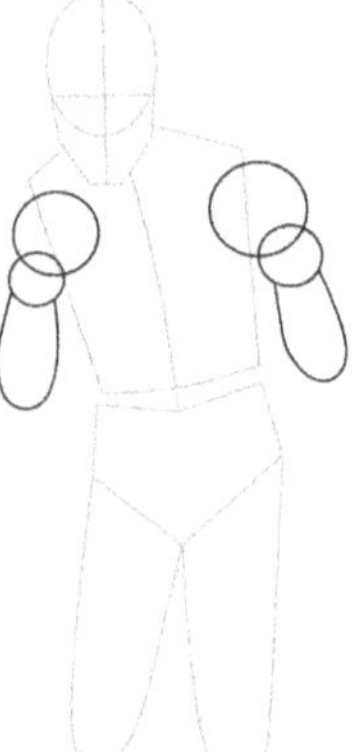

04

05

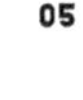
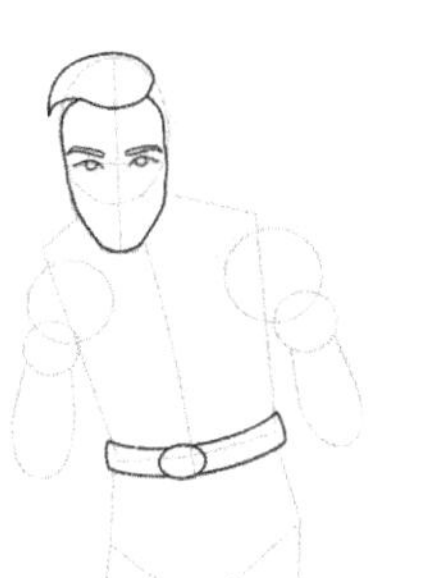
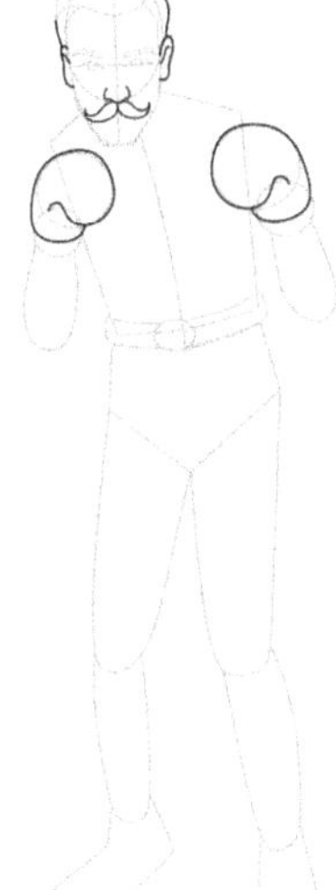

06

07

08

09

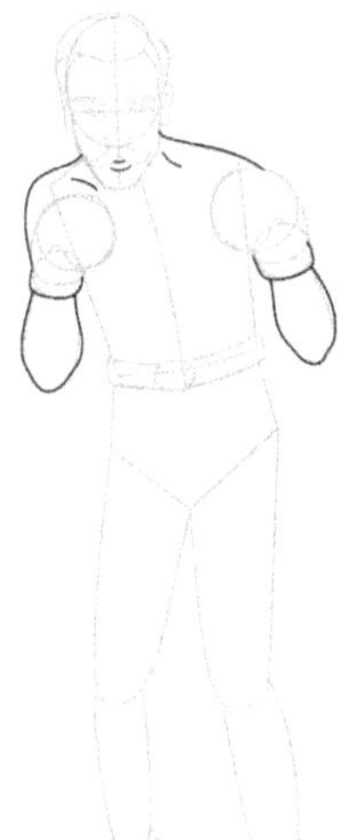
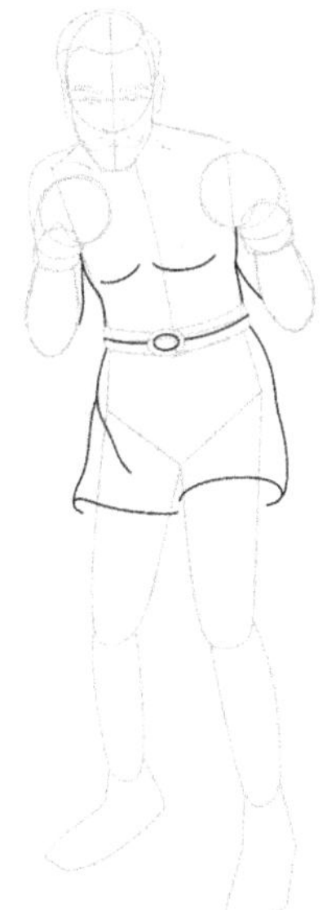
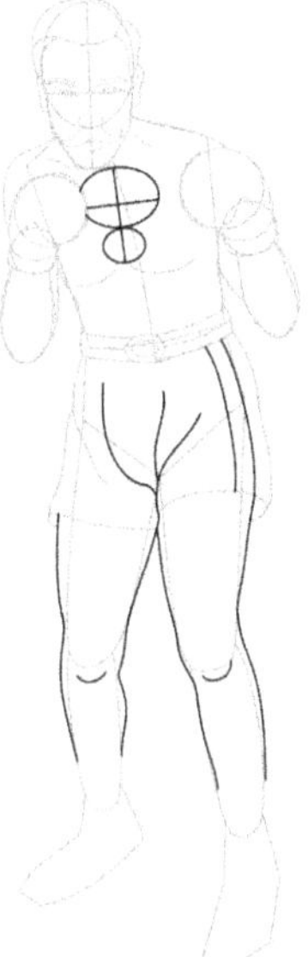

10

11

12

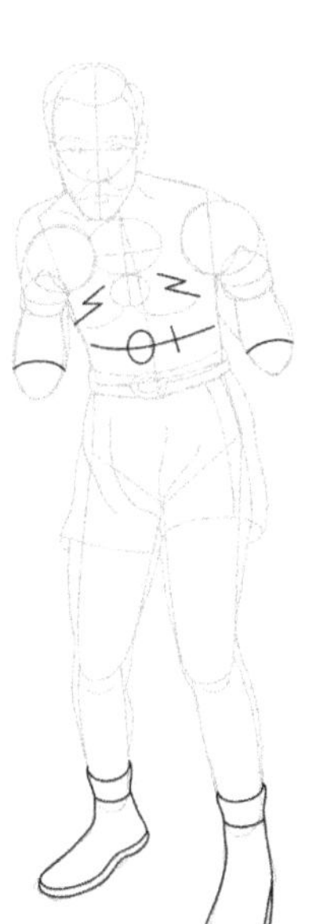
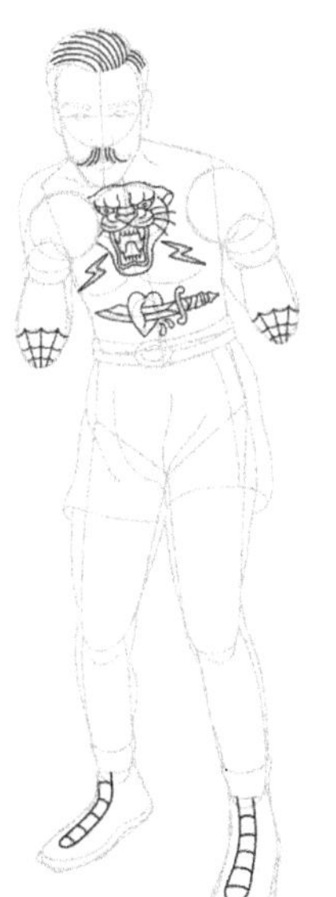
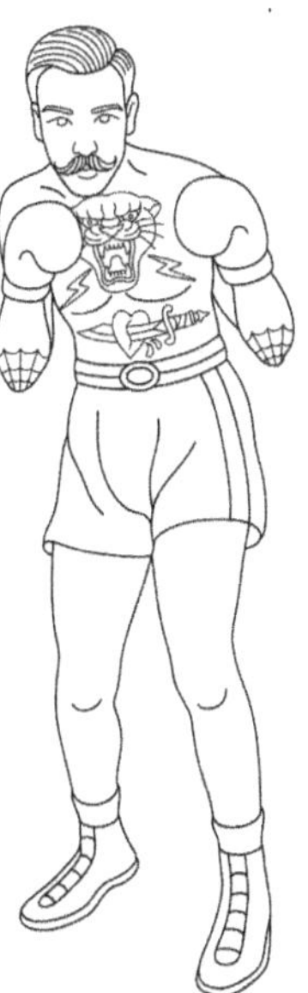

ANCHOR

Pro tip: Start with a central line to anchor your design

Begin by drawing a strong vertical centre line. This line acts as the backbone of the anchor, ensuring perfect symmetry on both sides. All elements, including the shank, crossbar and flukes, can then be built out from this central axis, making it easier to keep the proportions balanced and the curves mirrored accurately.

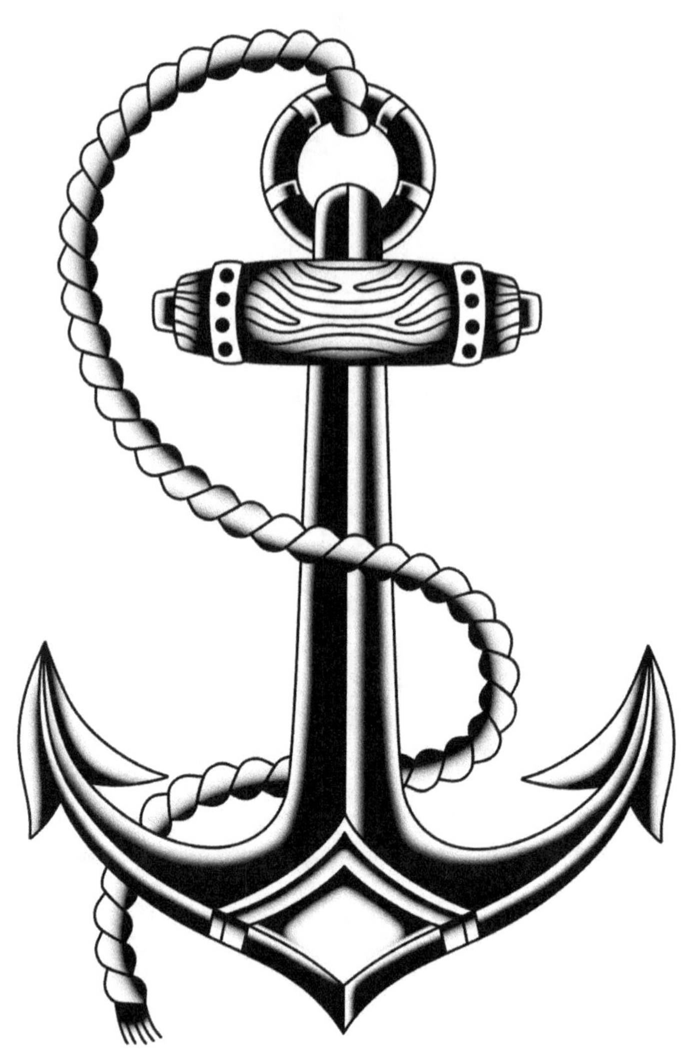

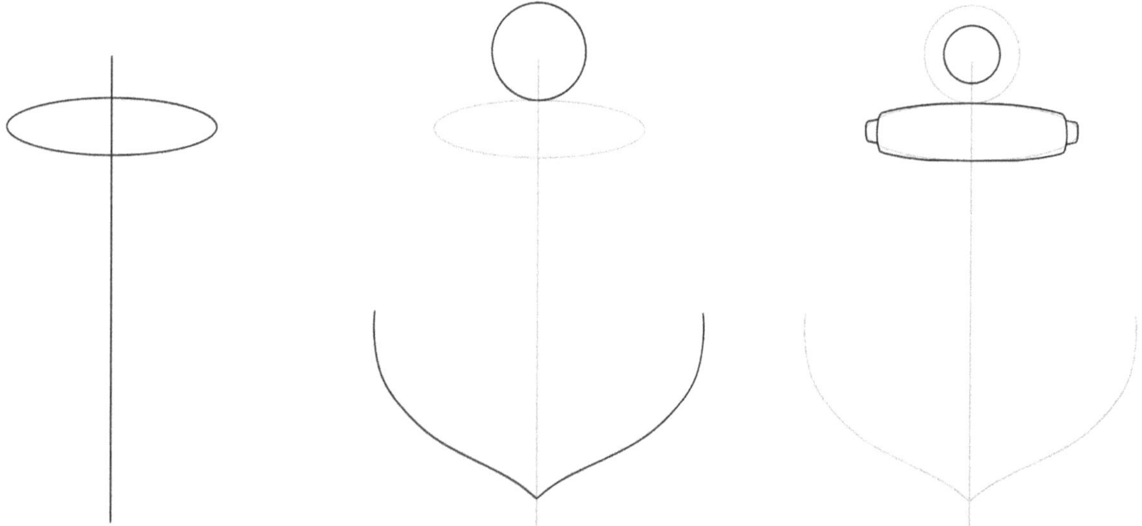

01   02   03

04

05

06

07

08

09

10

11

12

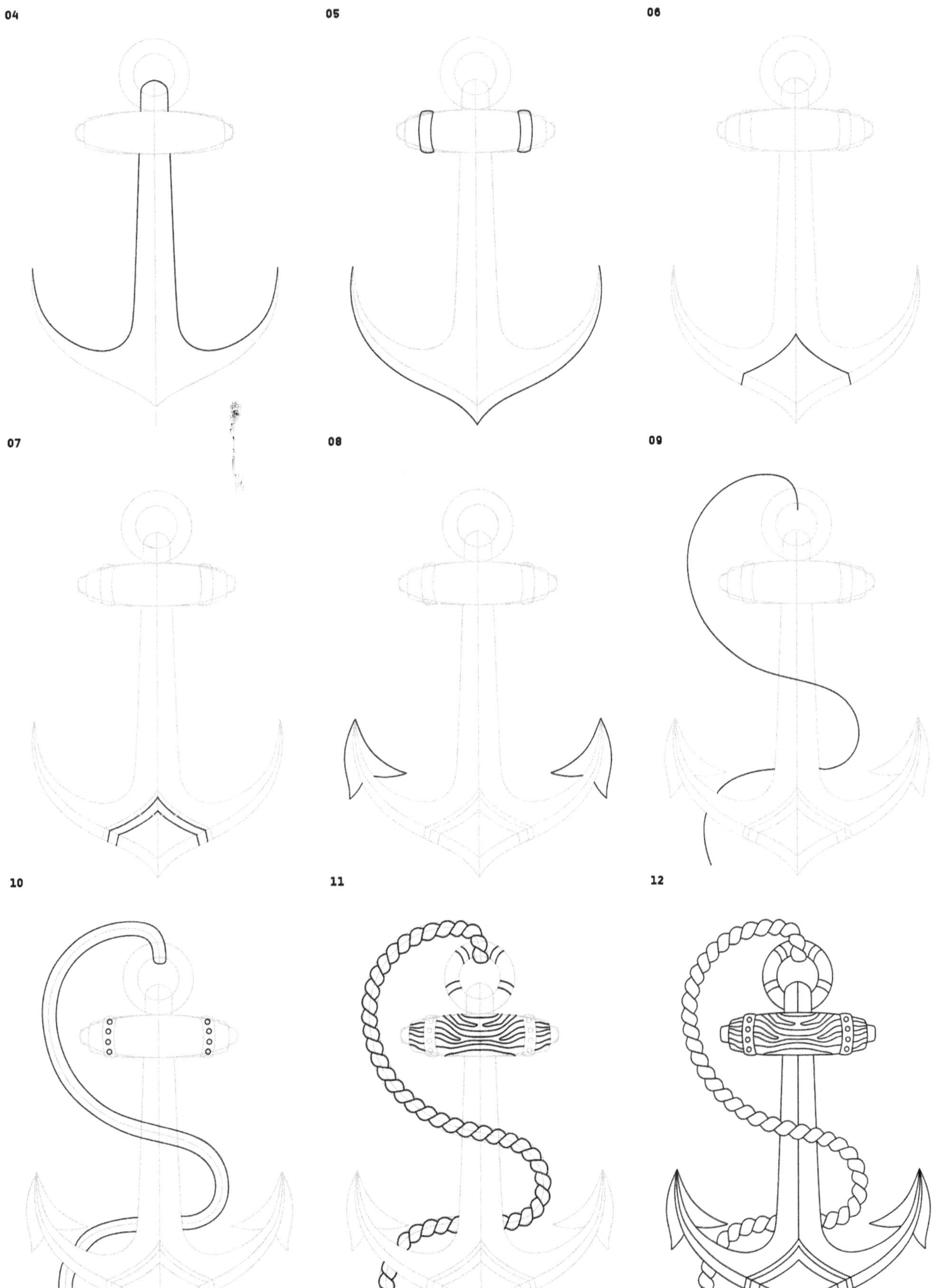

SKULL RACER

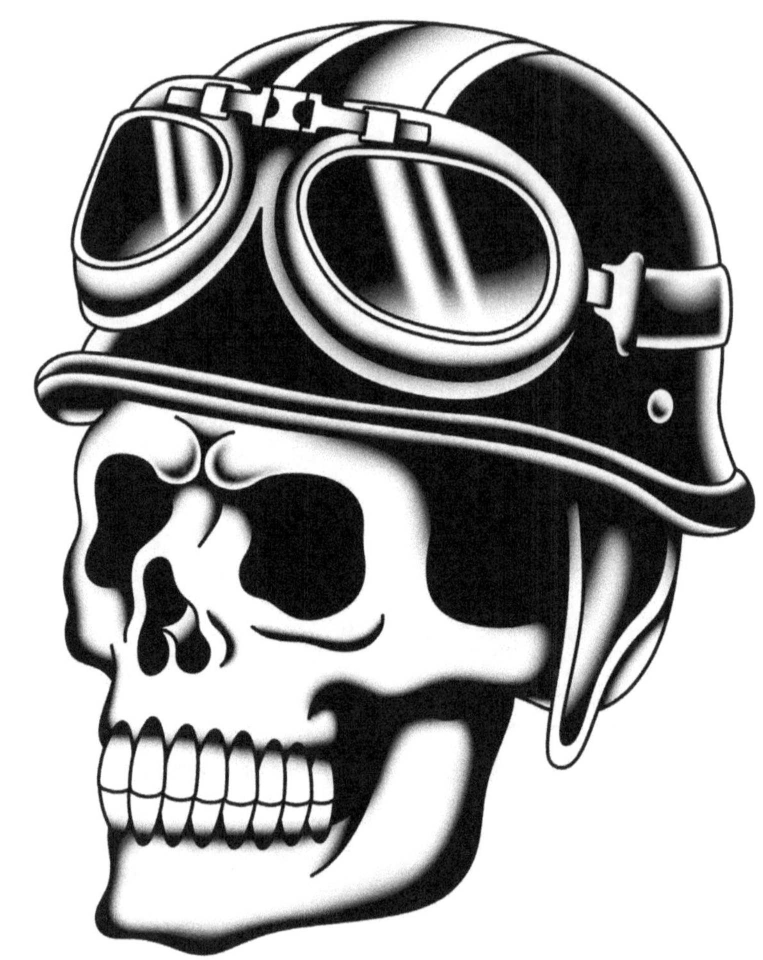

Pro tip: Use the base of the jaw to position the teeth

The placement of the teeth is determined by the jaw shape, not the circle. Draw a horizontal line through the middle of the jaw shape to mark the centre of the tooth row. Sketch evenly spaced ovals along this line to establish the teeth, making sure they sit securely within the jaw's structure. This keeps the teeth correctly anchored and proportioned.

01

02

03

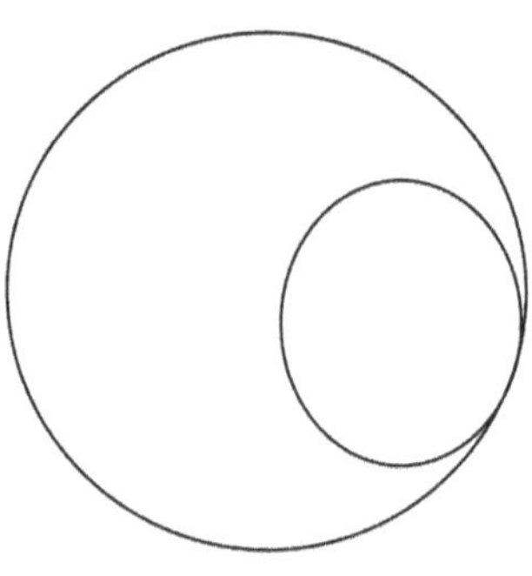

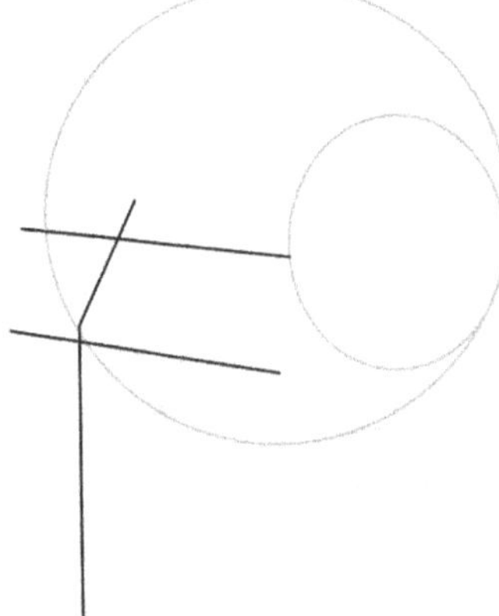

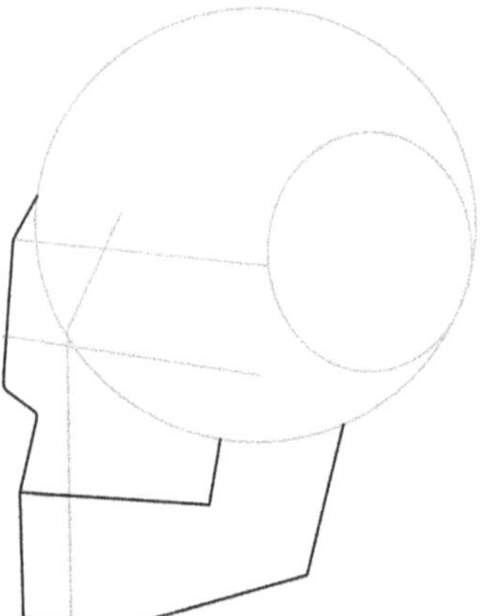

04

05

06

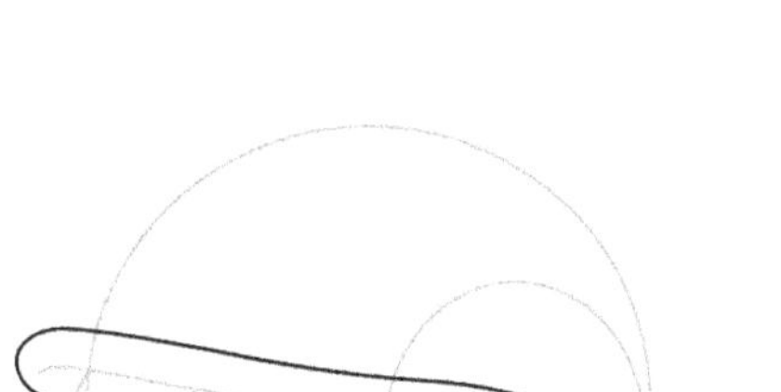

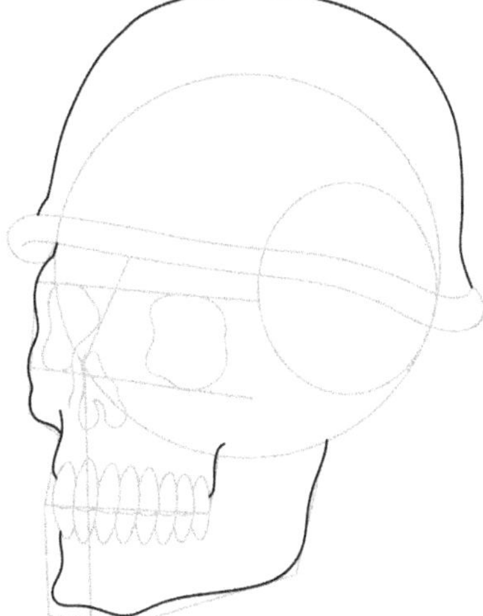

07

08

09

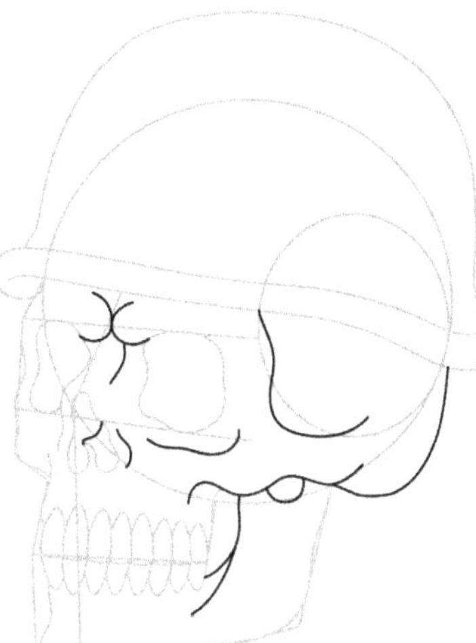

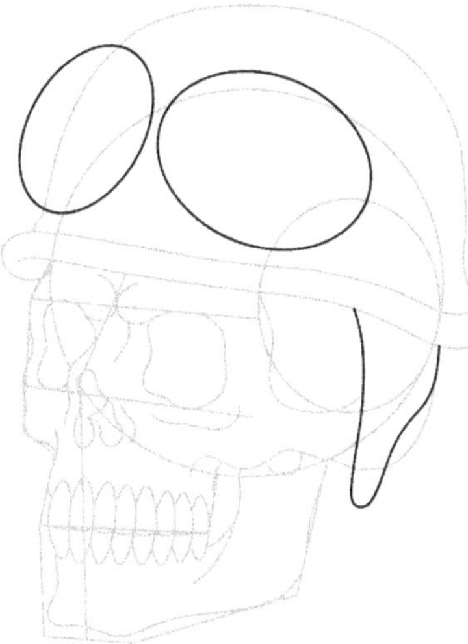

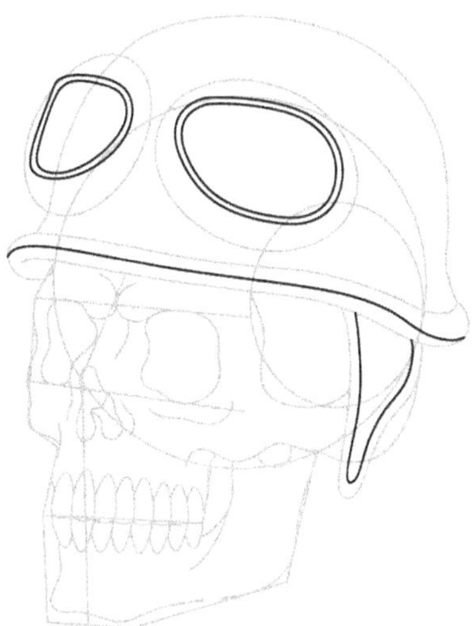

10

11

12

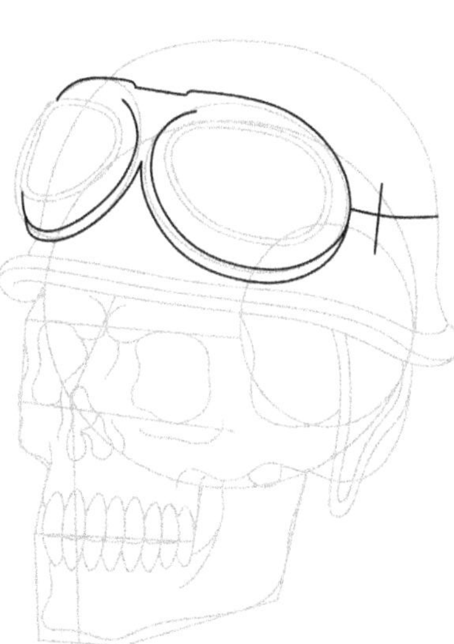

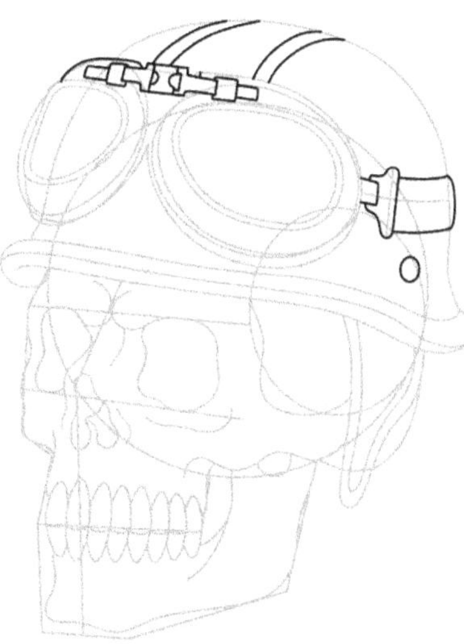

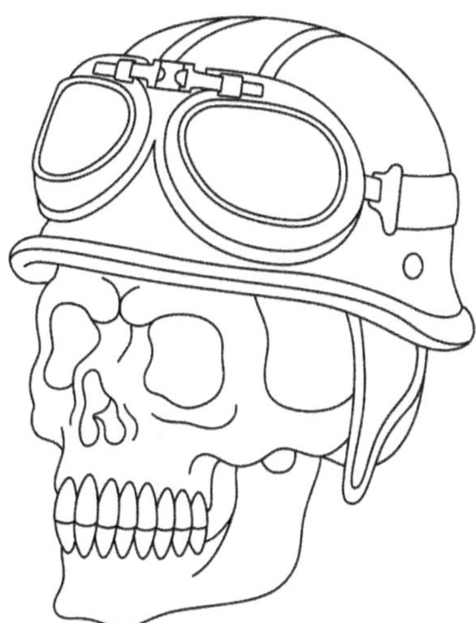

HOW TO DRAW TRADITIONAL TATTOOS

BARBED WIRE

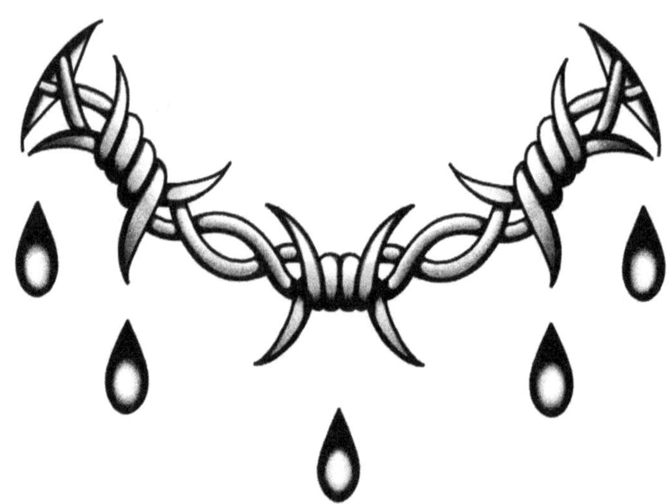

Pro tip: Keep your barbs consistent using the guide curve

Use the main curved guide as your anchor for spacing and symmetry. Each barb should be positioned evenly along this curve, mirroring the tilt and distance of the others. This ensures the wire flows naturally and keeps the twist pattern tight and believable across the design.

01

02

03

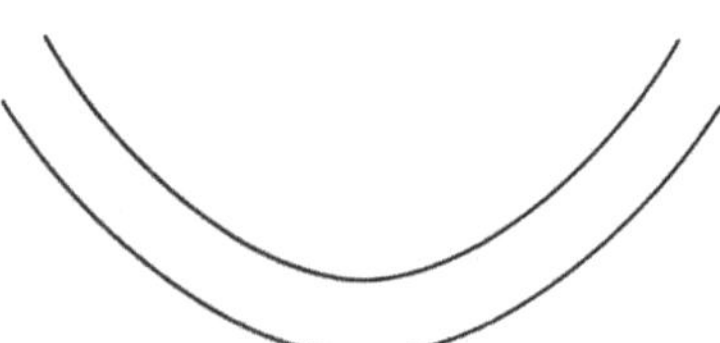

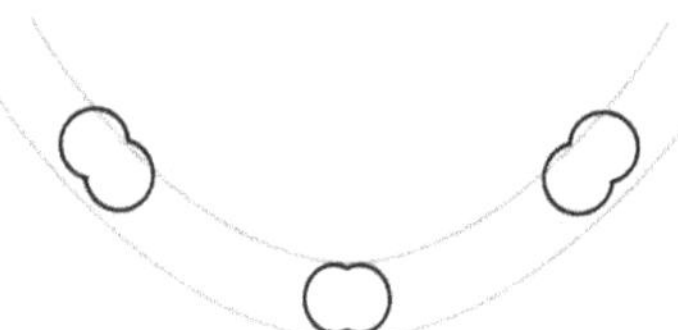

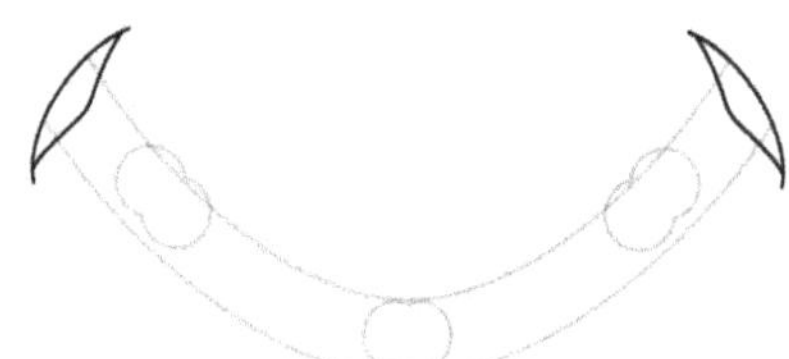

04

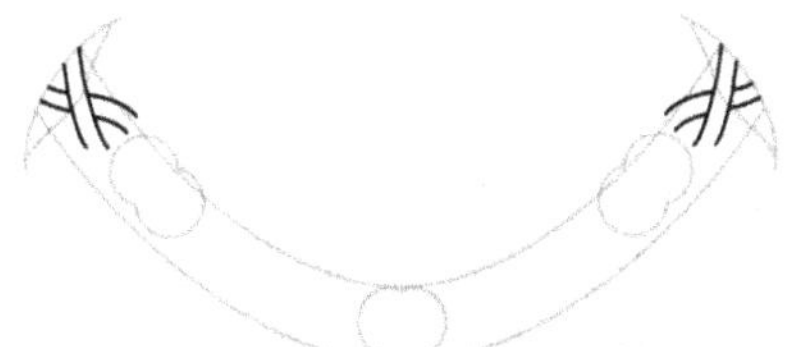

05

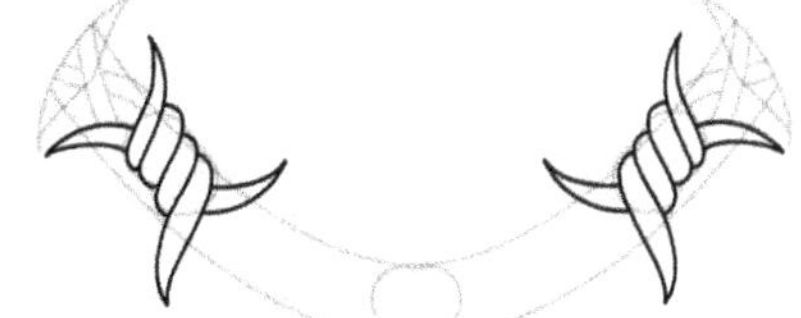

06

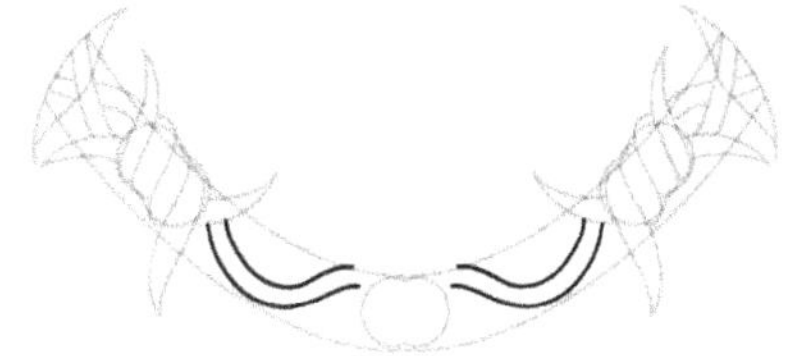

07

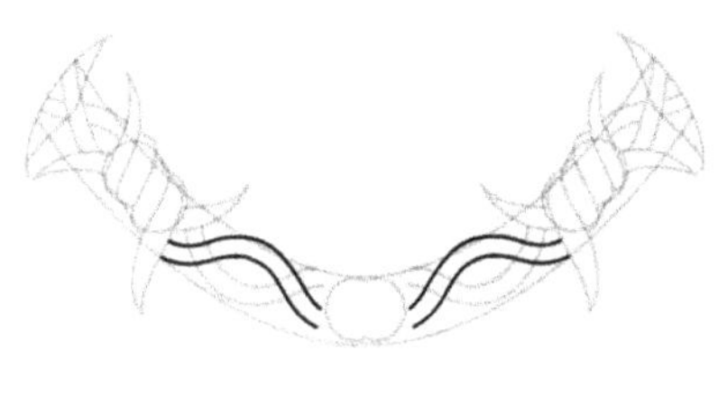

08

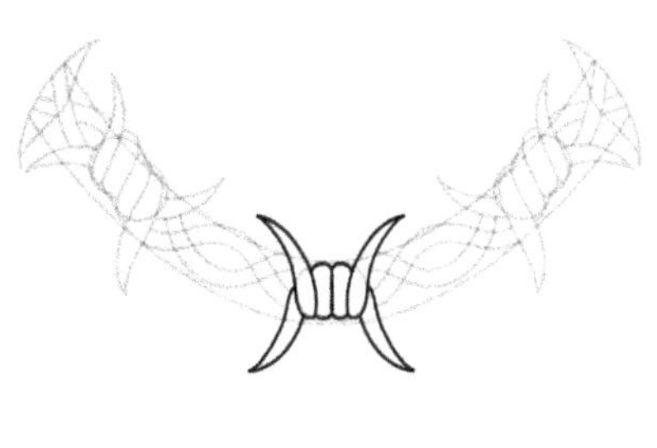

09

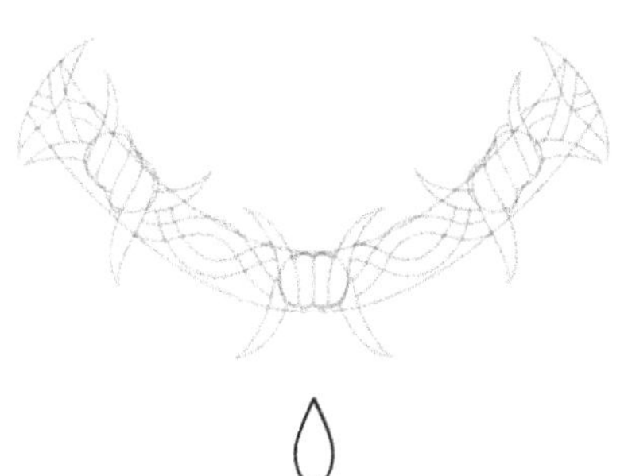

10

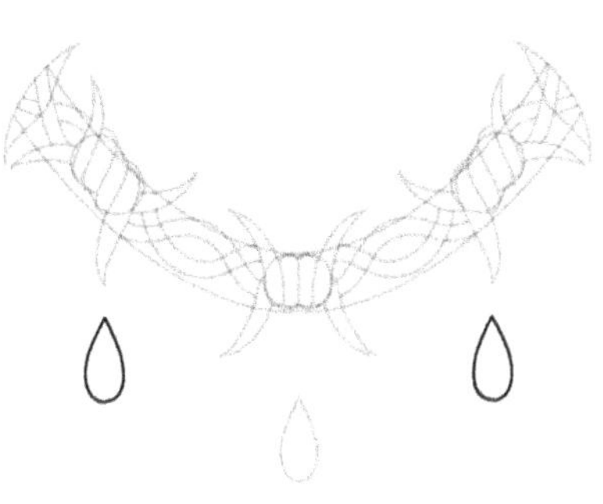

11

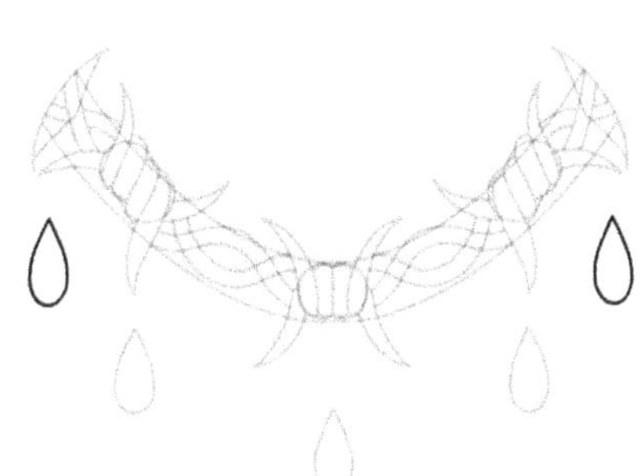

12

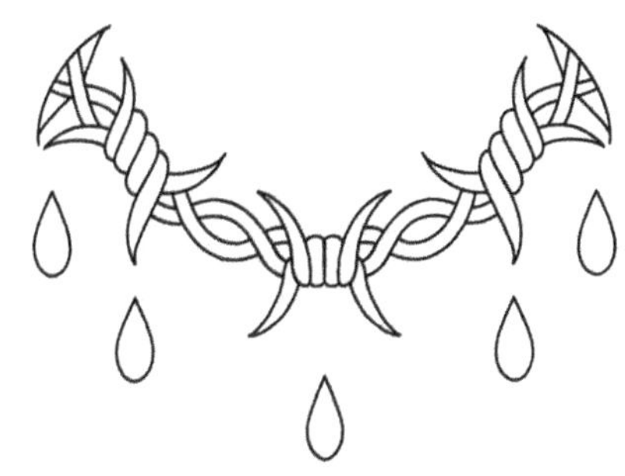

APE & SNAKE

Pro Tip: Use the main circle to align the snake and ape

Use the large head circle as your anchor point for the composition. The snake should wrap naturally around this shape, following its curve to create balance and rhythm. Keep the snake's body thickness consistent relative to the circle, and ensure its flow leads the viewer's eye toward the ape's face.

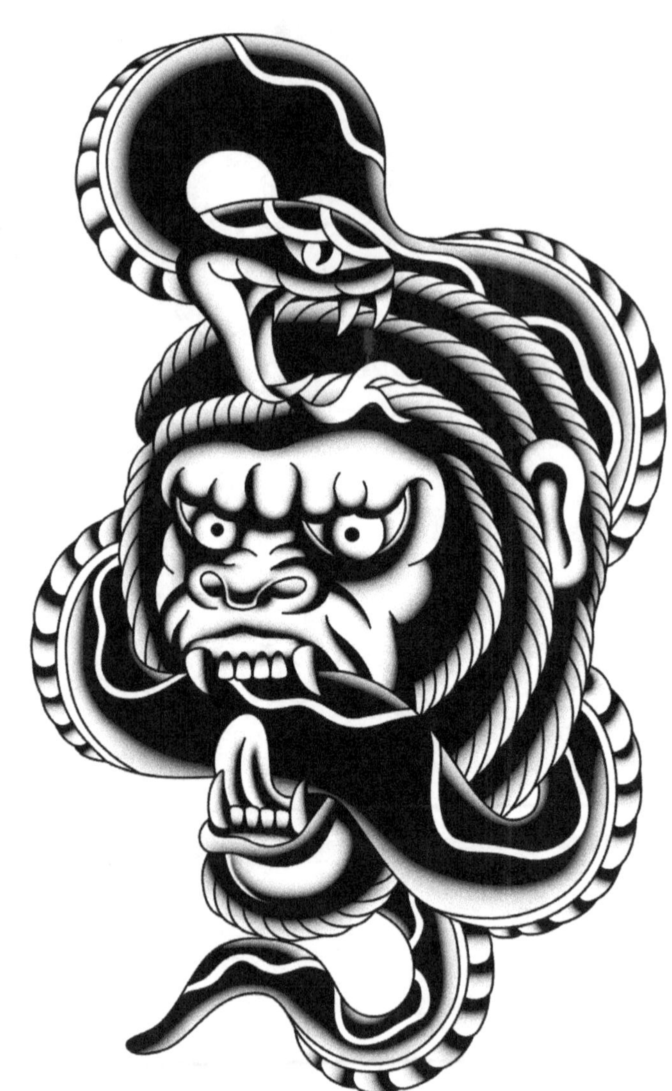

01

02

03

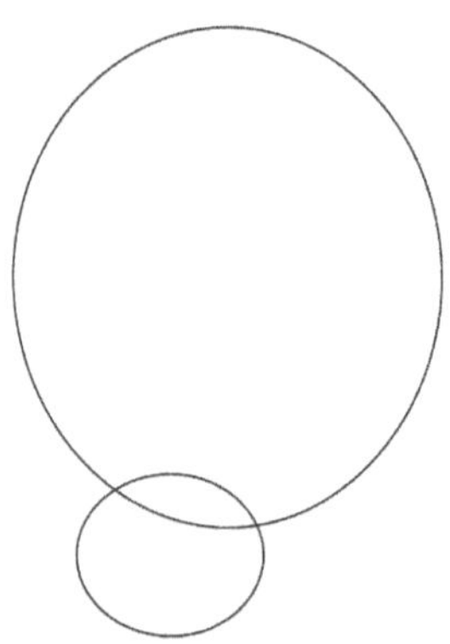

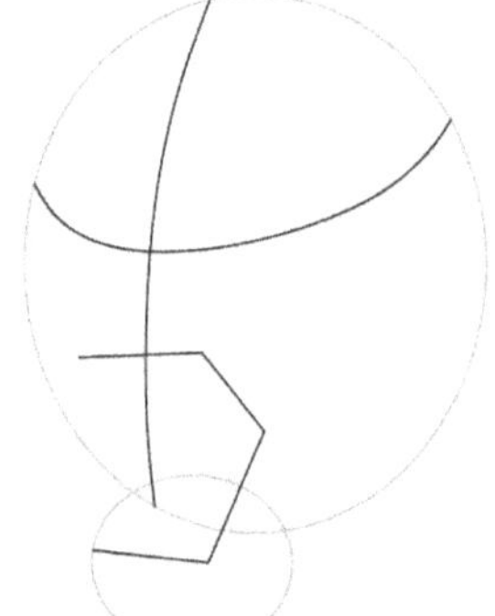

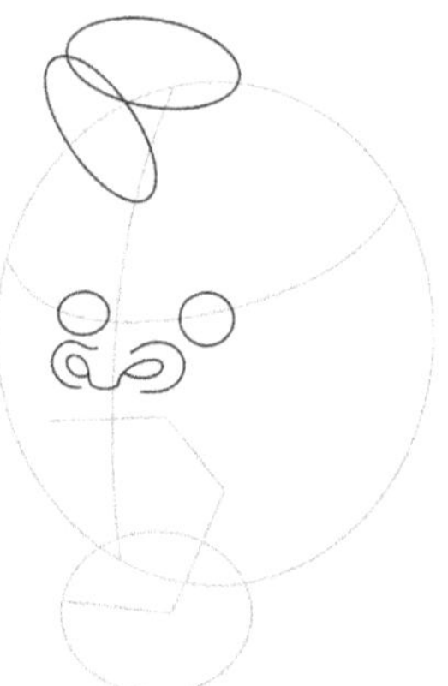

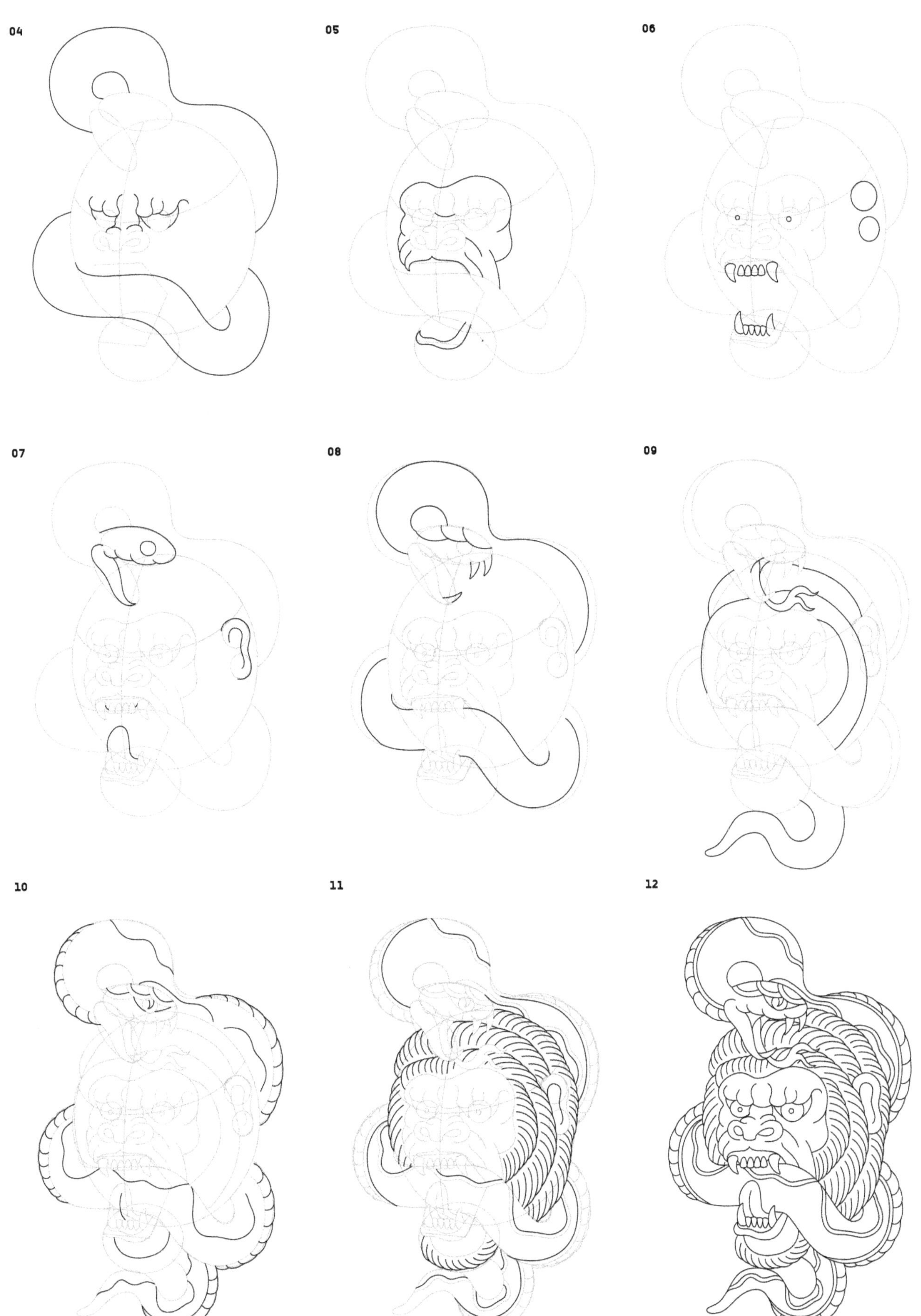

DEVIL & SKULL

Pro tip: Use halves to position the nose and mouth

Draw a horizontal line halfway down the lower section of the head to mark the position of the mouth. Then divide the space between the top of the bottom section and the mouth line in half again. The bottom of the nose should sit on this halfway mark, giving you accurate and proportional placement for both features.

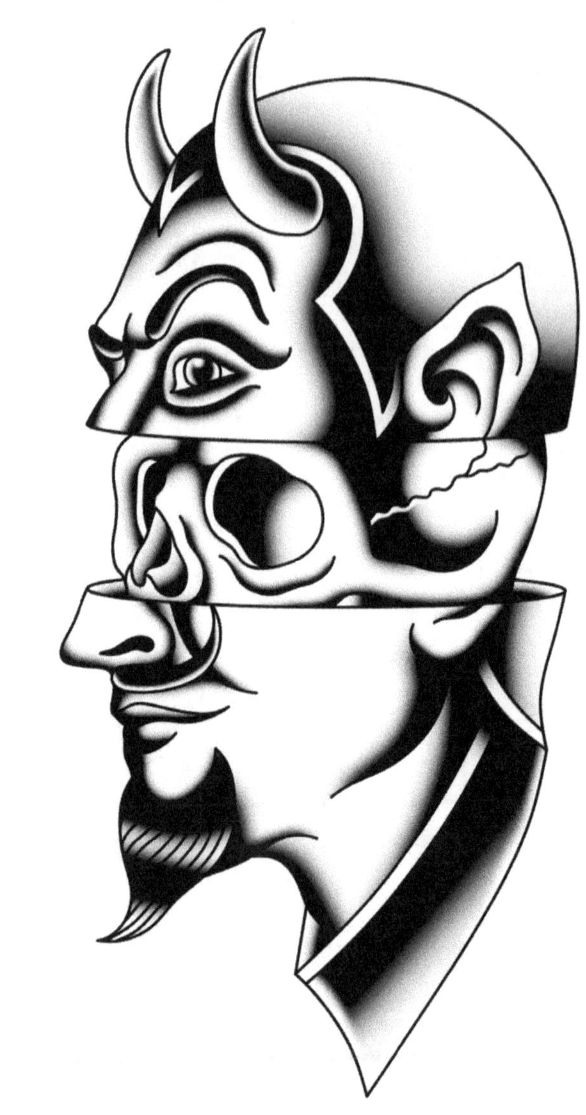

01

02

03

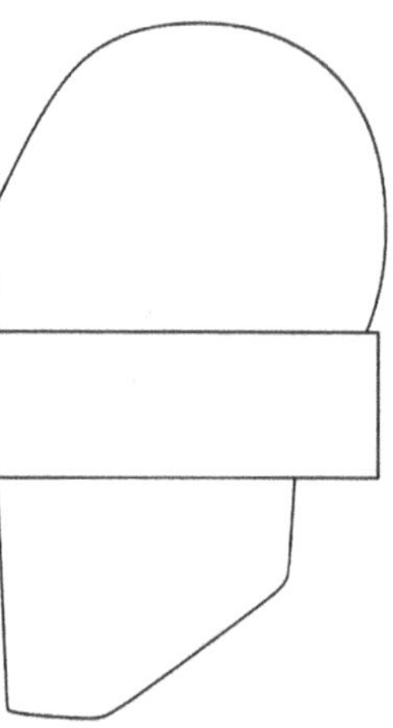

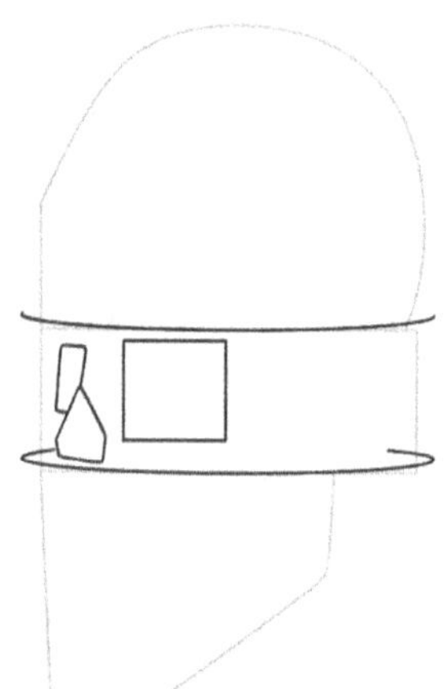

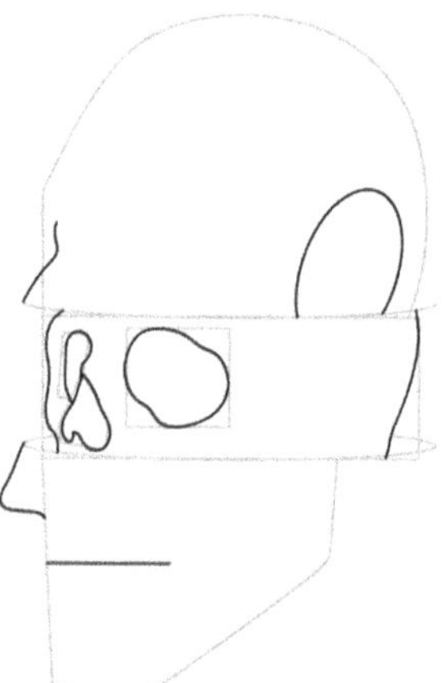

04

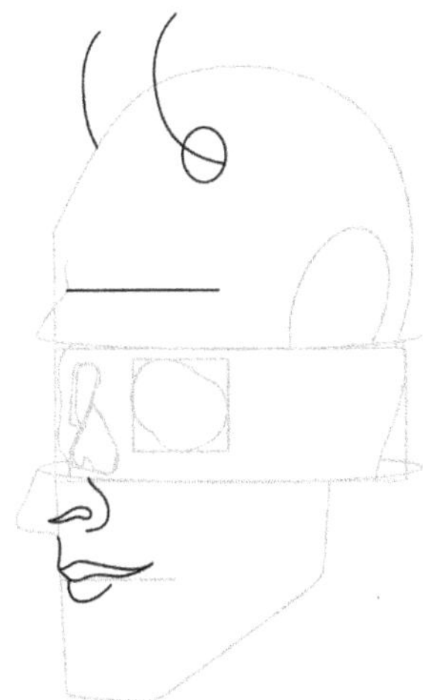

05

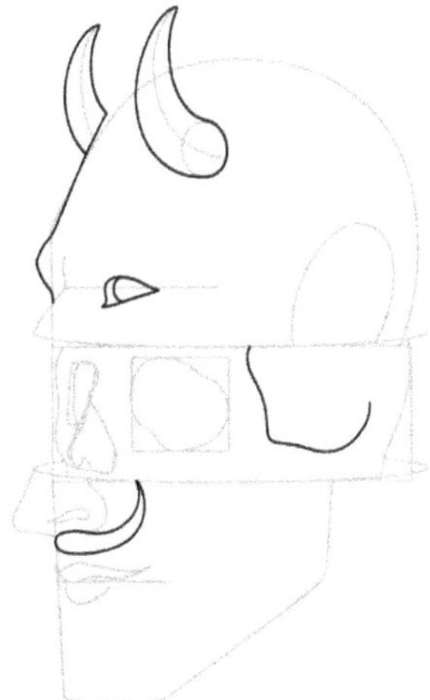

06

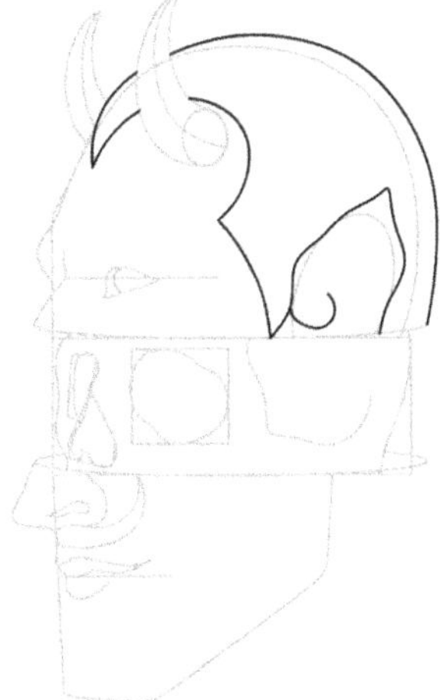

07

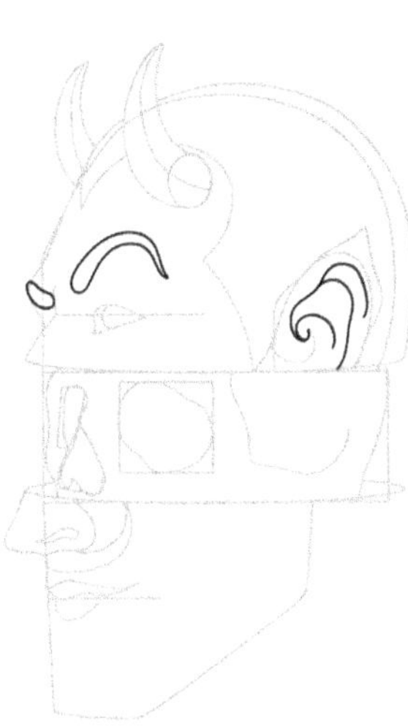

08

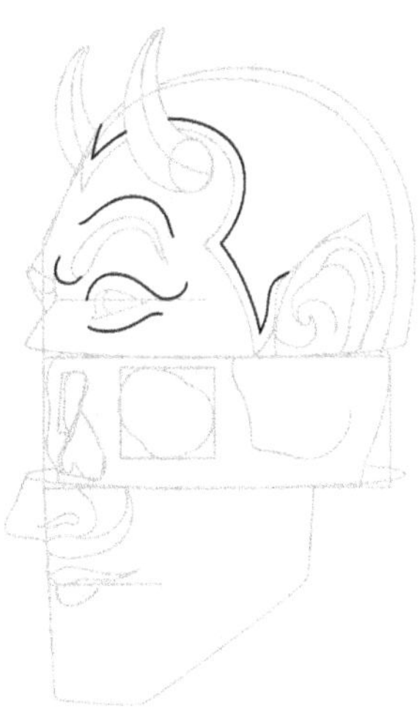

09

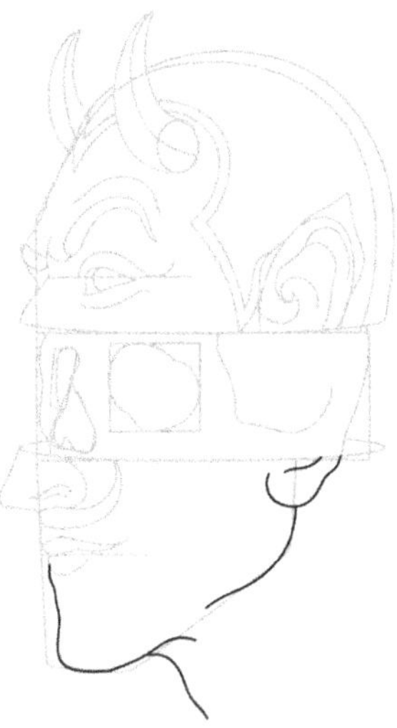

10

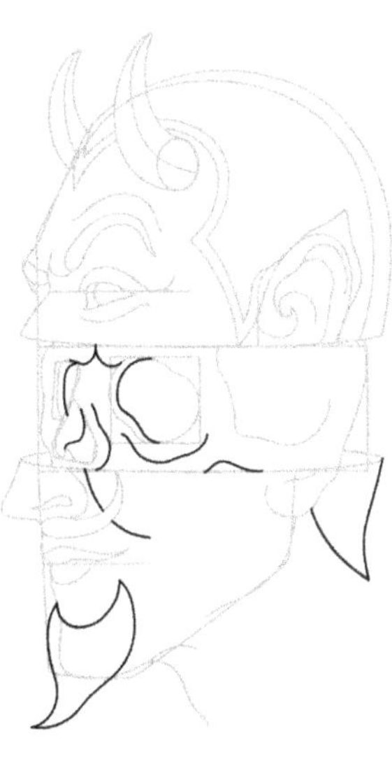

11

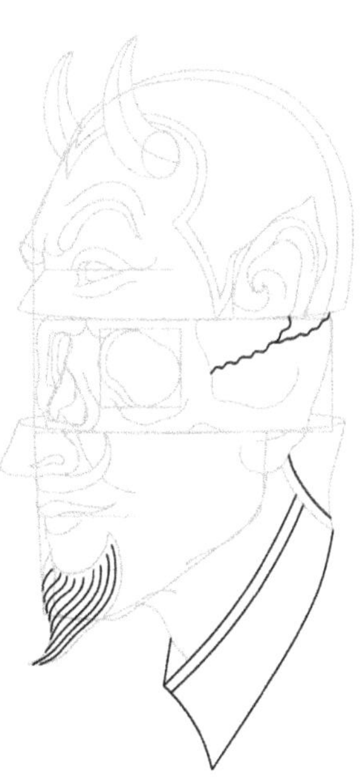

12

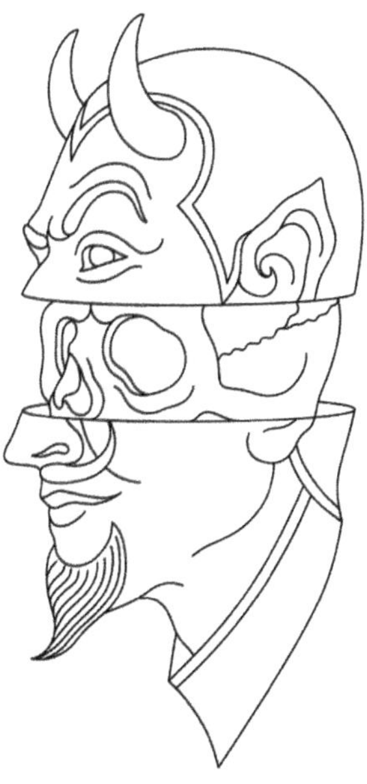

SKULL IN COFFIN

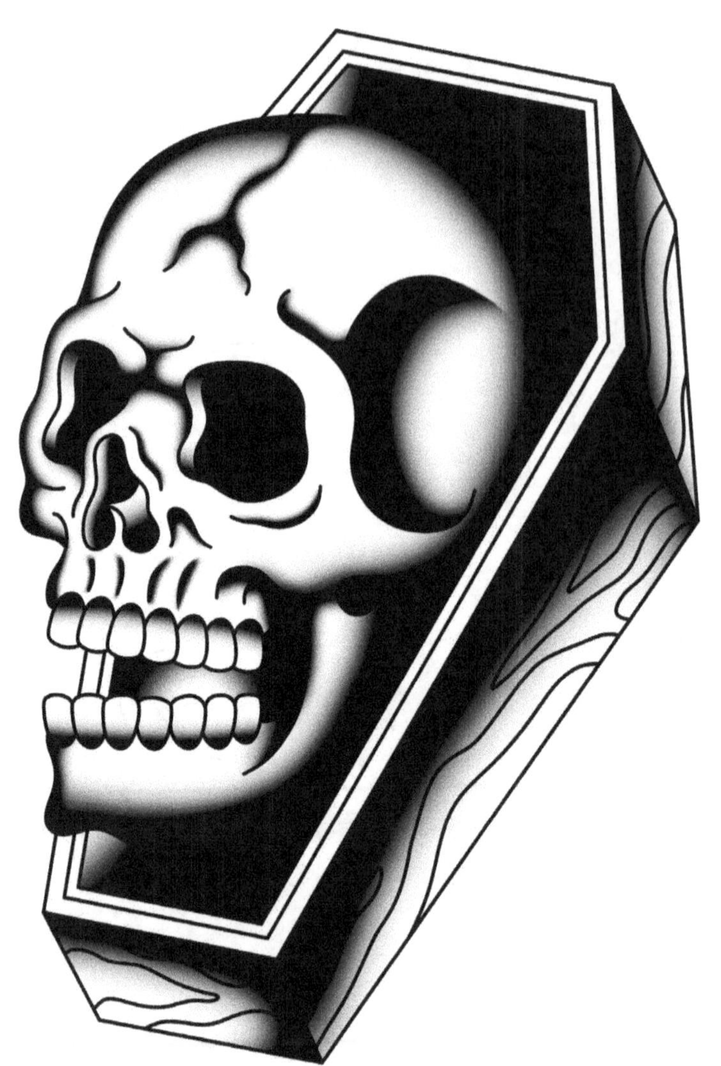

Pro tip: Centre the skull within the coffin for balance

To position the skull accurately, place it centrally within the upper third of the coffin shape. The base of the skull should sit just above the horizontal line that defines the coffin lid, ensuring the circle of the cranium overlaps the coffin's edges slightly so it appears to be emerging.

01

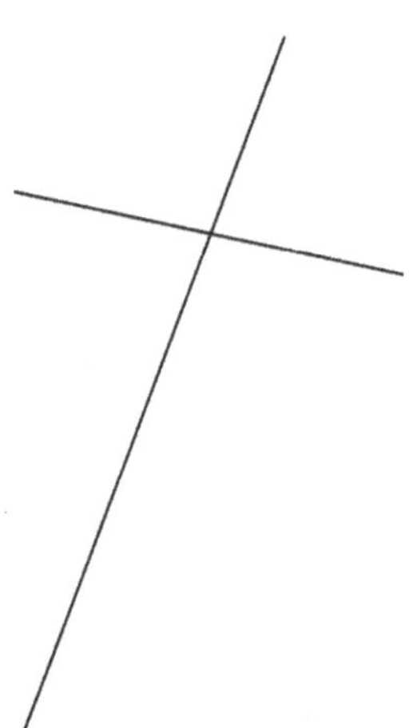

02

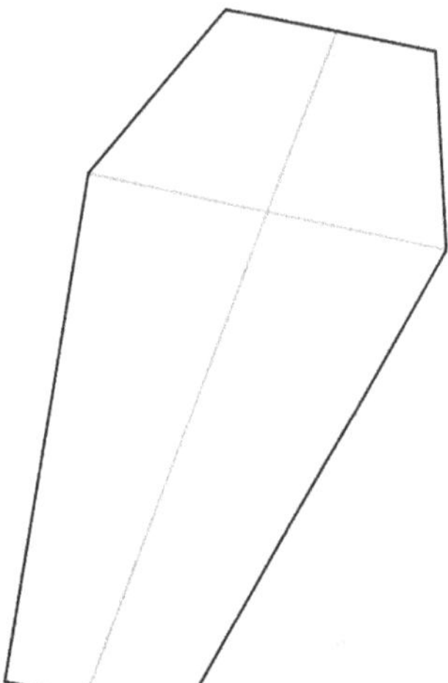

03

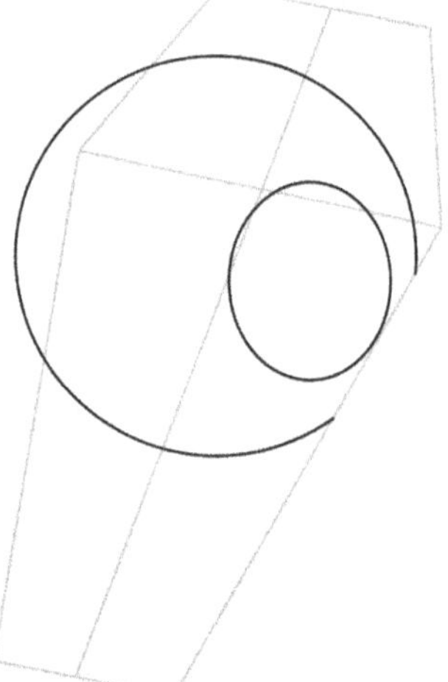

04

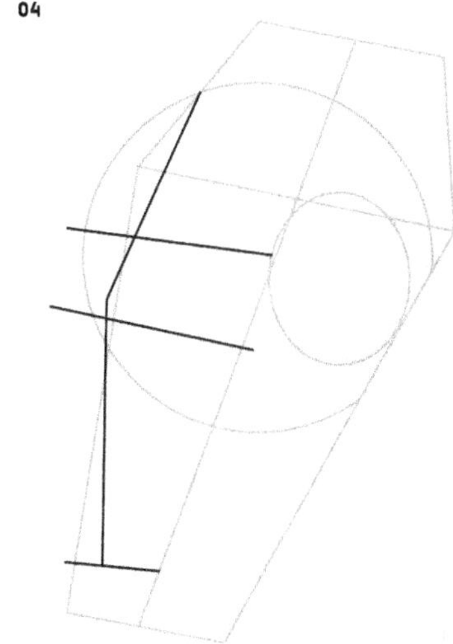

05

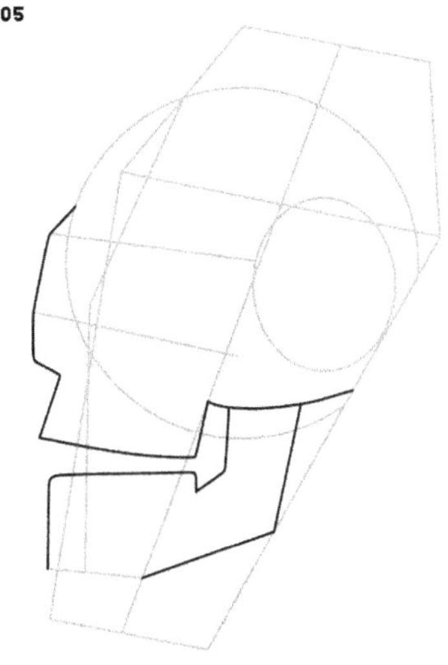

06

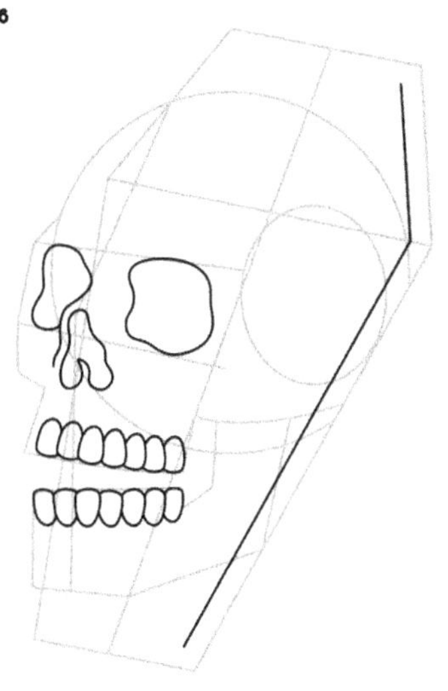

07

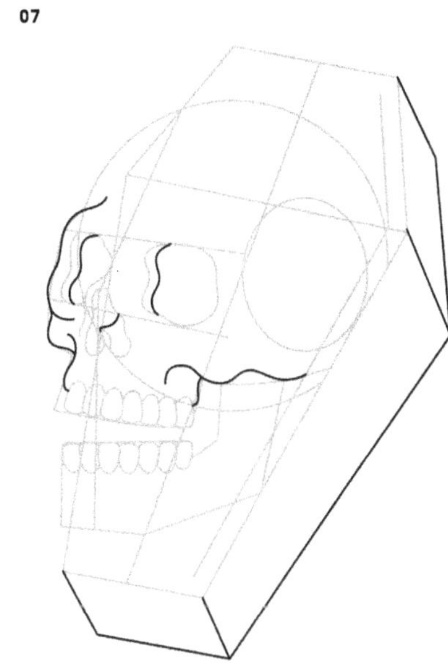

08

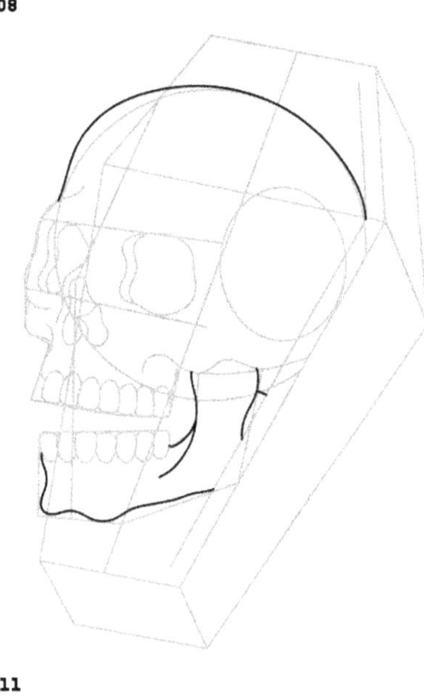

09

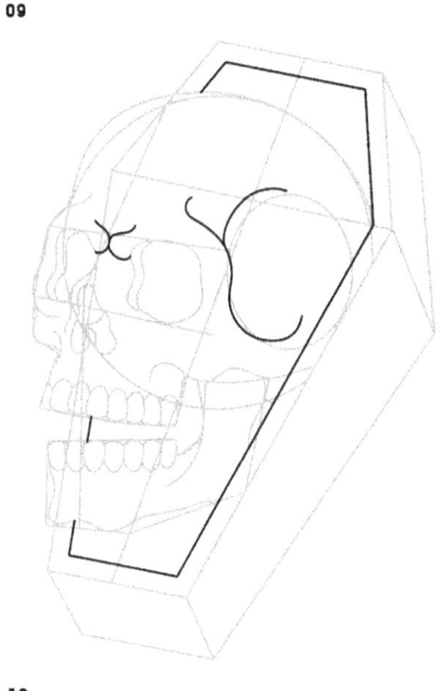

10

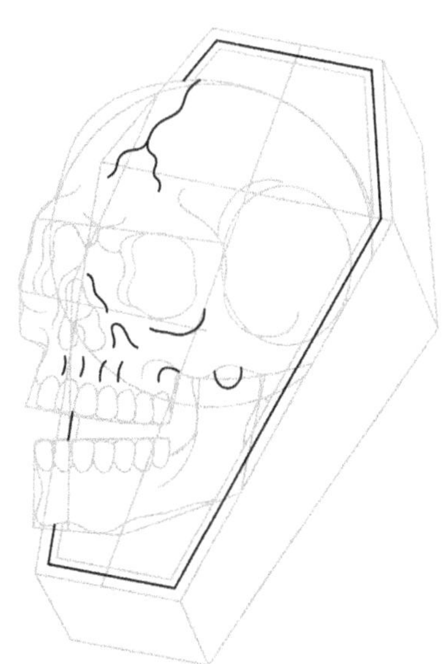

11

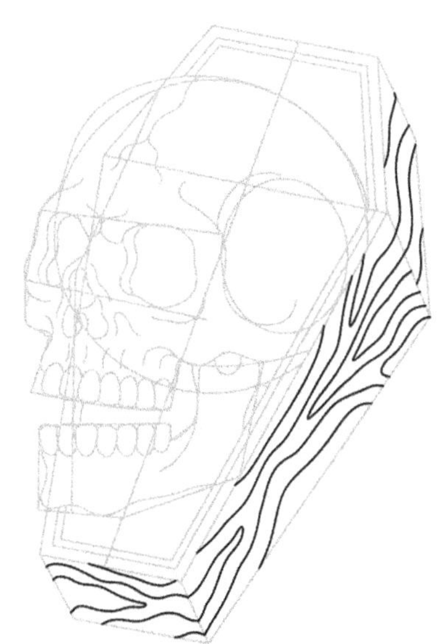

12

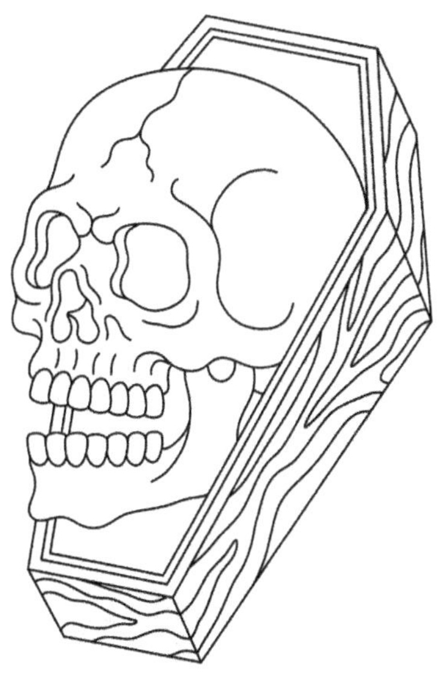

HOW TO DRAW TRADITIONAL TATTOOS

EAGLE & SNAKE

Pro tip: Use the snake's curve to lead the composition

Position the snake so that its body weaves naturally through the eagle's wings and body. Start the curve from the upper wing area, looping behind and around the eagle's torso before extending out. The tail should balance the composition by echoing the wing shapes without overwhelming them.

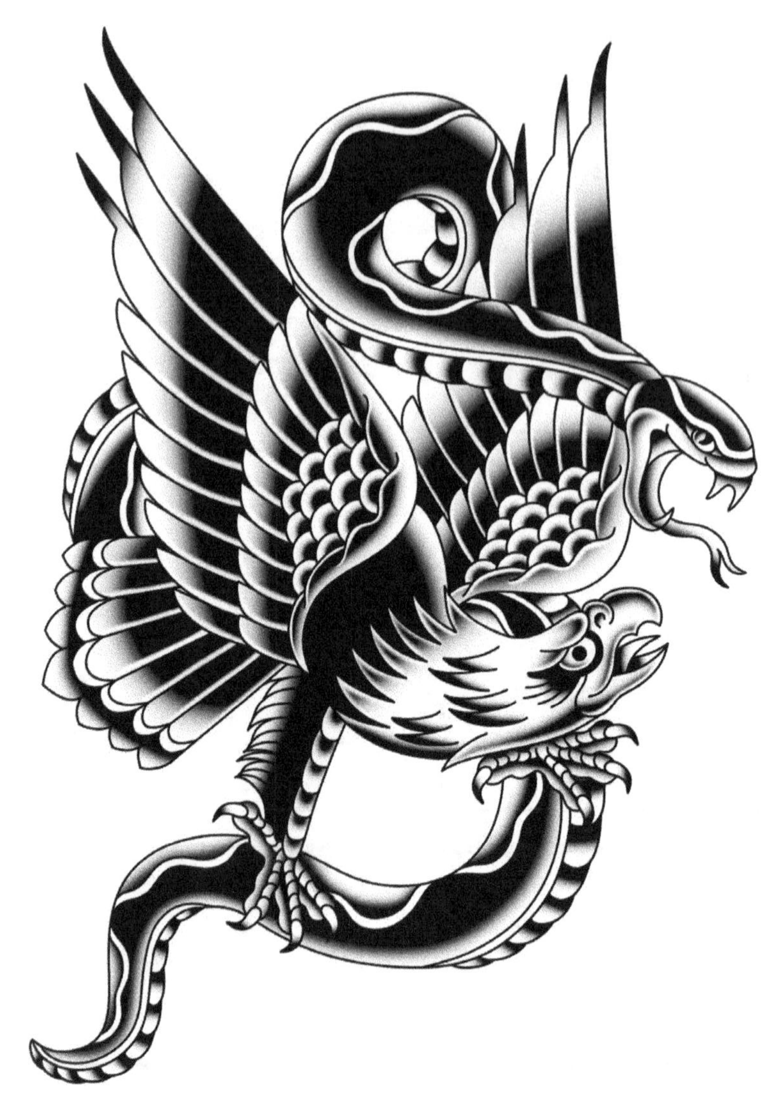

01

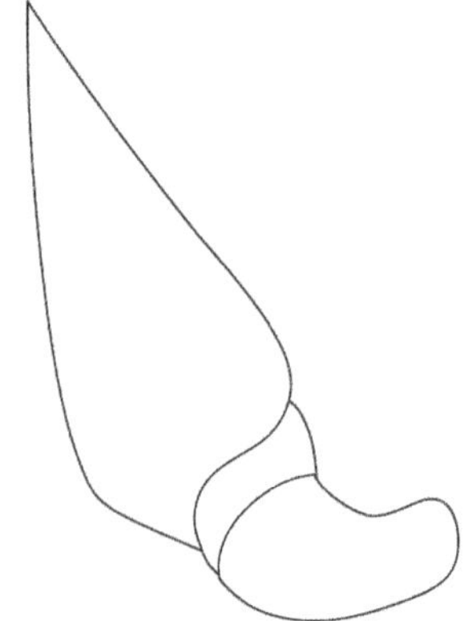

02

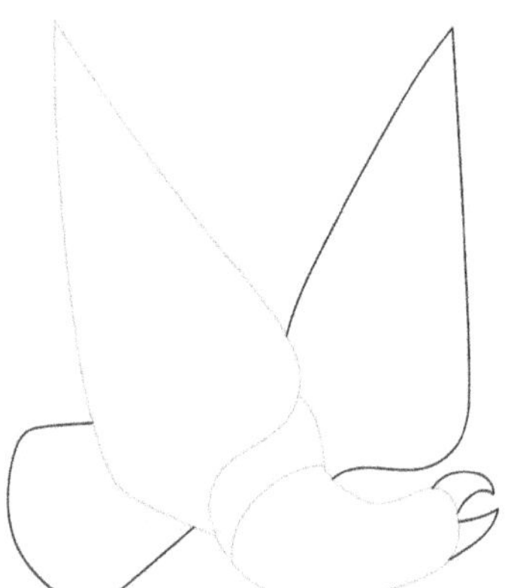

03

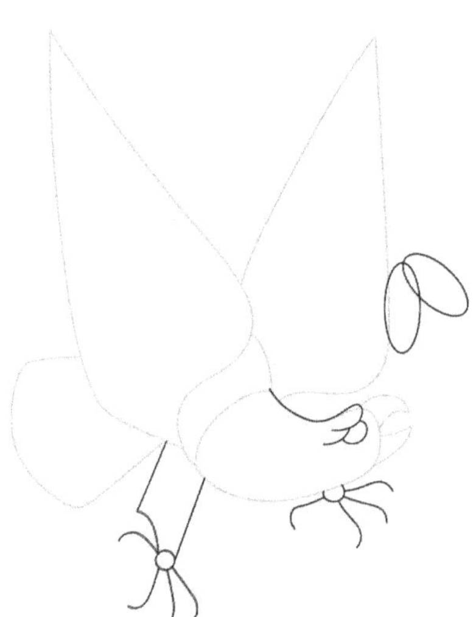

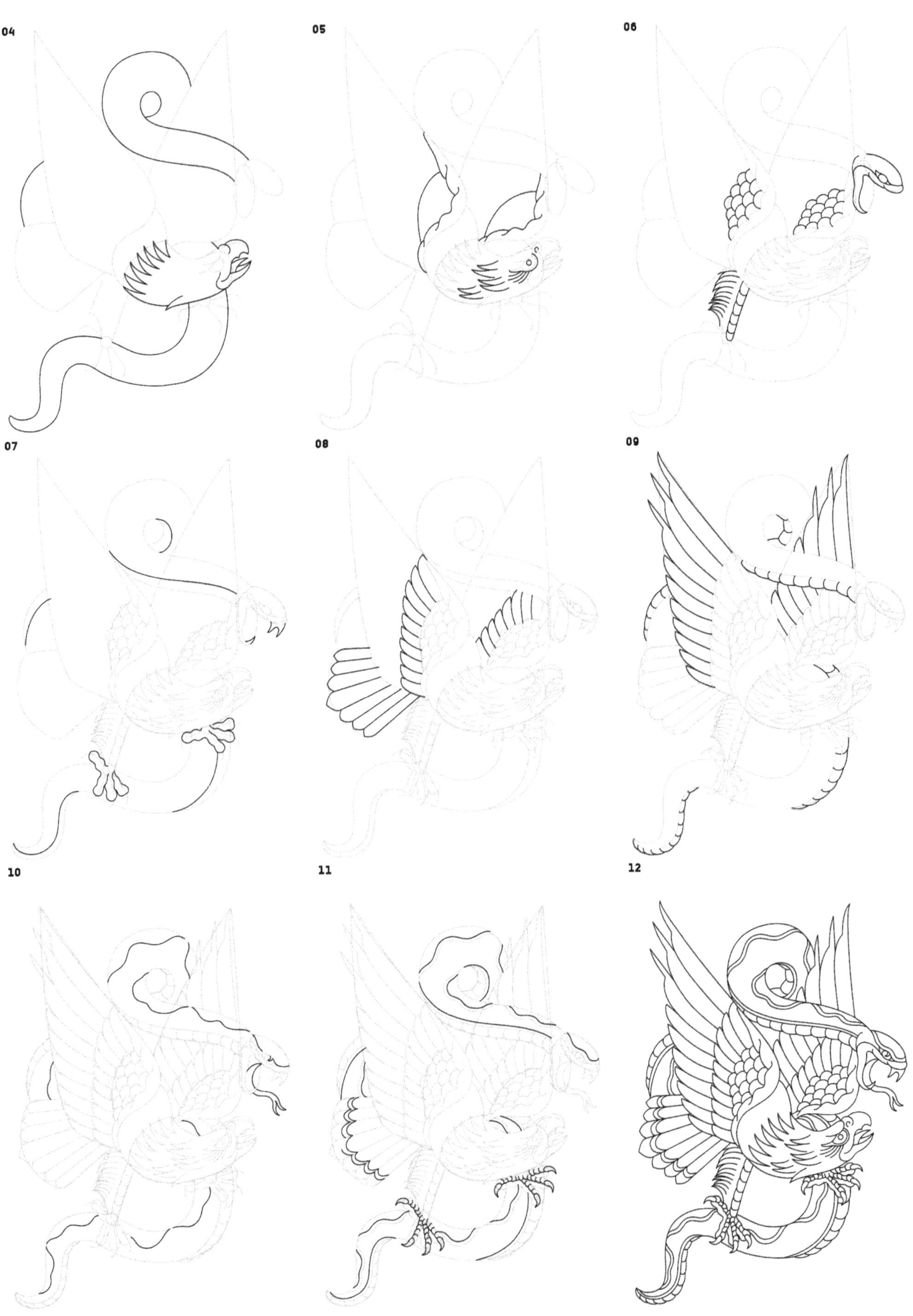
04
05
06
07
08
09
10
11
12
HOW TO DRAW TRADITIONAL TATTOOS

EAGLE & DAGGER

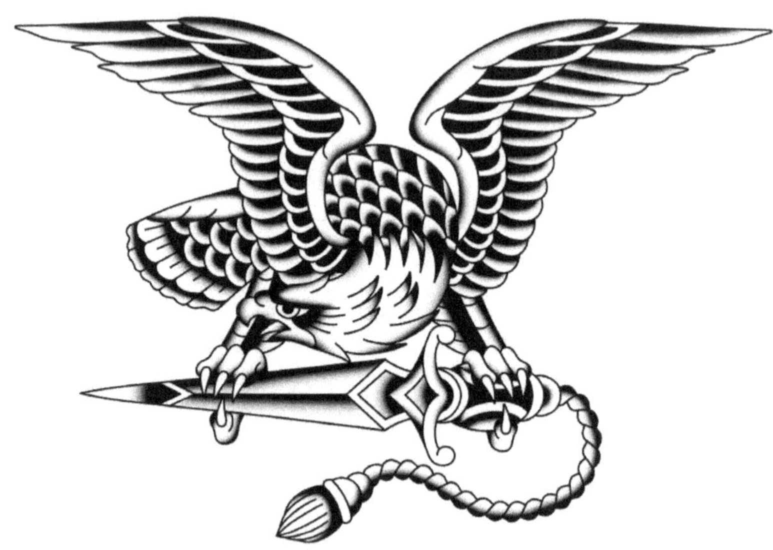

Pro tip: Use crosshatching to map the scale pattern

Crosshatch the eagle's back with diagonal lines to establish a clear guide for the scale pattern. Start by laying one set of lines that follow the curve of the back, then add a second set in the opposite direction to form a neat grid. This structure helps keep each scale uniform in size and evenly aligned, ensuring the finished pattern flows naturally with the body's form.

01

02

03

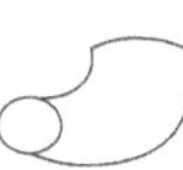

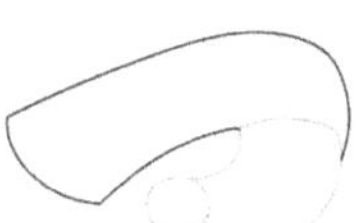

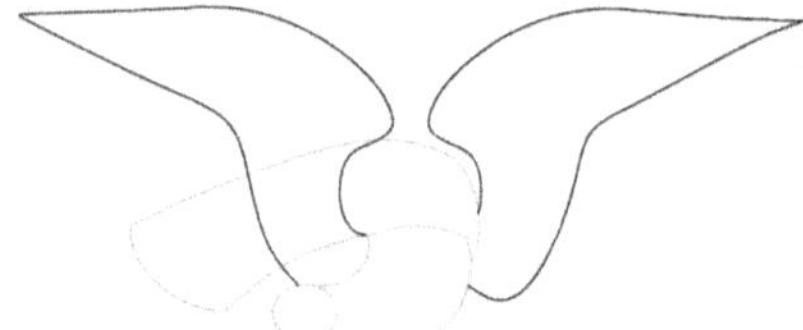

04

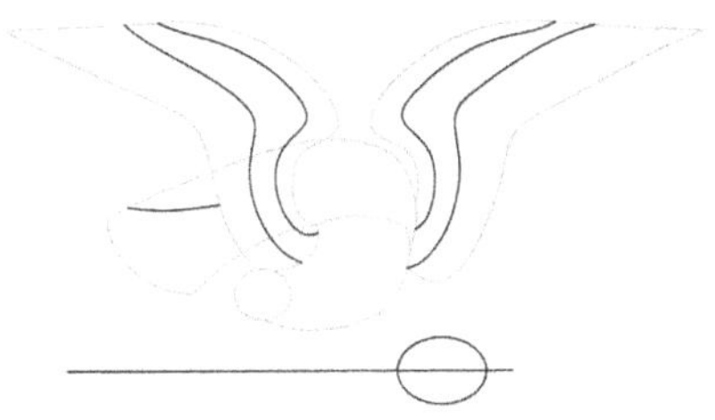

05

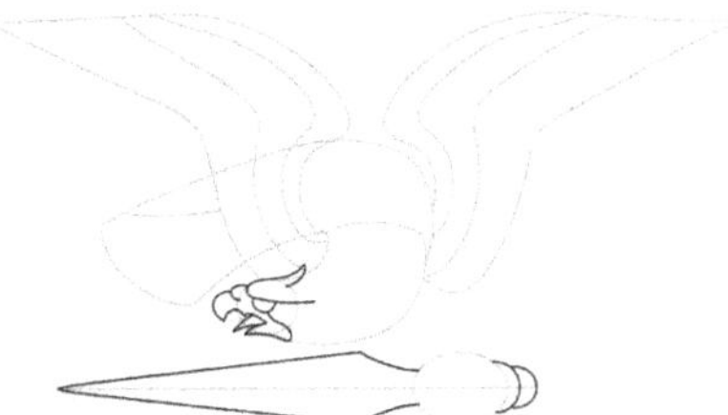

06

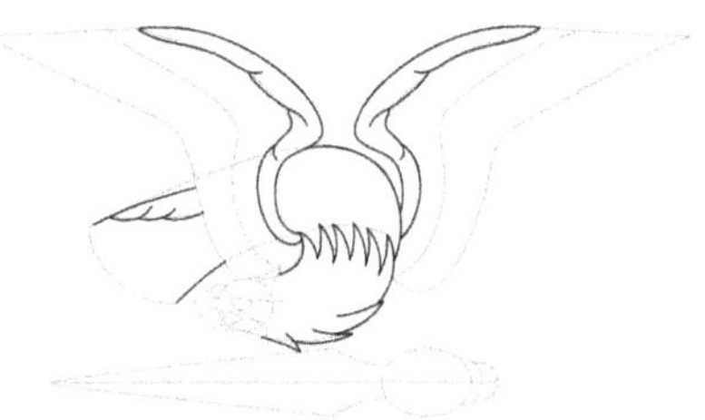

07

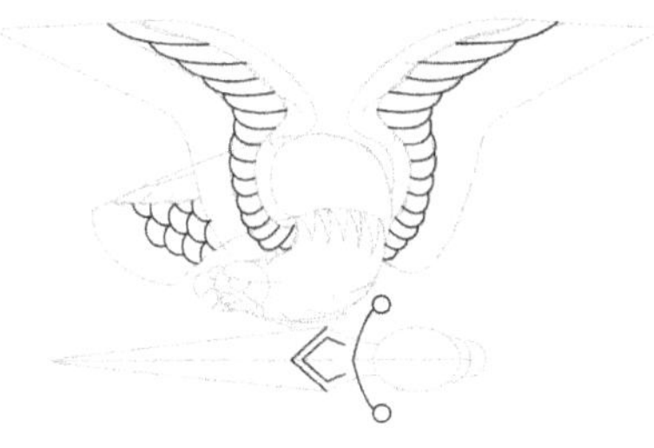

08

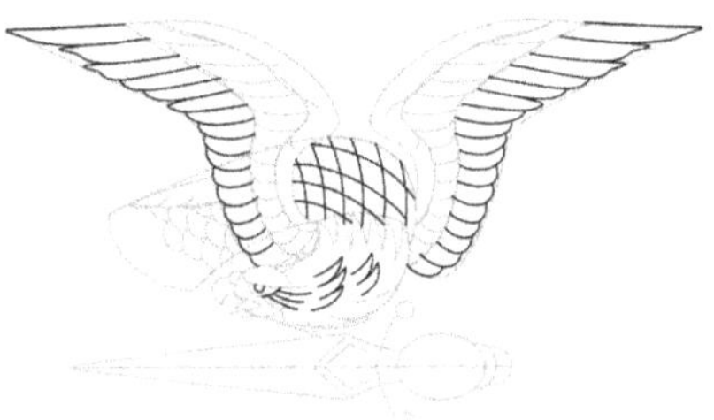

09

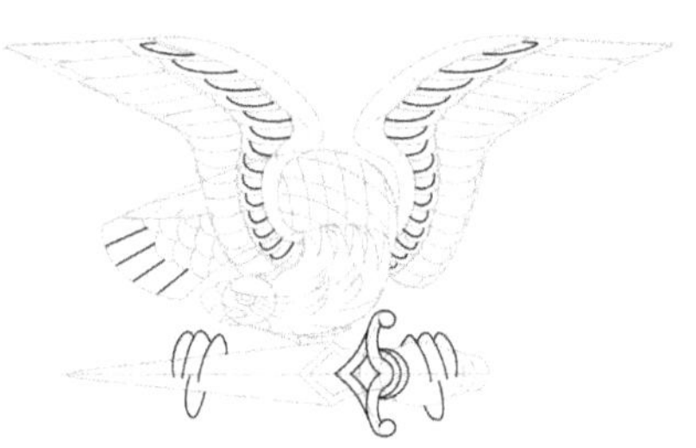

10

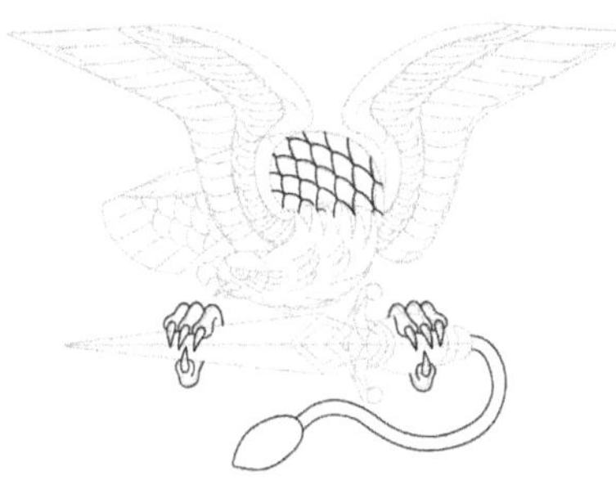

11

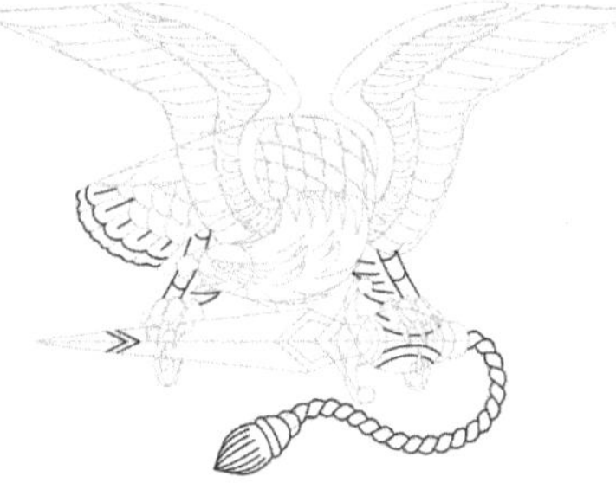

12

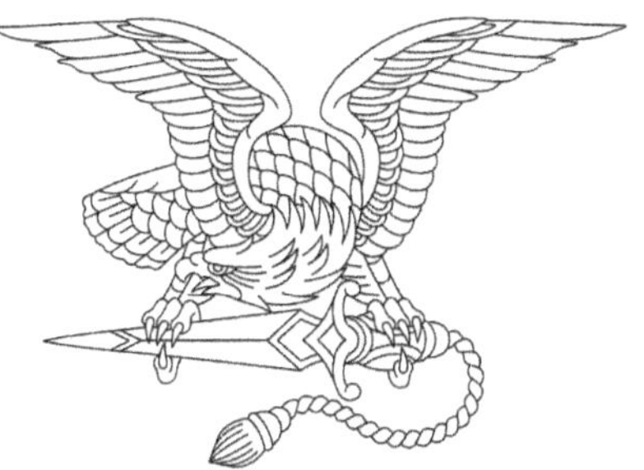

EASTERN DRAGON

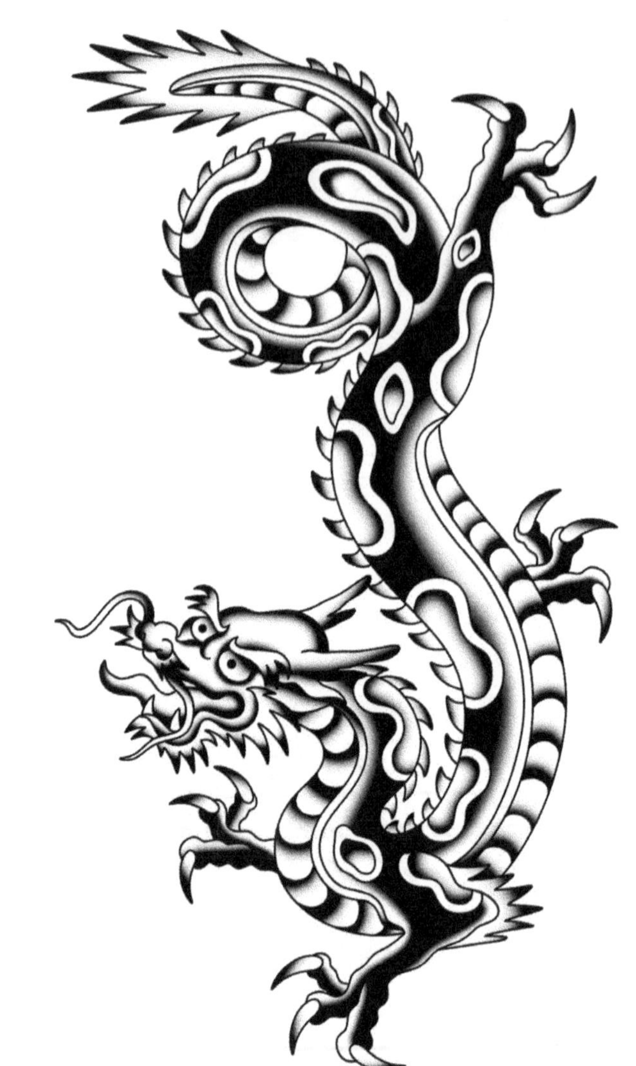

Pro Tip: Building the Dragon's Body Curve

Use the head as your anchor, then draw the main body line so it sweeps upward and away before curving back down. This long, fluid motion gives the dragon its characteristic elegance and sense of movement. Keep the curve wide and balanced—avoid tight loops at this stage to maintain a natural, flowing rhythm through the body.

01

02

03

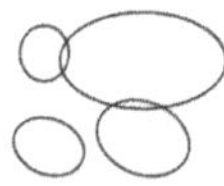

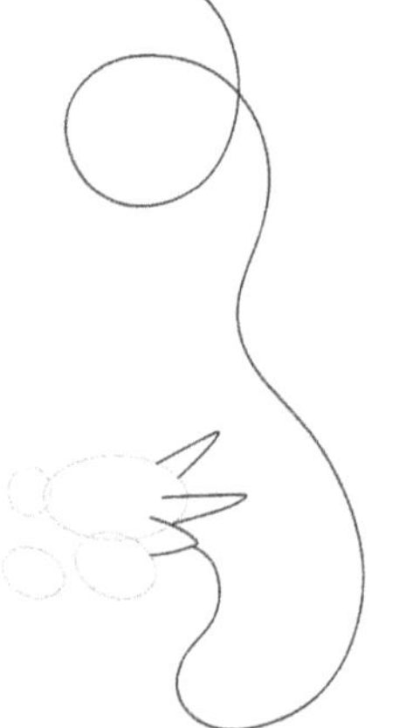

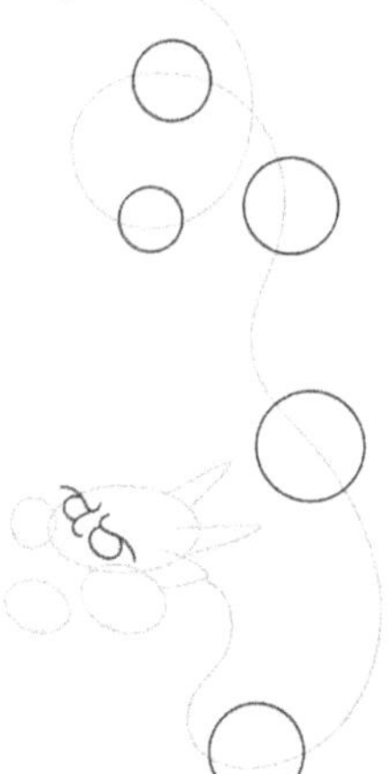

04

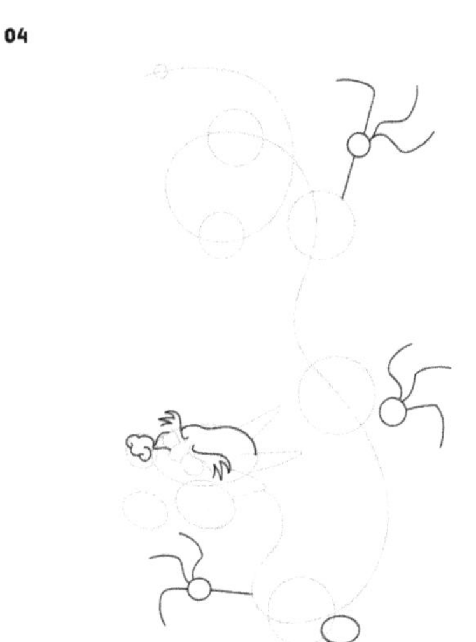

05

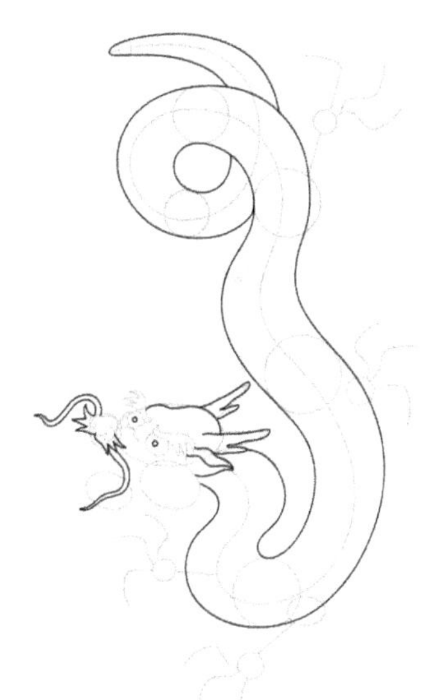

06

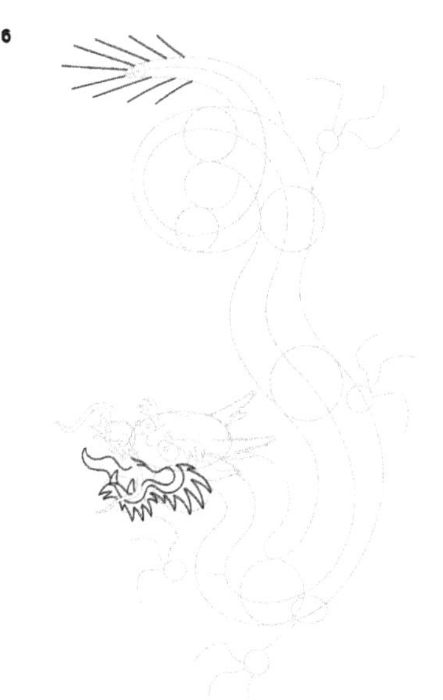

07

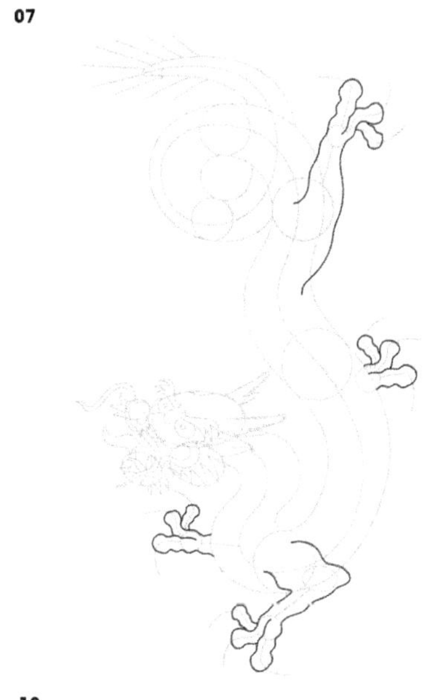

08

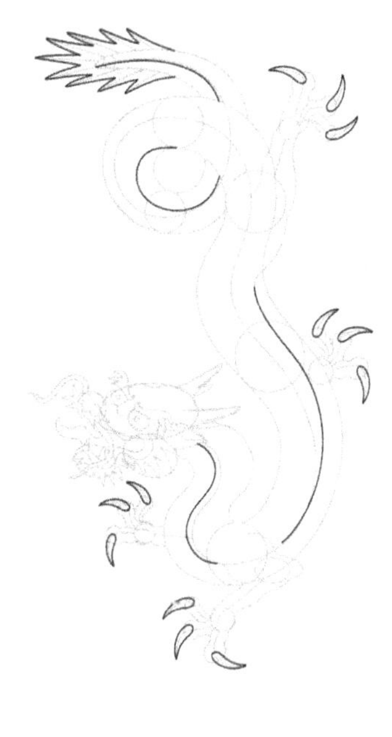

09

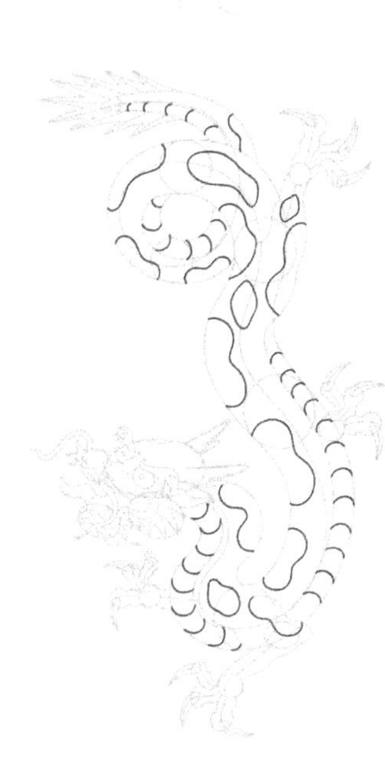

10

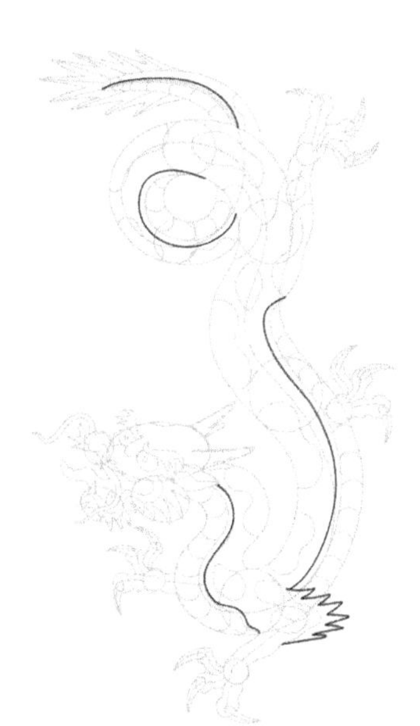

11

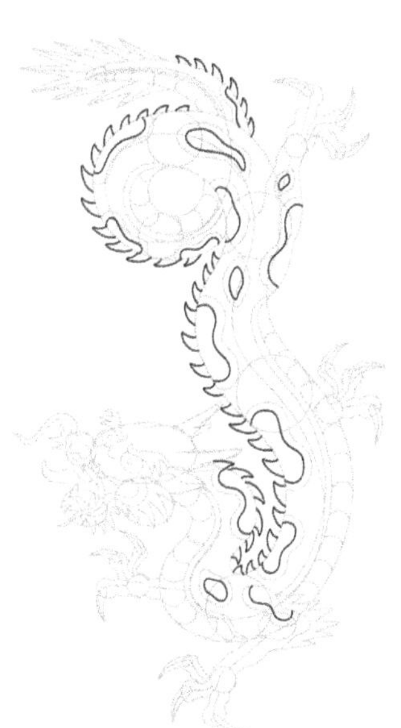

12

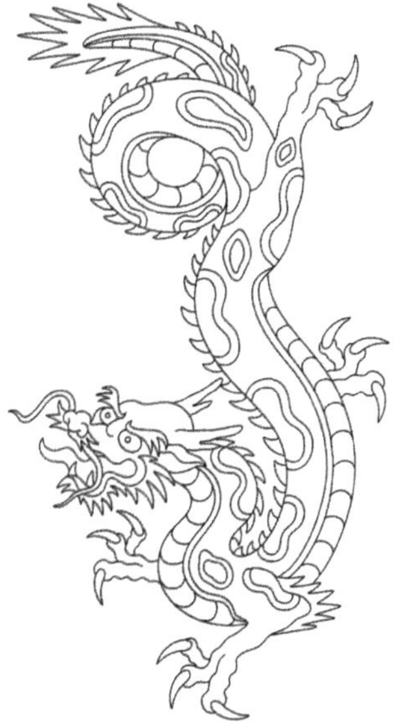

GUN & ROSE

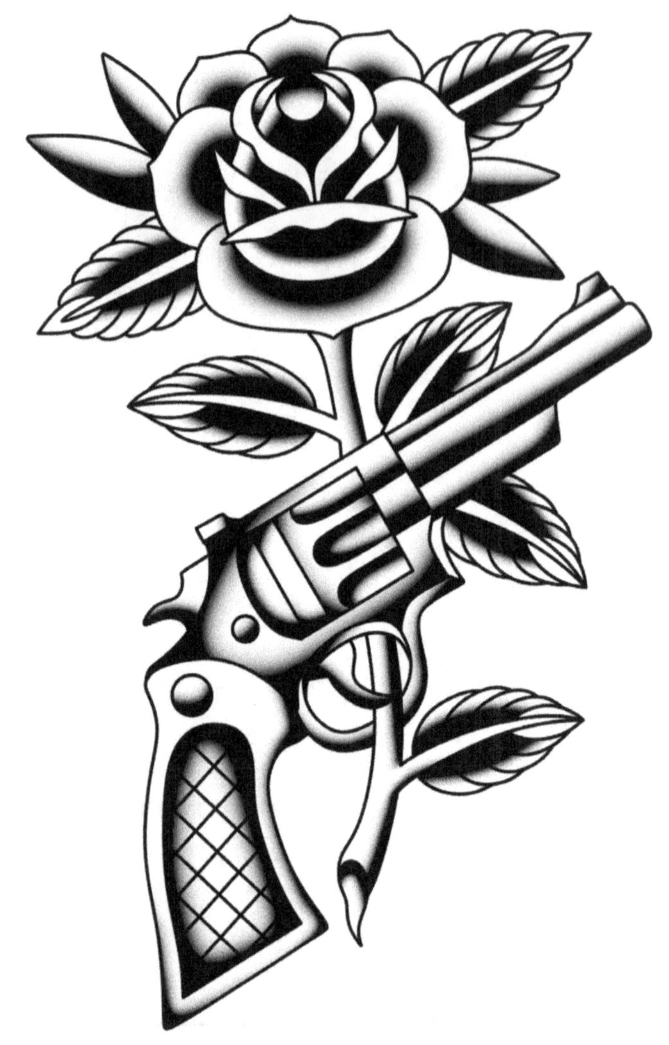

Pro tip: Use the inner circle to map the rose's core petals

The smaller circle inside the main rose shape acts as a guide for the central cluster of petals. Begin by sketching the tight, overlapping petal shapes within this boundary, using the curve of the circle to maintain even spacing and natural symmetry. This helps you keep the rose's core compact and defined before expanding outward with larger petals.

01

02

03

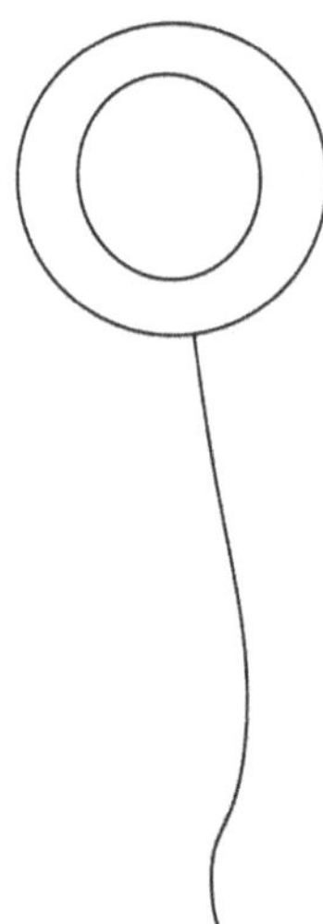

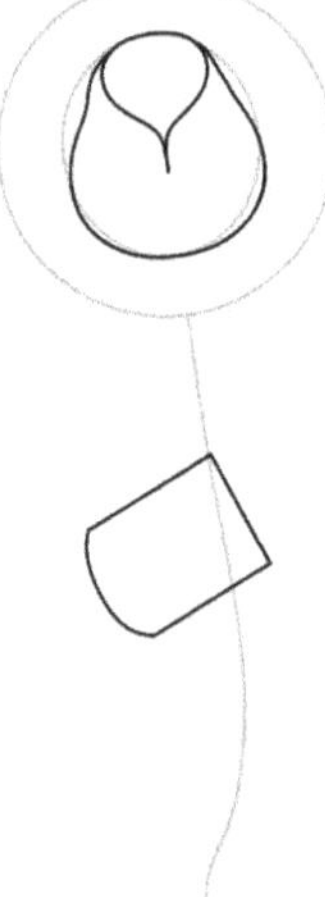

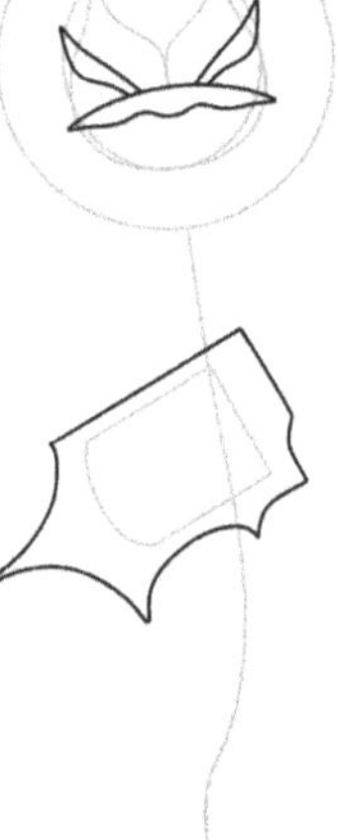

04

05

06

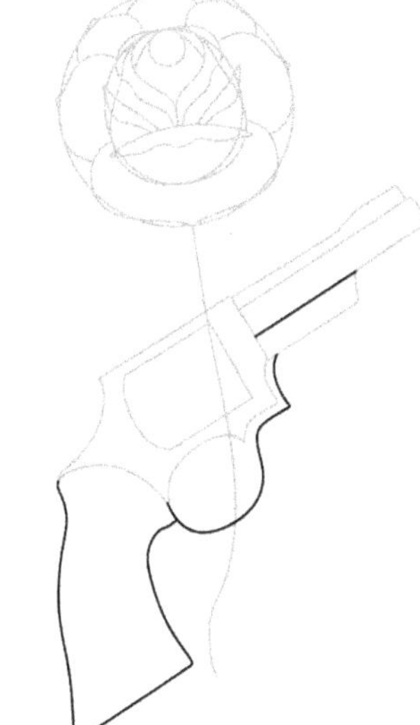

07

08

09

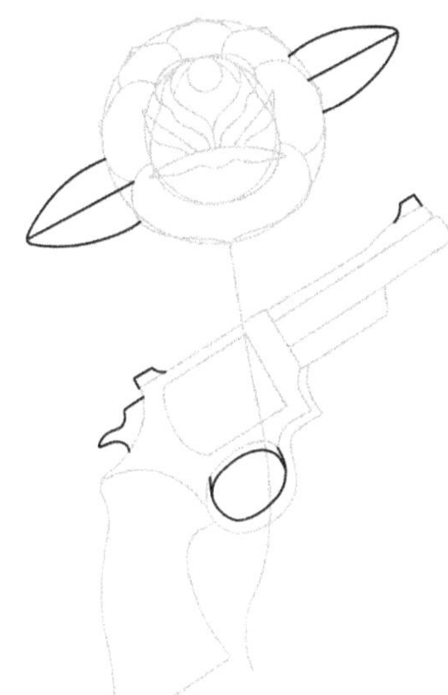

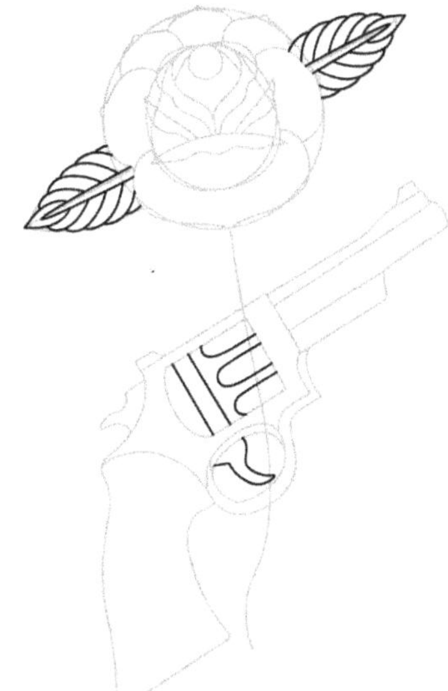

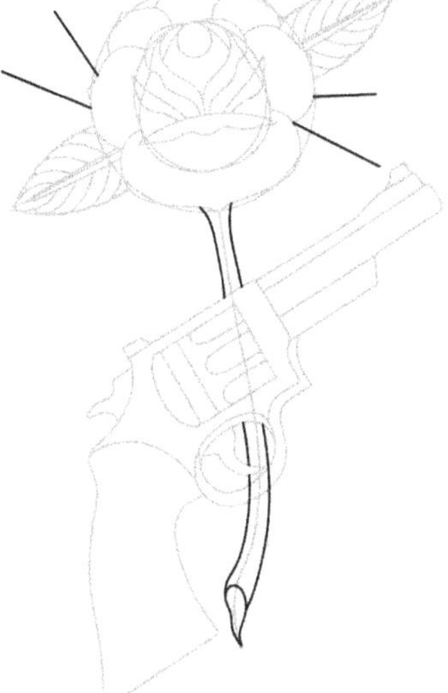

10

11

12

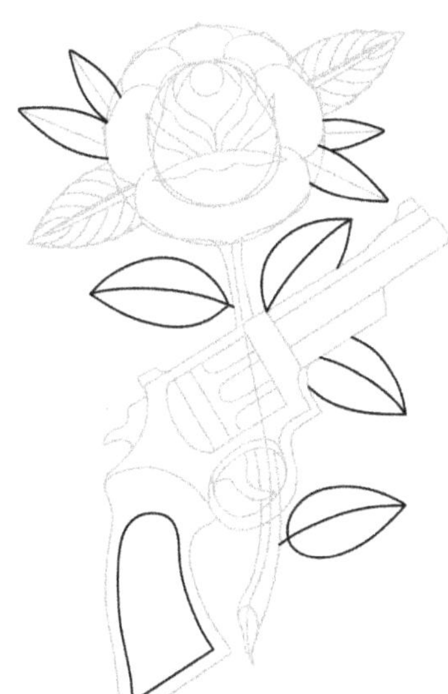

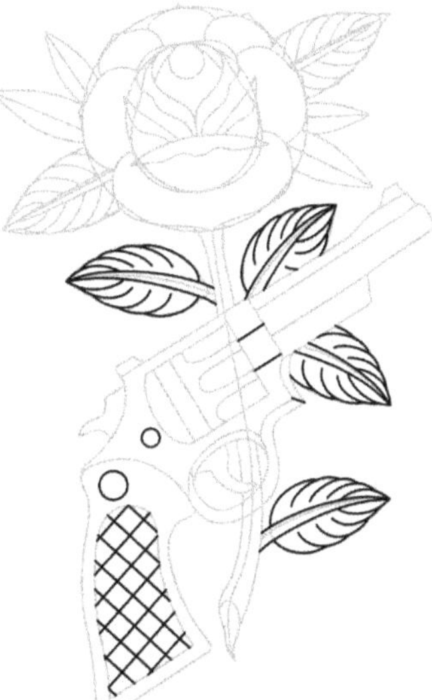

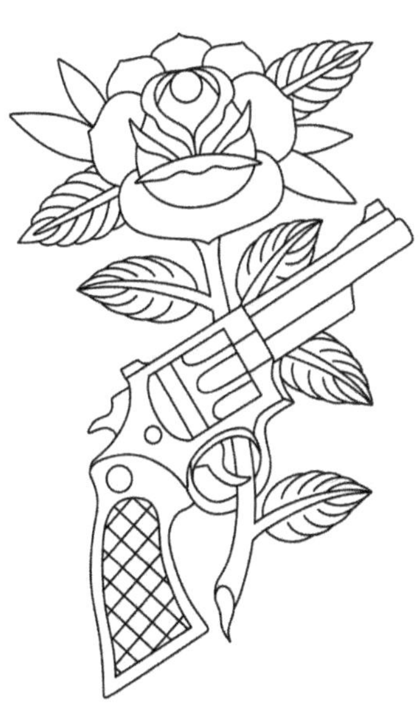

SWALLOW

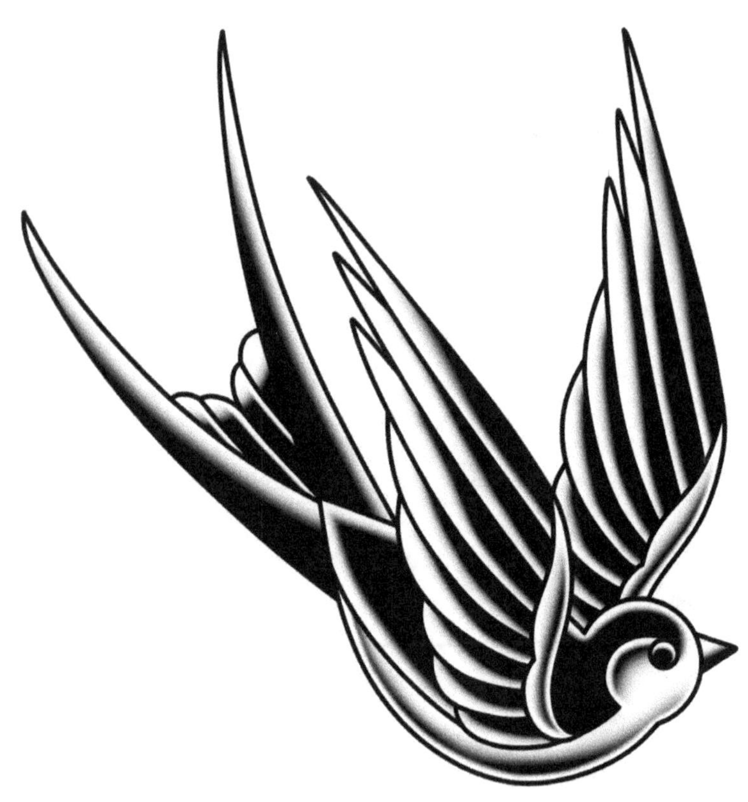

Pro tip: Use the head as a unit of measurement for wing size

To establish the correct proportions, use the head as your measuring guide. Each wing should extend roughly three head lengths outwards from the body, with the highest point of the wing starting about one head height above the top of the head. This simple ratio helps you achieve balanced, natural-looking wings with an elegant upward sweep typical of traditional swallow designs.

01

02

03

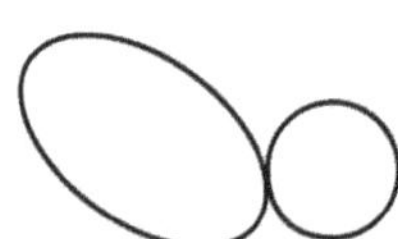

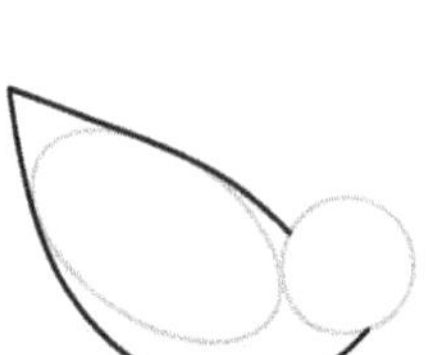

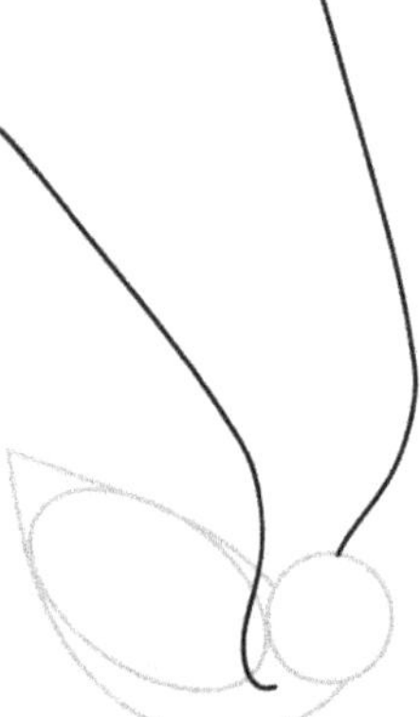

04

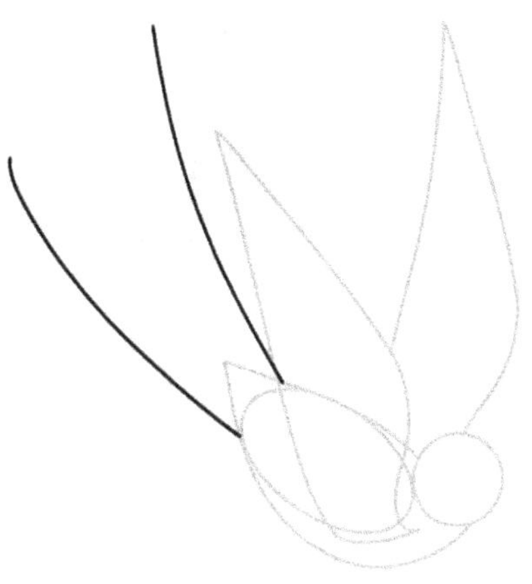

05

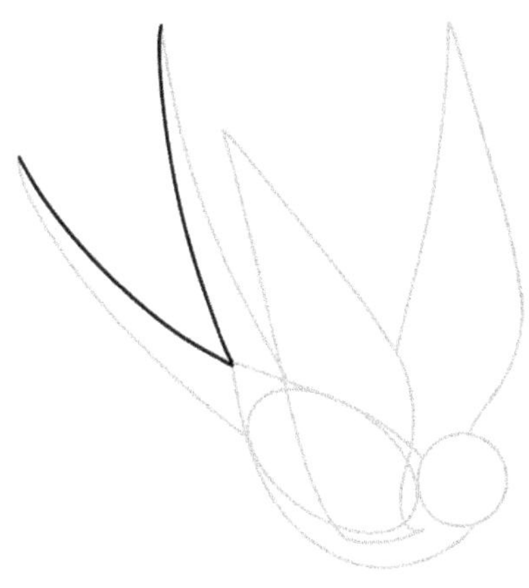

06

07

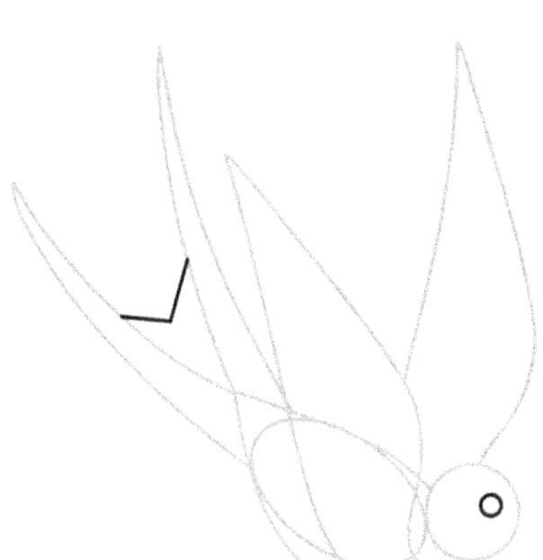

08

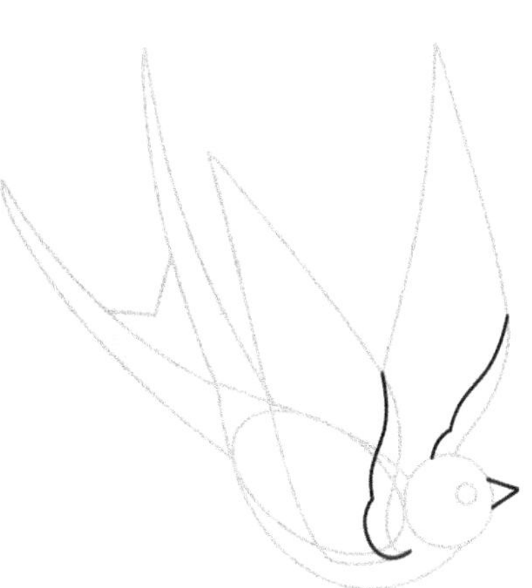

09

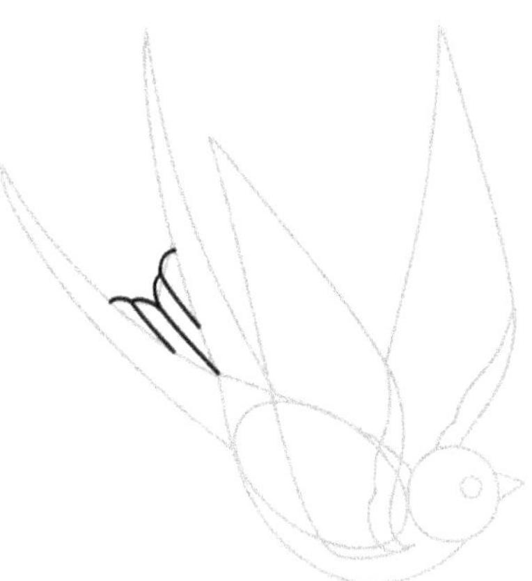

10

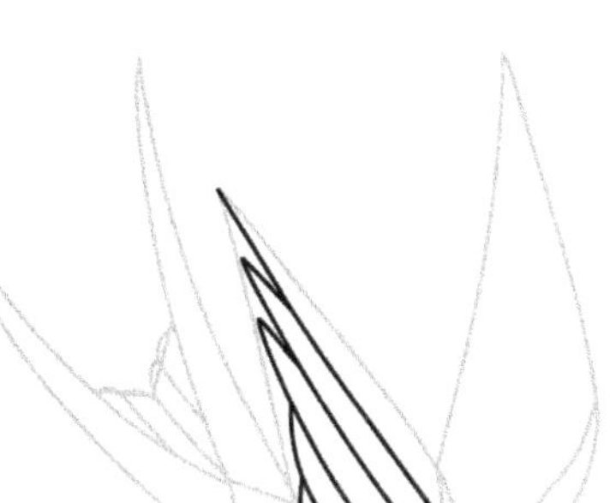

11

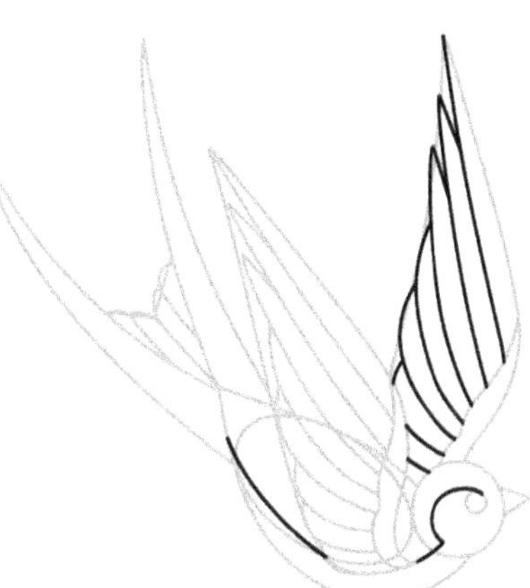

12

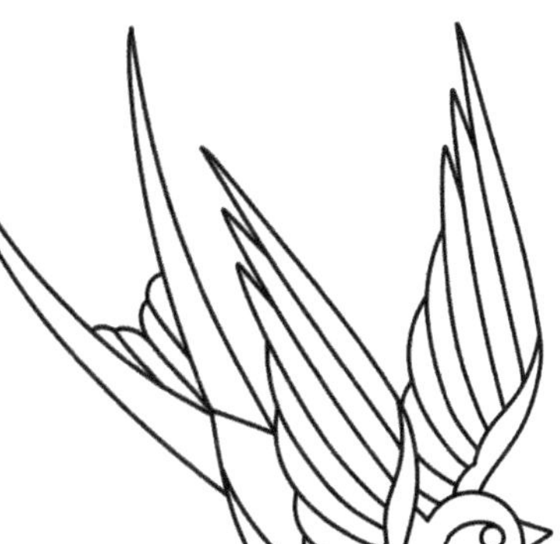

HOW TO DRAW TRADITIONAL TATTOOS

ONI & SNAKE

Pro tip: Use the centre line and eye guide to establish the oni's structure

Start by drawing a vertical central line to anchor the symmetry of the head. Then, position a curved horizontal line through the lower third of the circle to define the brow and eye level. The jawline should taper from the base of the circle, angling inward to form a strong, slightly elongated chin.

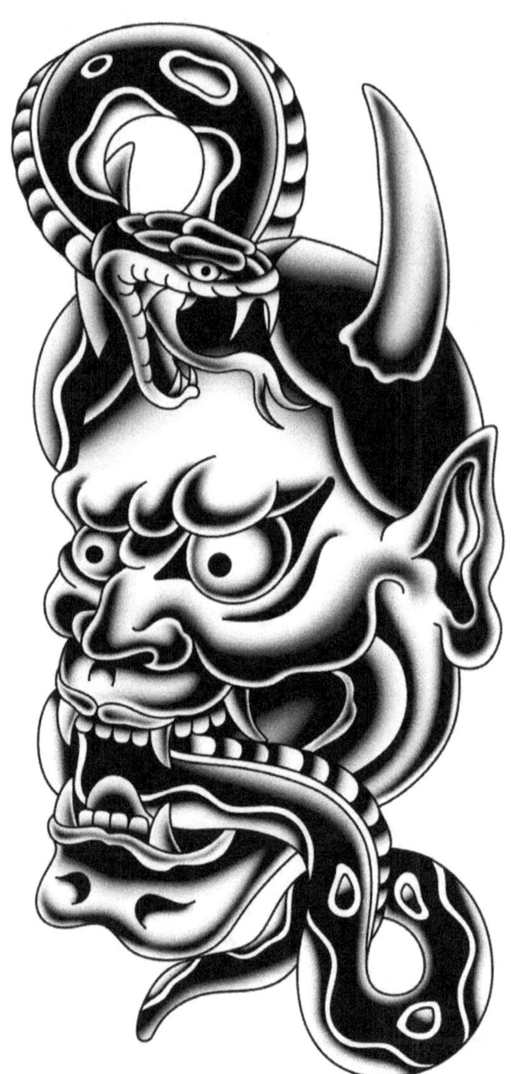

01

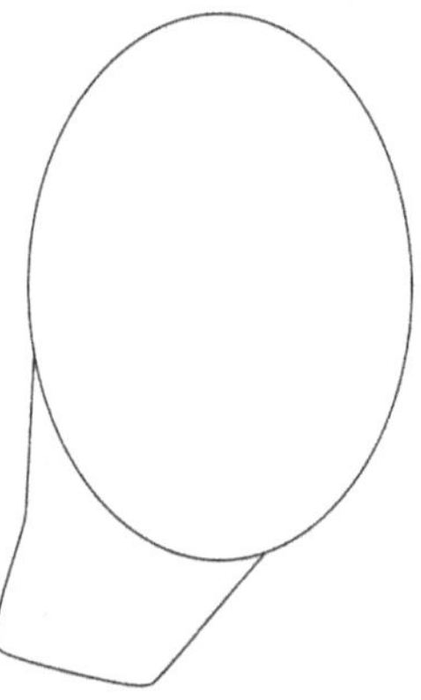

02

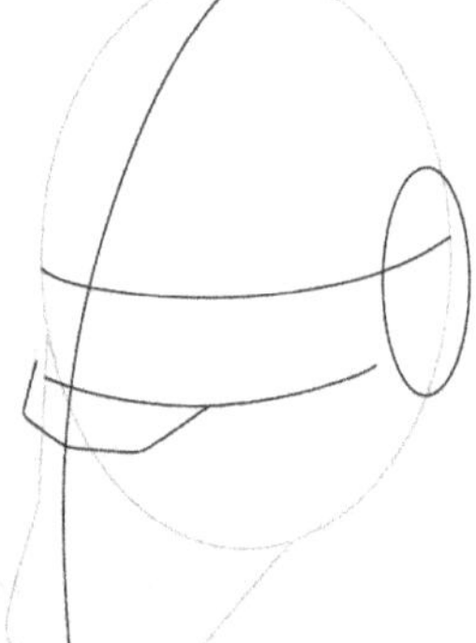

03

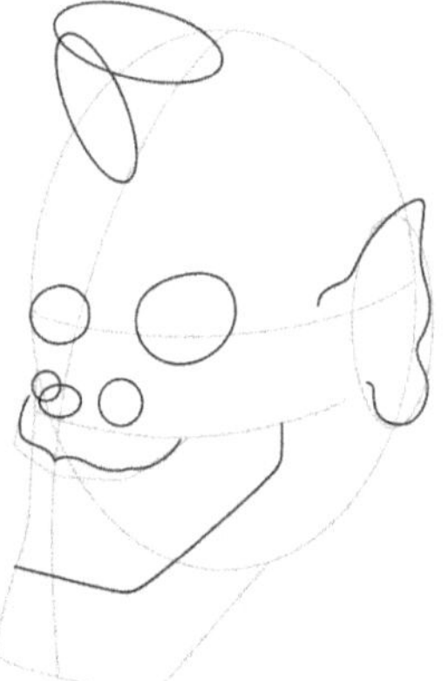

04

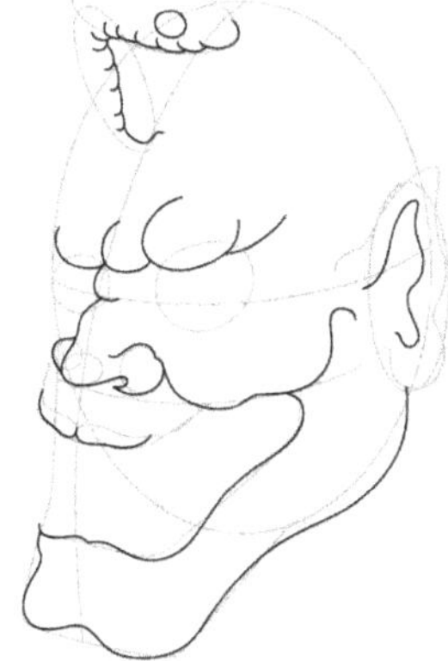

05

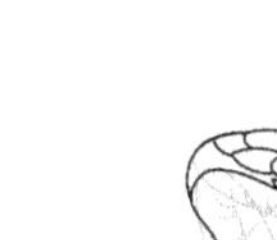

06

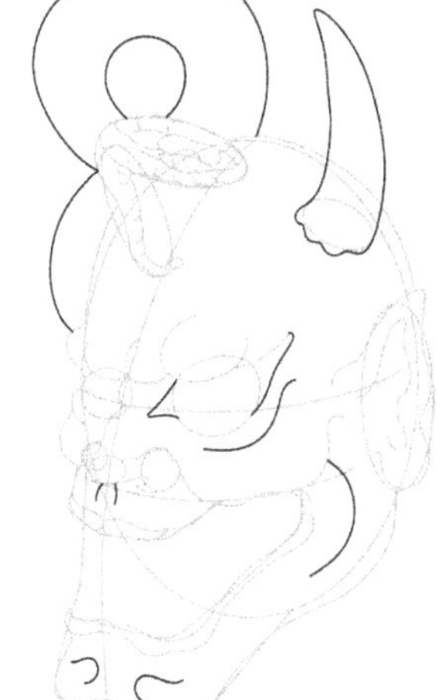

07

08

09

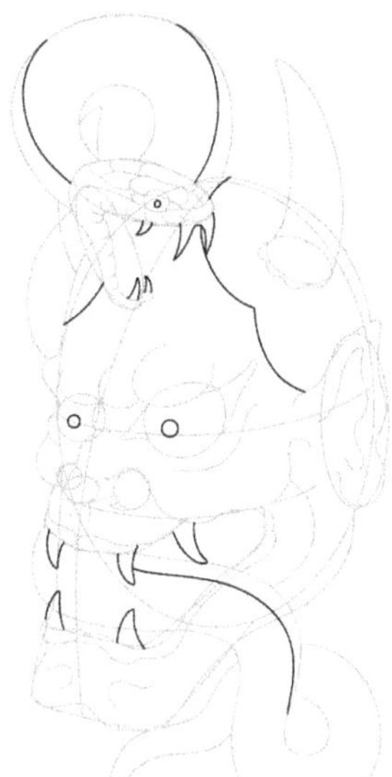

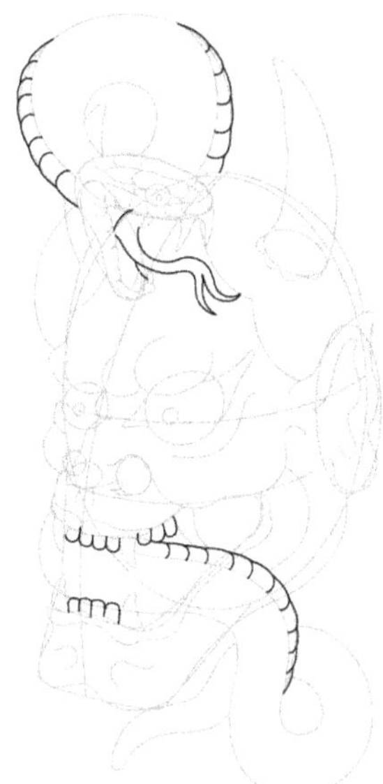

10

11

12

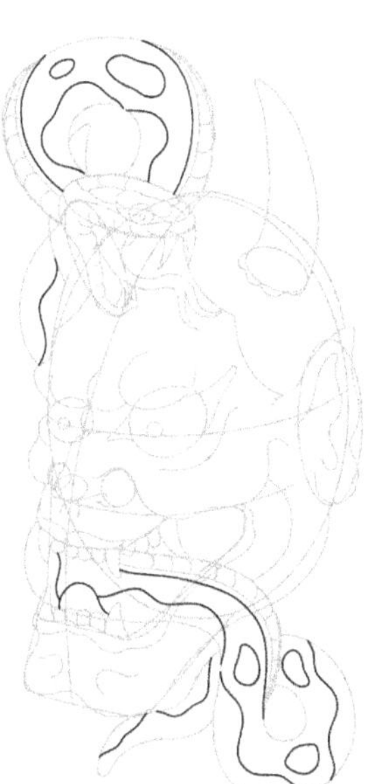

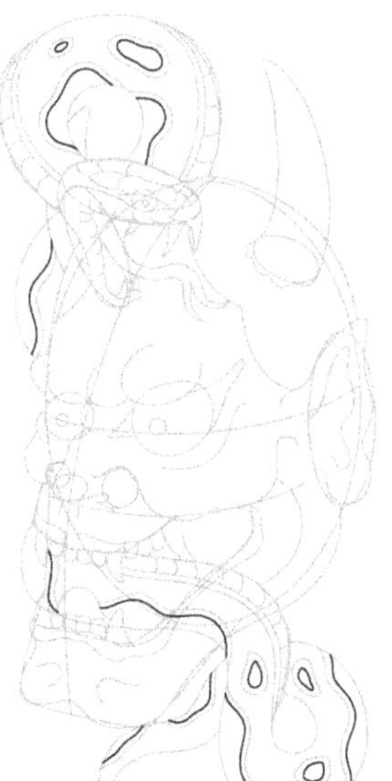

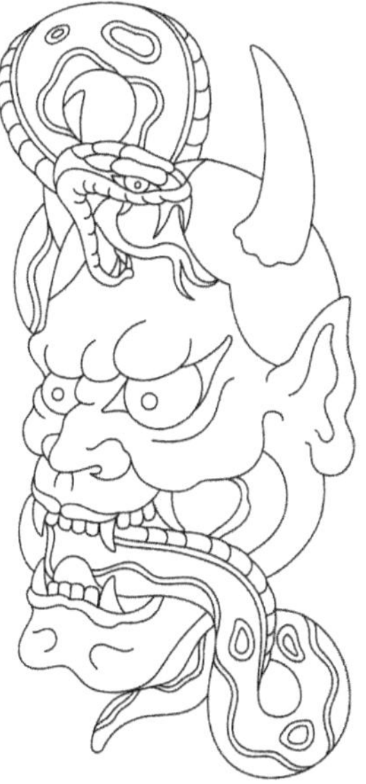

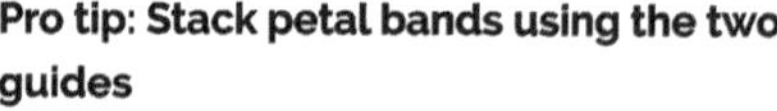

ROSE

Pro tip: Stack petal bands using the two guides

Use the inner oval to size the bud core, then build the "collar" petals around it. Place the top band so its widest points touch the sides of the inner oval and its arc follows the curve of the outer oval.

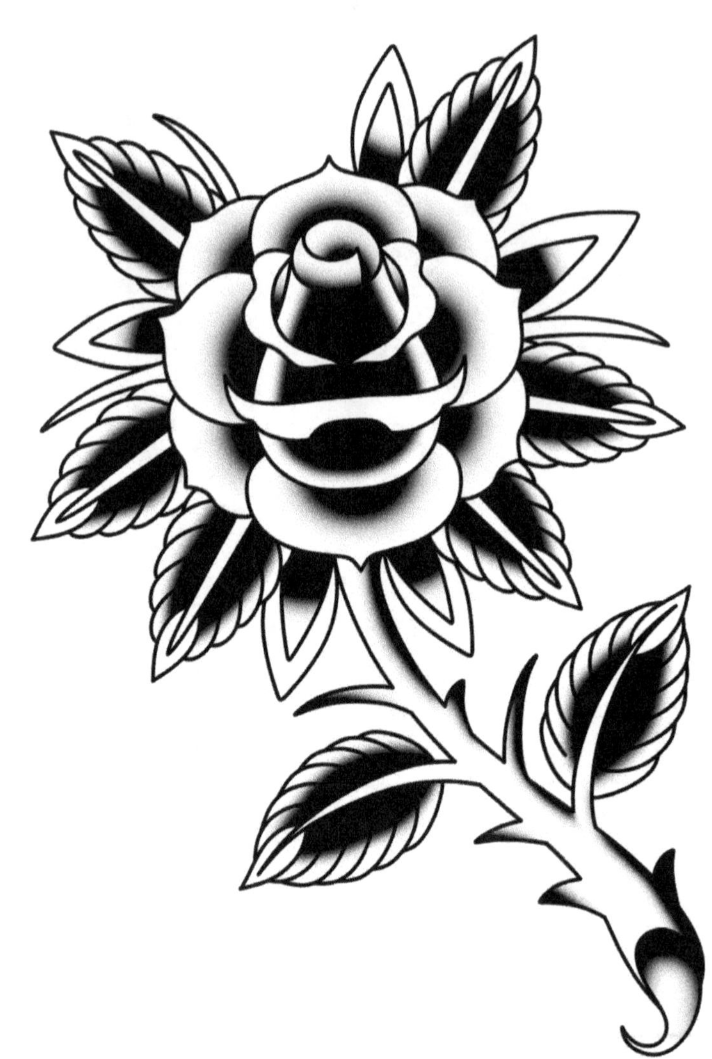

01

02

03

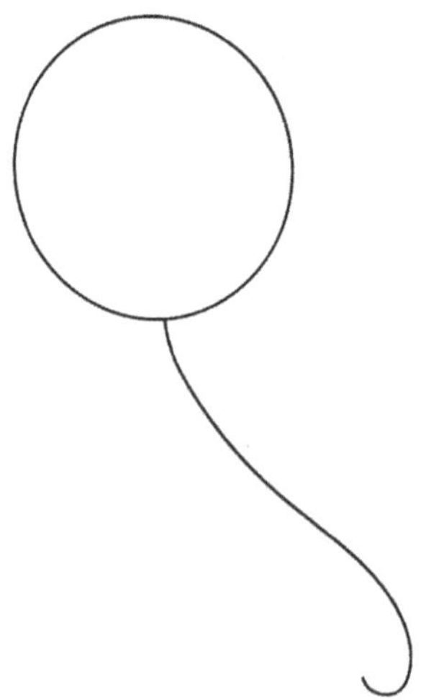

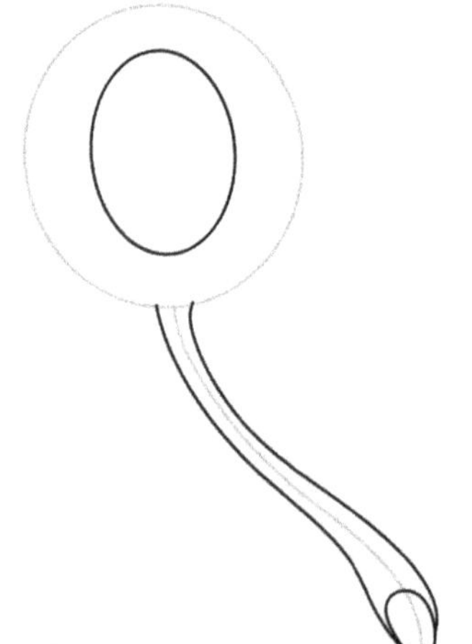

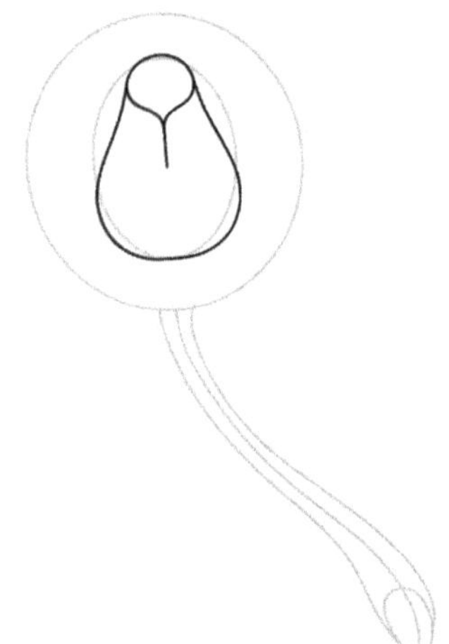

04

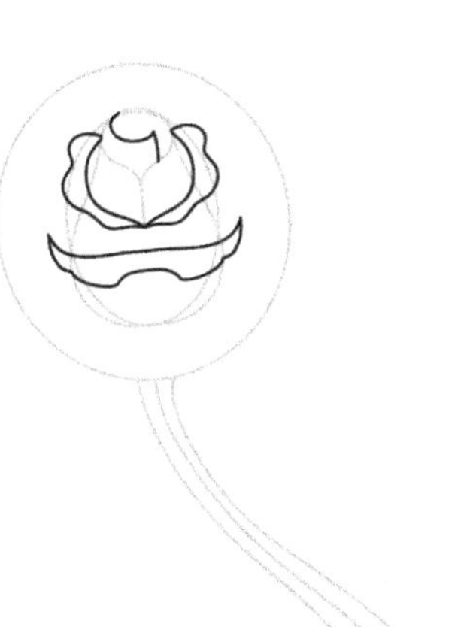

05

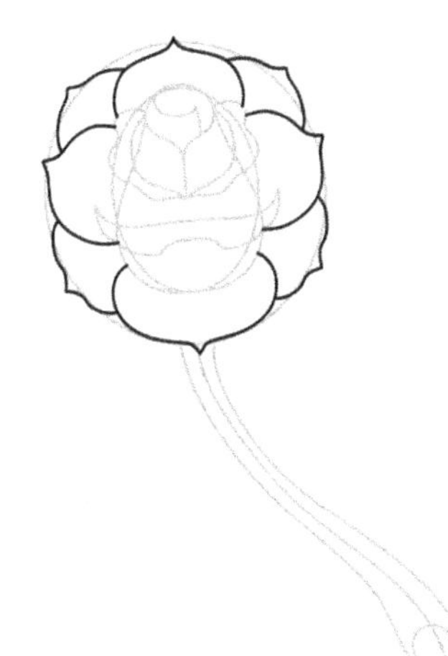

06

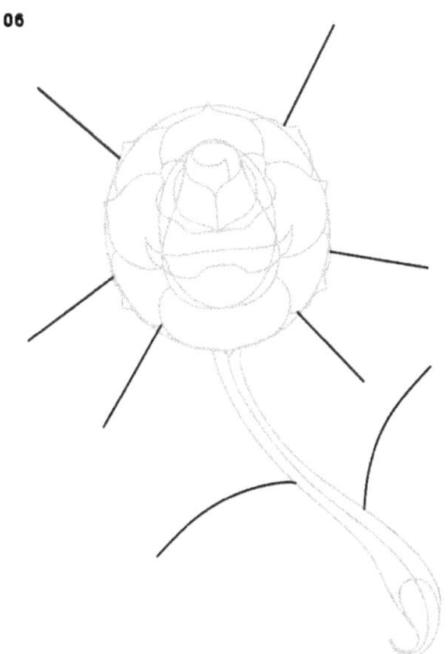

07

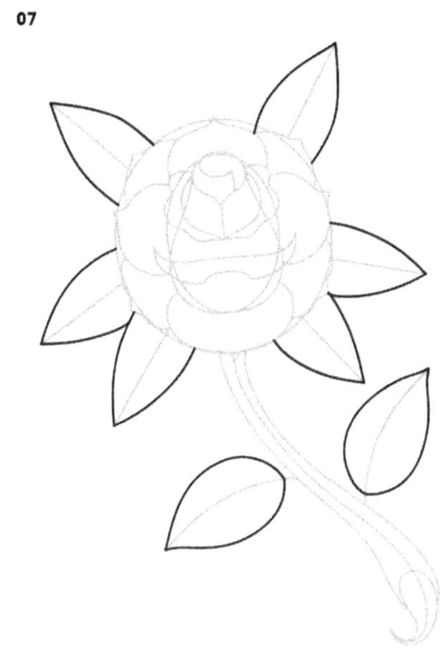

08

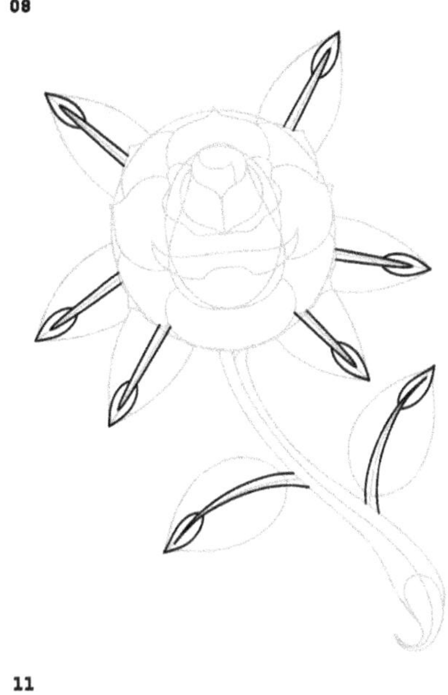

09

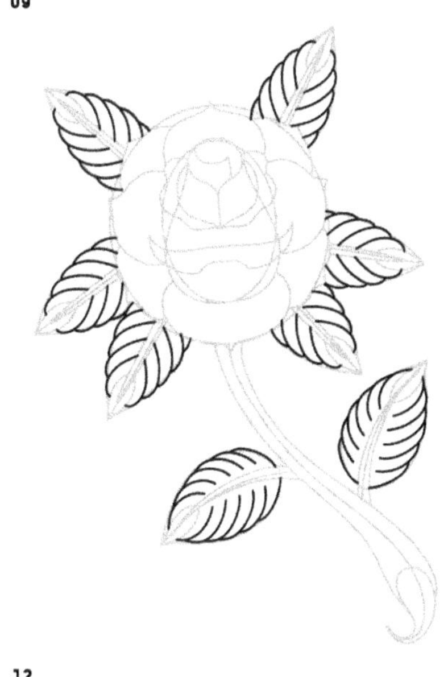

10

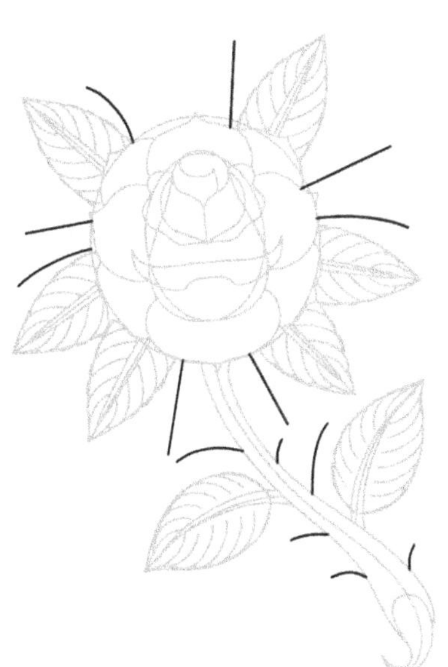

11

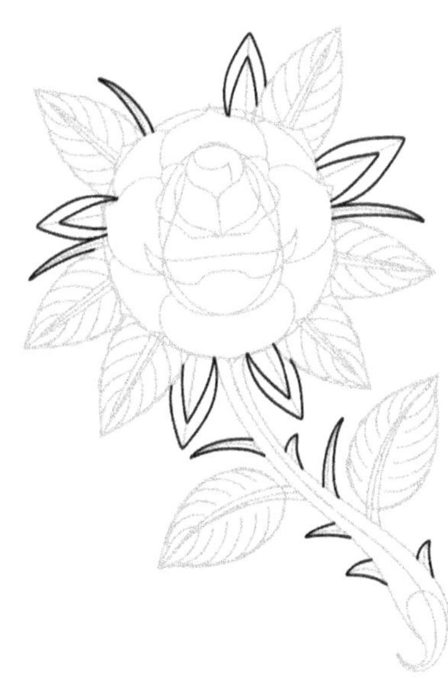

12

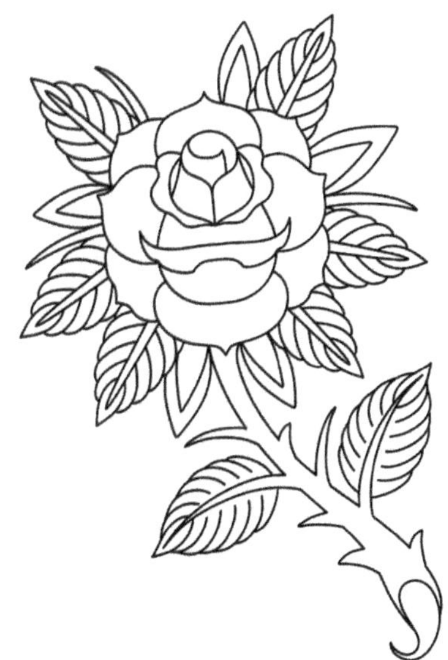

HOW TO DRAW TRADITIONAL TATTOOS

SAMURAI TIGER

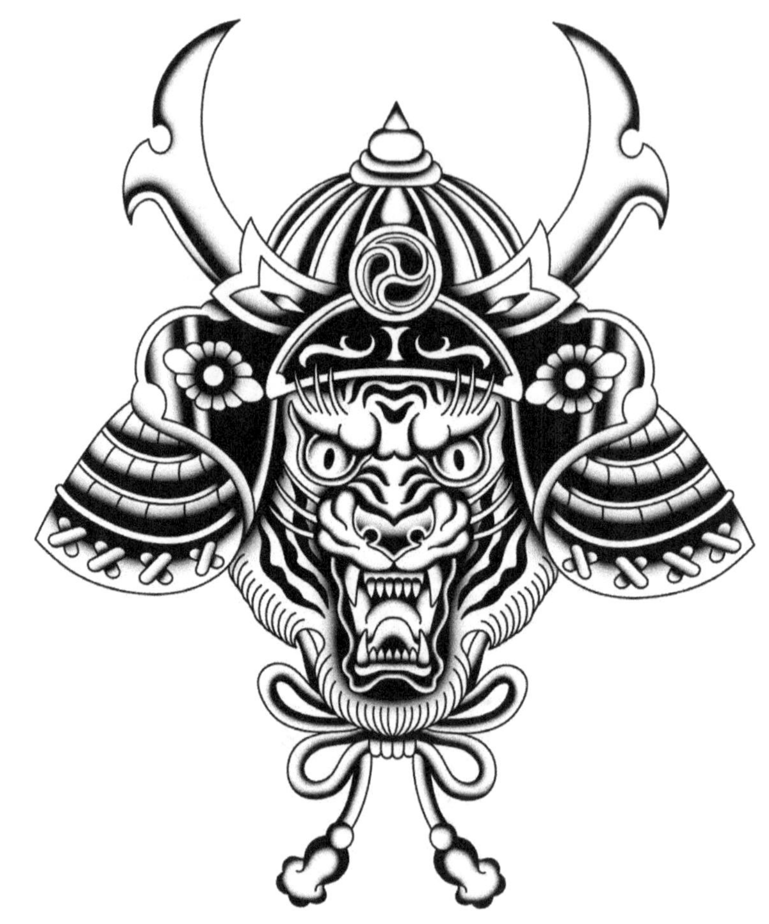

Pro tip: Use the circle and centre line to align the tiger's facial features

Use the central circle as the foundation for the tiger's head. The vertical centre line will help you evenly position the nose, eyes, and forehead details, while the horizontal guide defines the brow and snout angle. Keep the eyes just above the midline of the circle and the nose sitting slightly below it, making sure both features stay symmetrical on either side of the centre line.

01   02   03

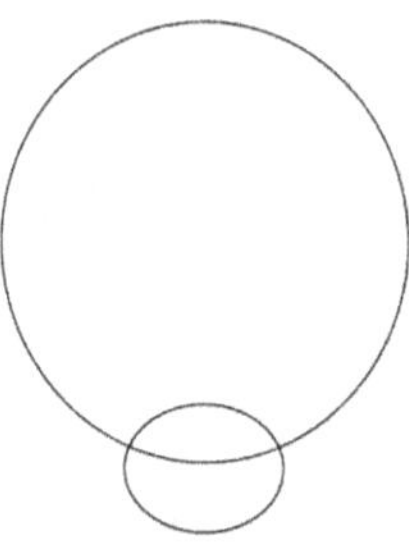

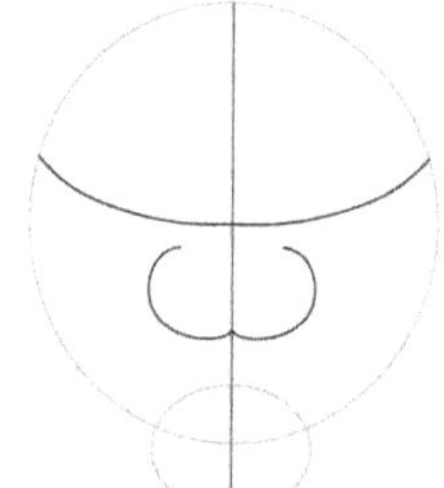

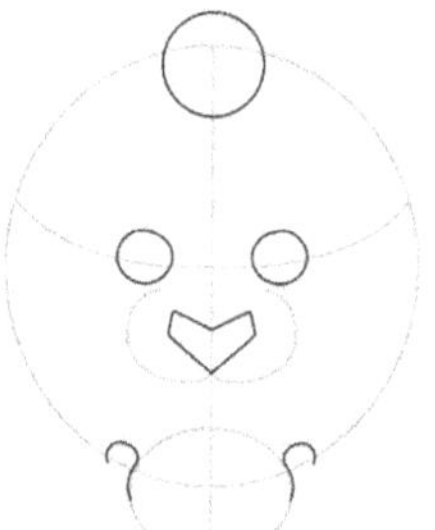

04

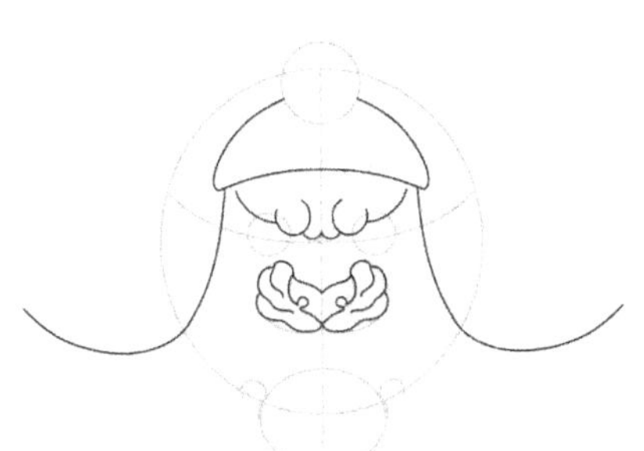

05

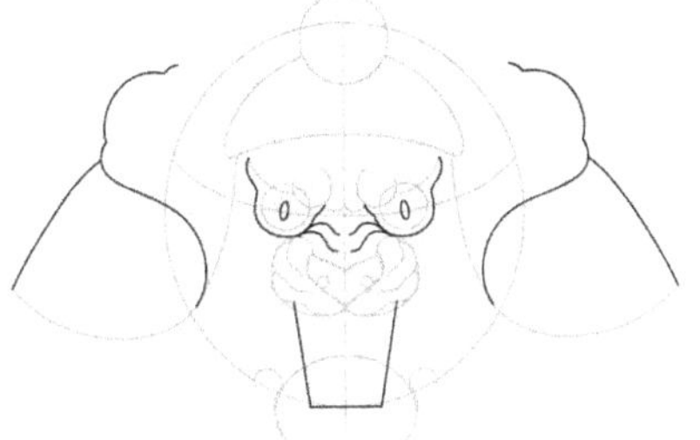

06

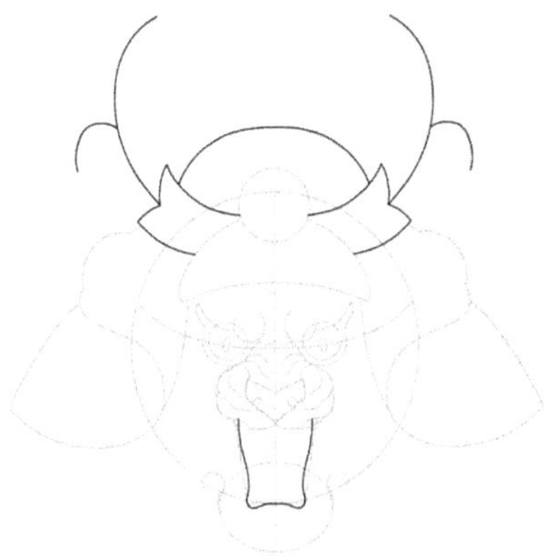

07

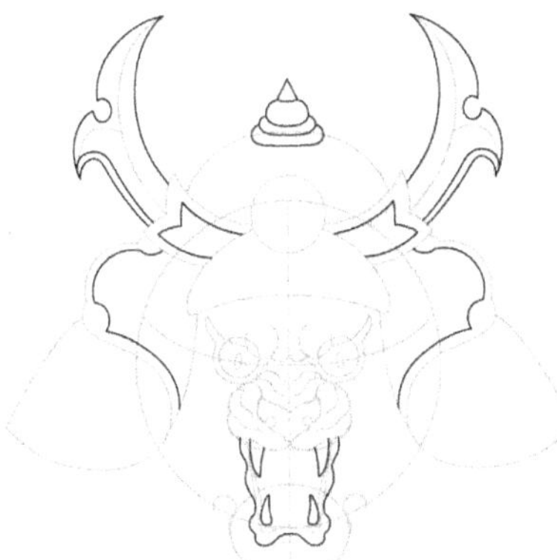

08

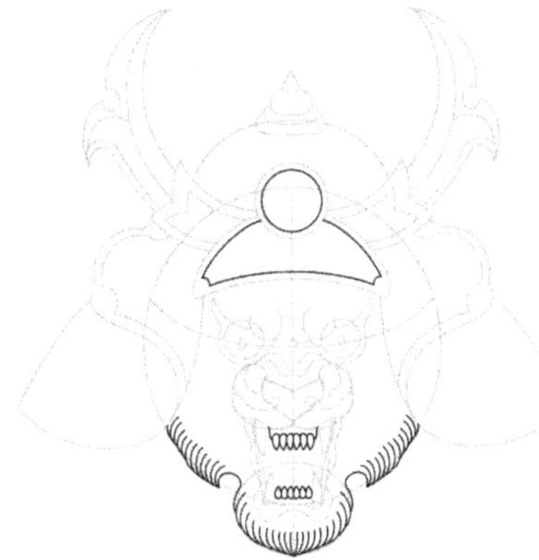

09

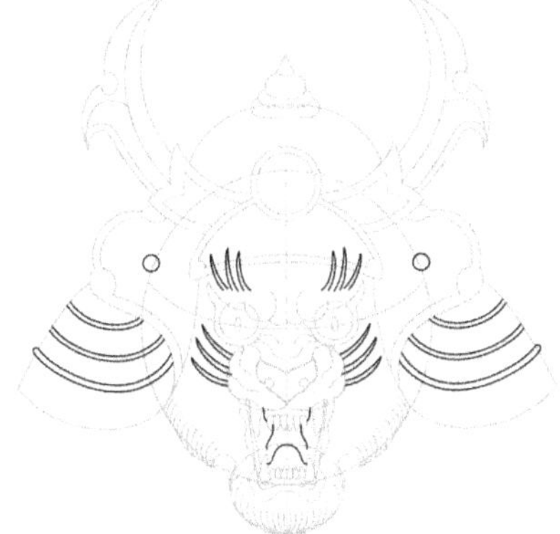

10

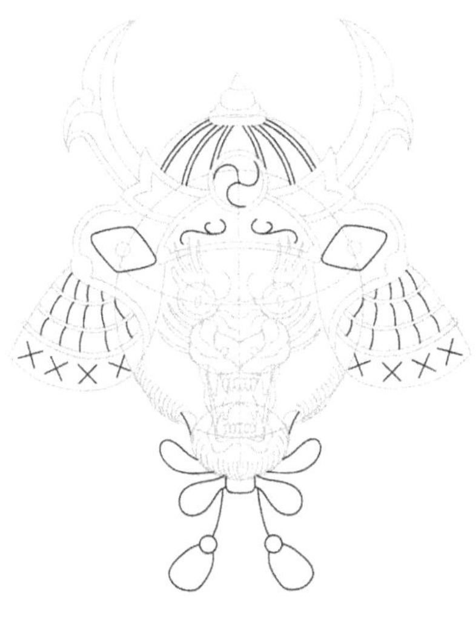

11

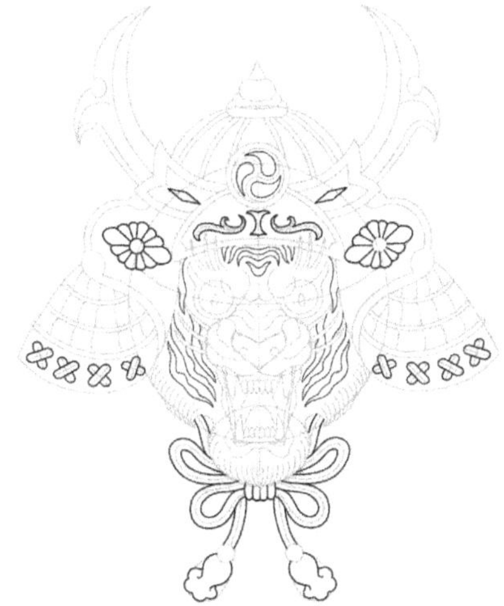

12

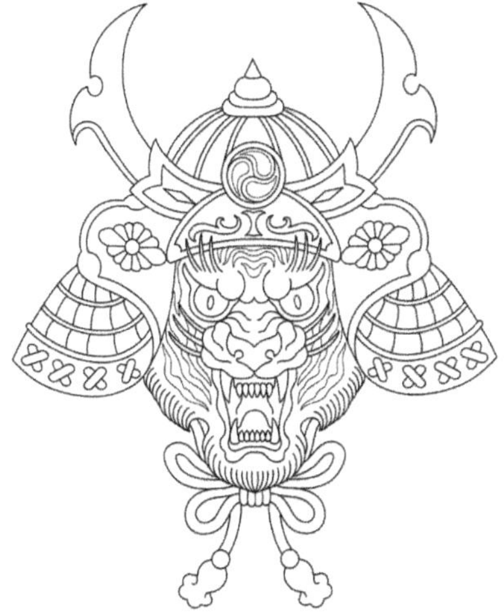

SKULL & COBRA SNAKE

HOW TO DRAW TRADITIONAL TATTOOS

Pro tip: Use the circle and centre line to correctly position the eye

Start by dividing the lower half of the main circle in two with a horizontal line. This acts as your eye line. The eyes should first be drawn as equal squares that sit symmetrically on either side of the centre line, each beginning roughly half an eye width from the edge of the circle. The space between each eye should also be roughly half the width of one of the squares.

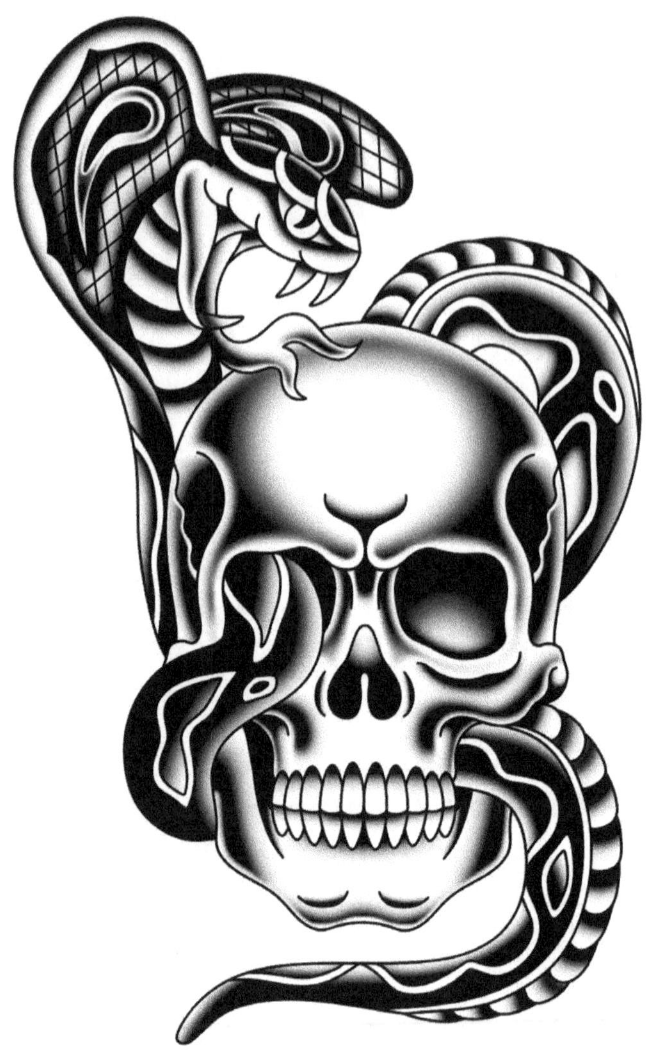

---

01   **02**   **03**

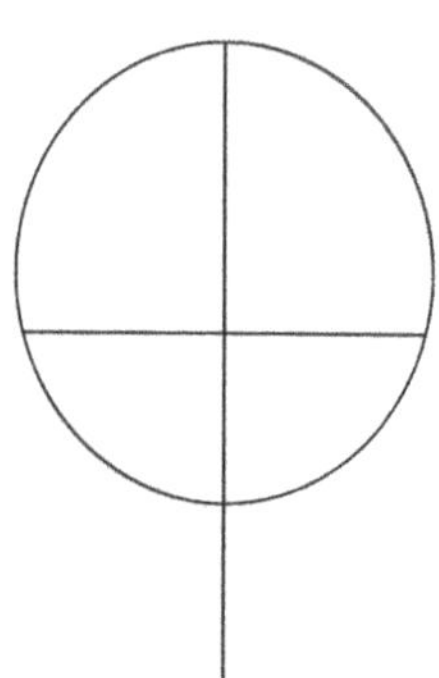

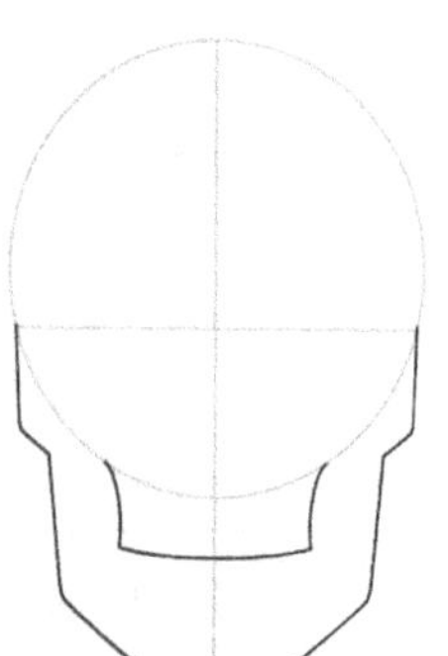

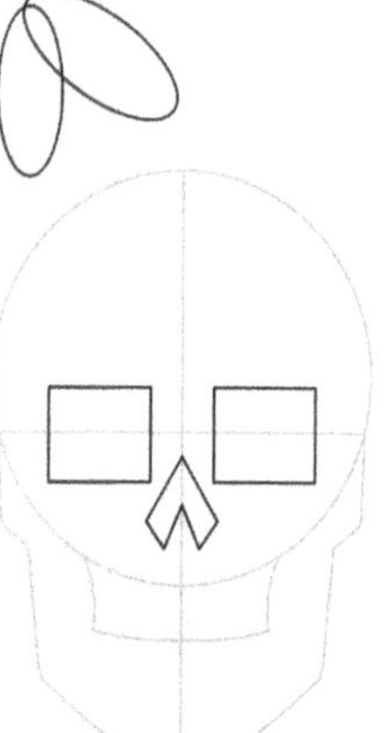

04

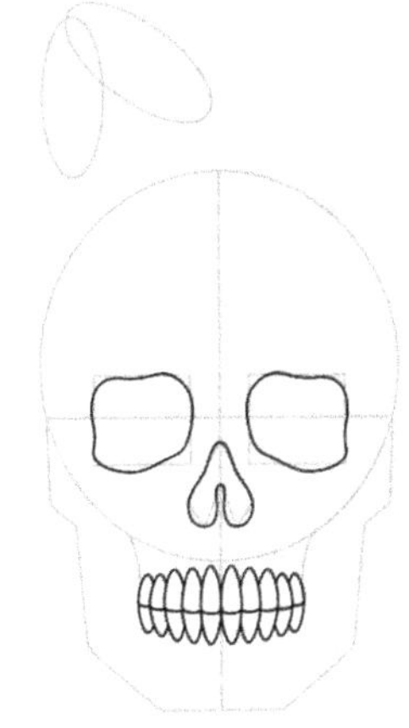

05

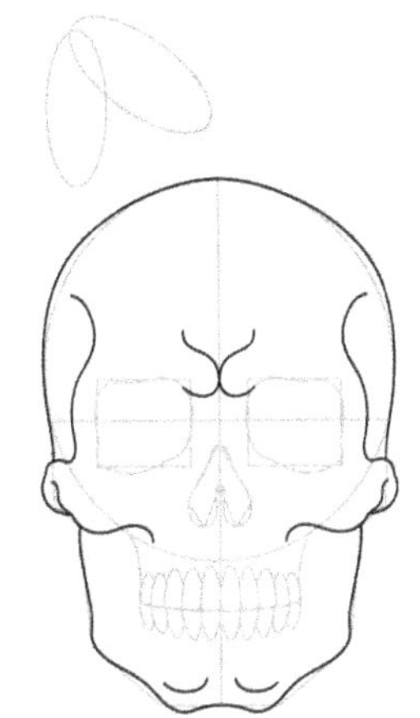

06

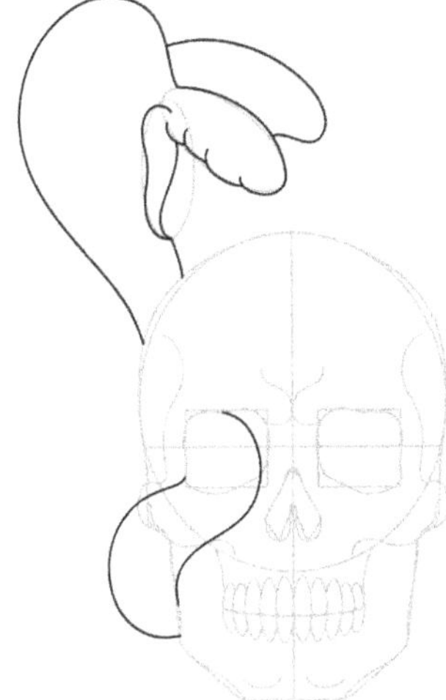

07

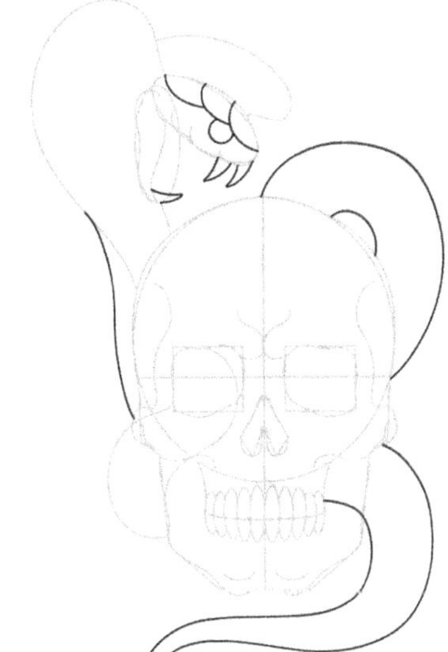

08

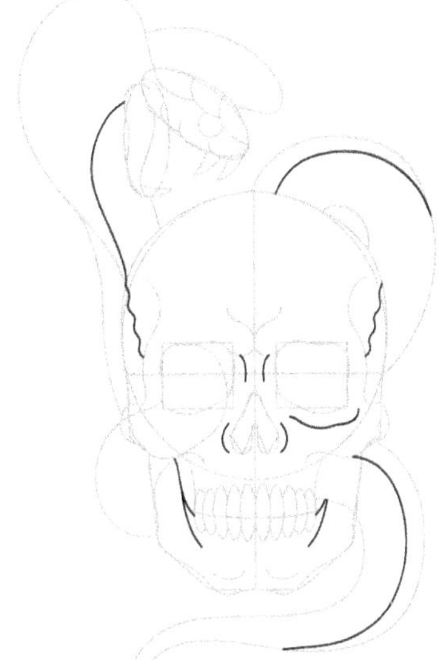

09

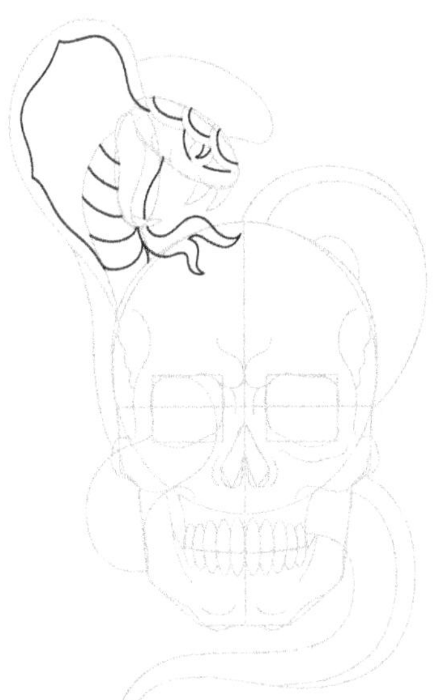

10

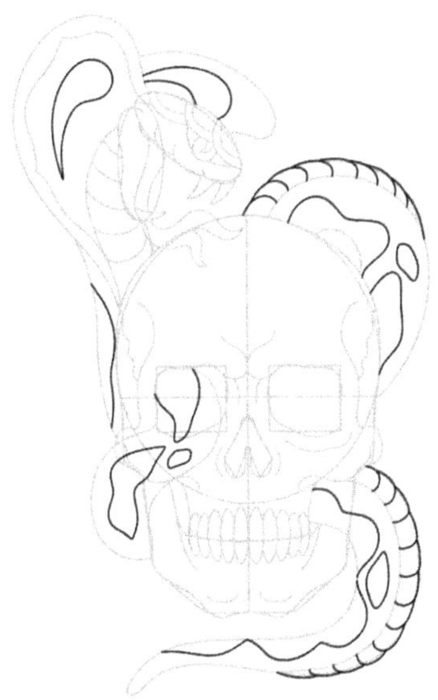

11

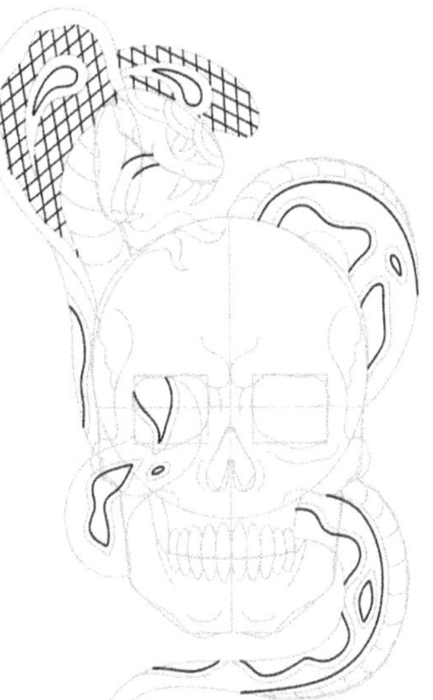

12

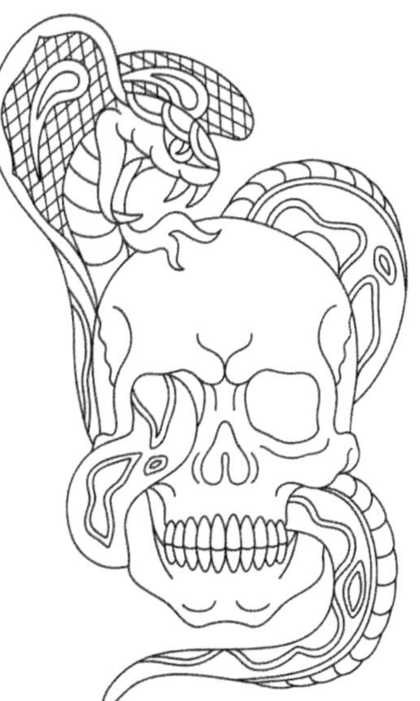

HOW TO DRAW TRADITIONAL TATTOOS

SKELETON HAND & ROSE

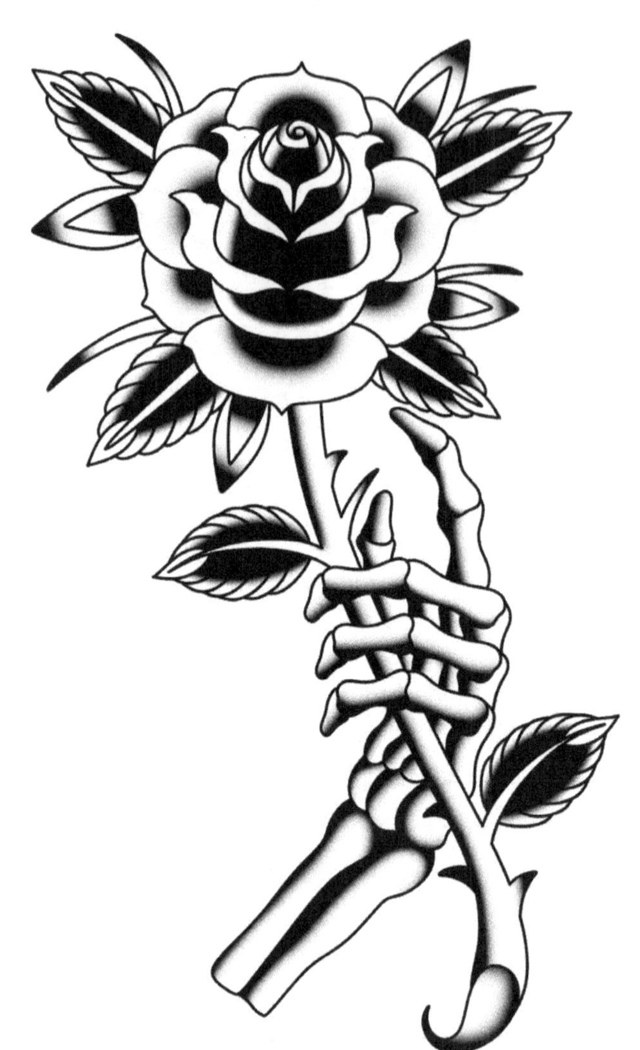

Pro tip: Use the outer oval as a guide for petal placement

The outer oval defines the full spread of the rose. Use it to position and shape the outermost petals so they follow the curve of the oval's edge. This ensures the flower feels full and symmetrical.

01

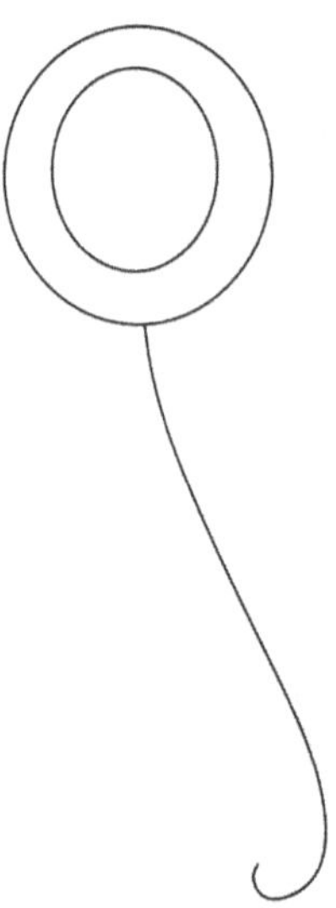

02

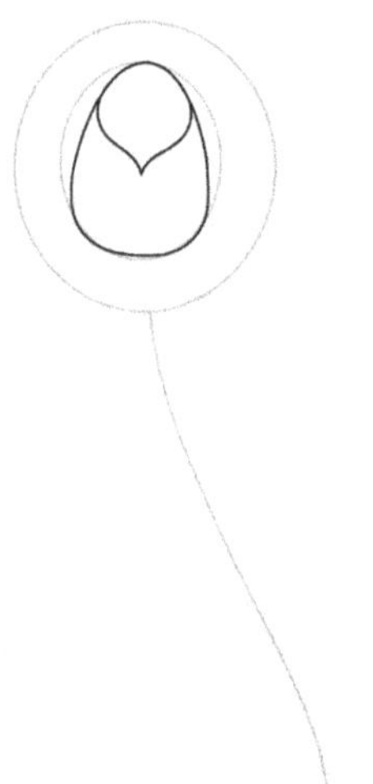

03

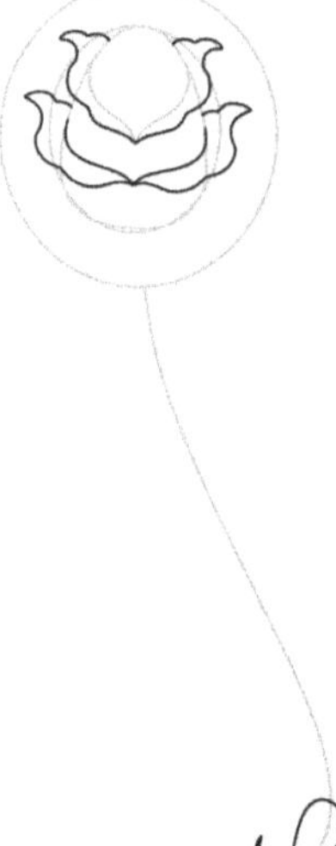

04

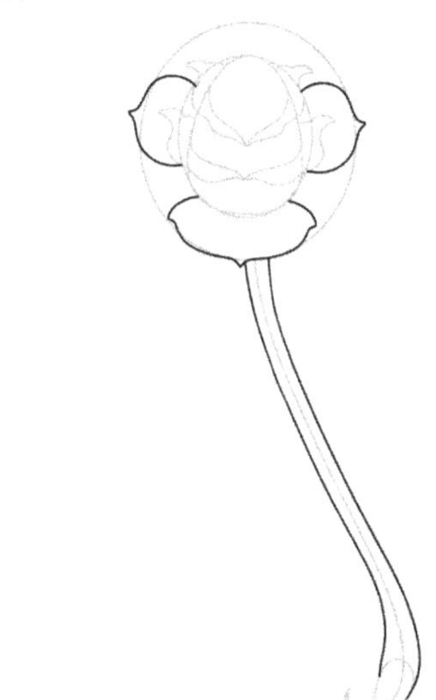

05

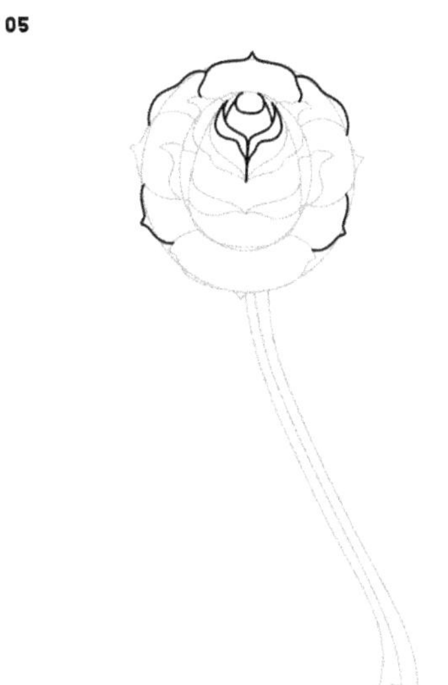

06

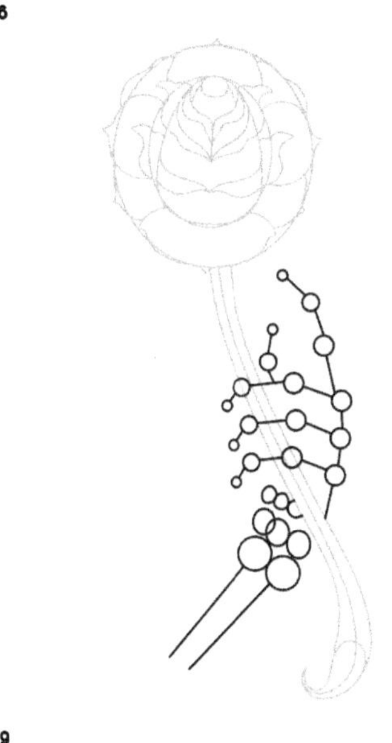

07

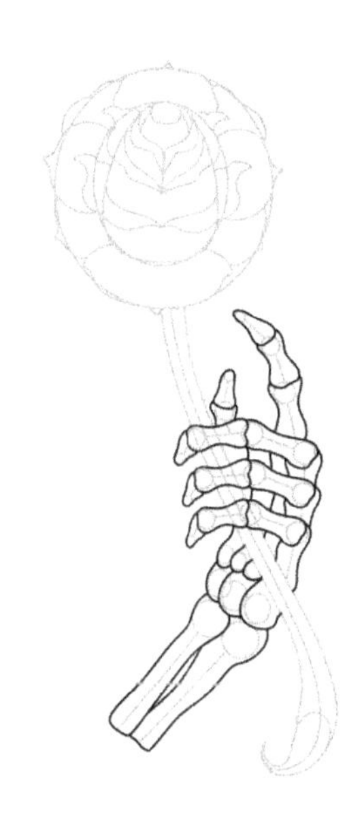

08

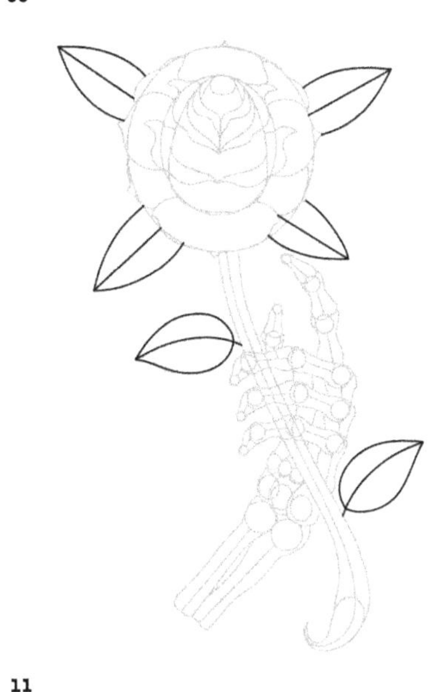

09

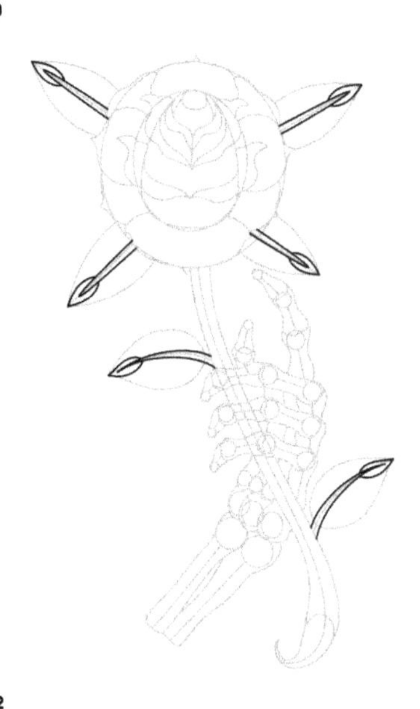

10

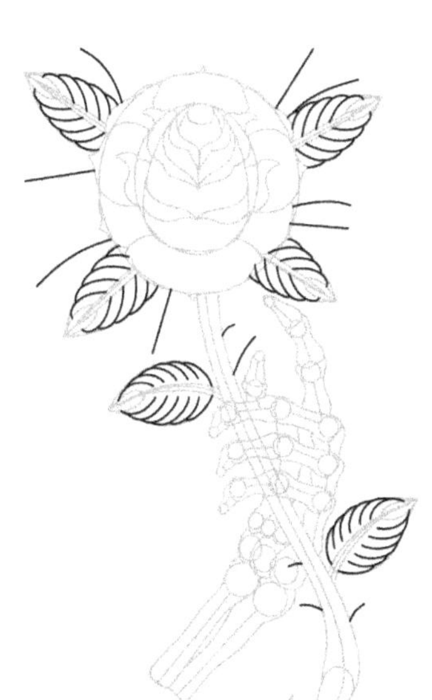

11

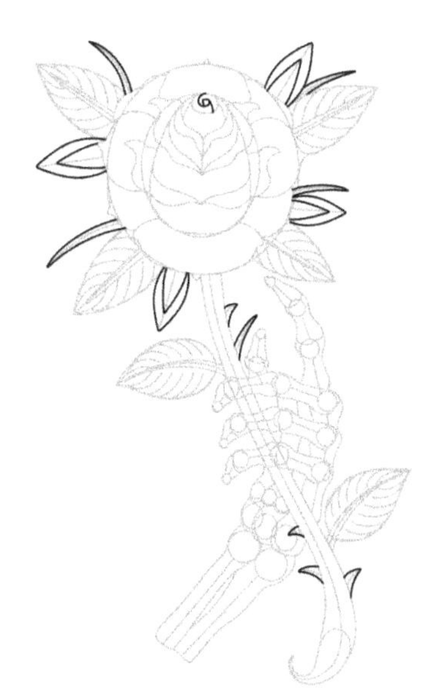

12

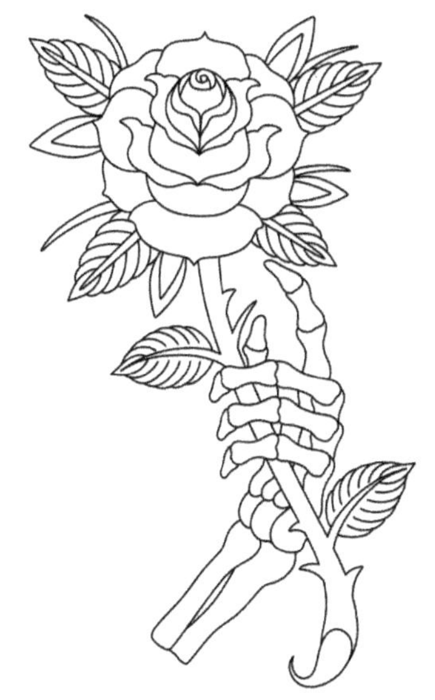

SKULL, DAGGER & SNAKE

Pro tip: Use the centre line and skull to position the dagger handle

Align the dagger's centre with the vertical line running through the skull to ensure balance and symmetry. The base of the handle should begin just above the top of the skull.

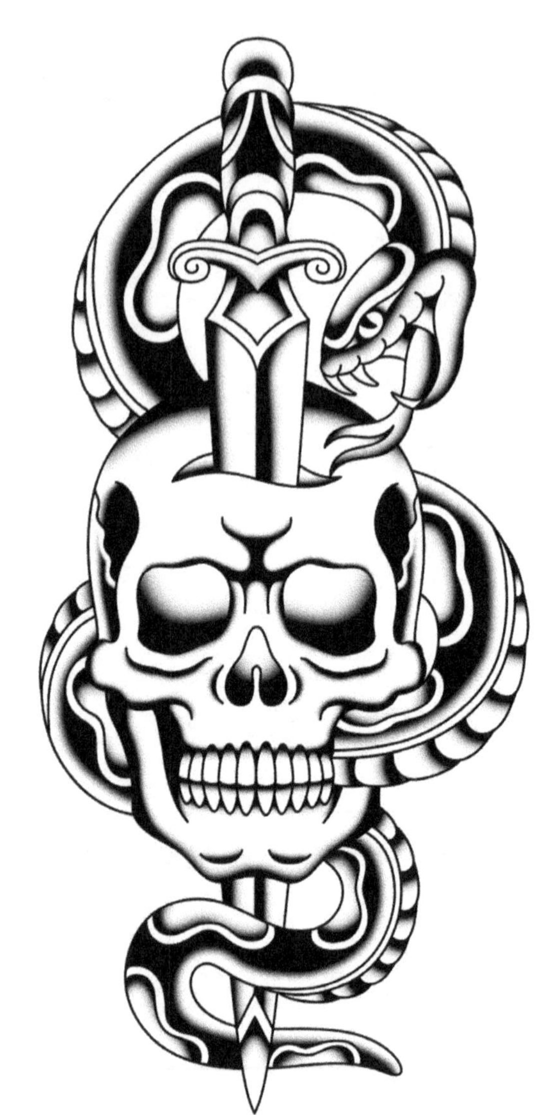

---

01   02   03

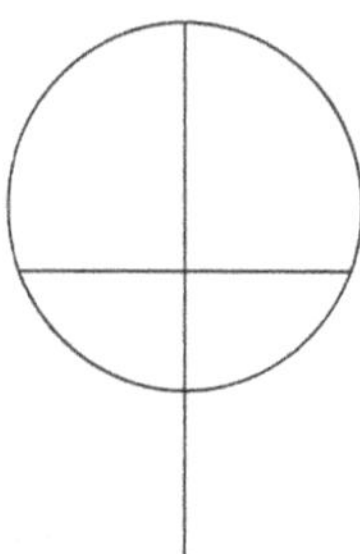

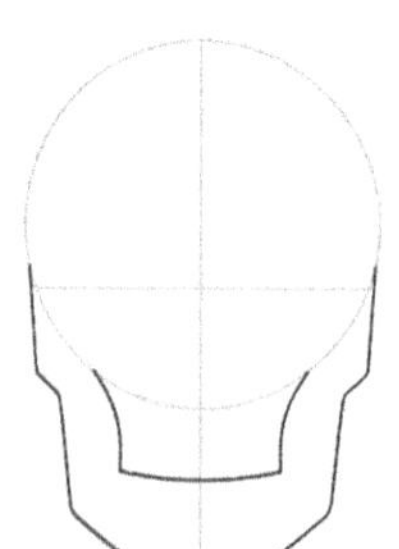

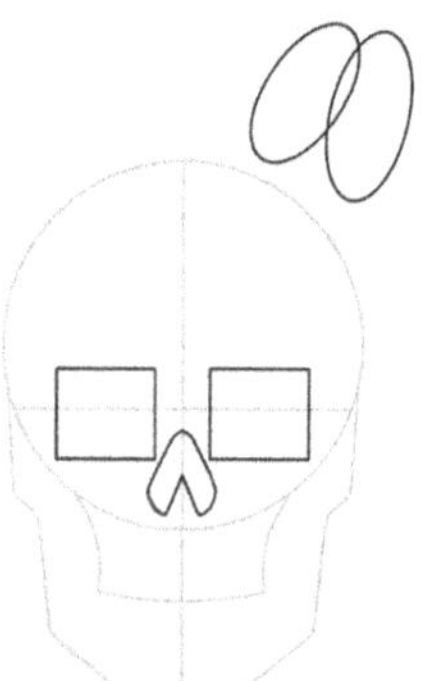

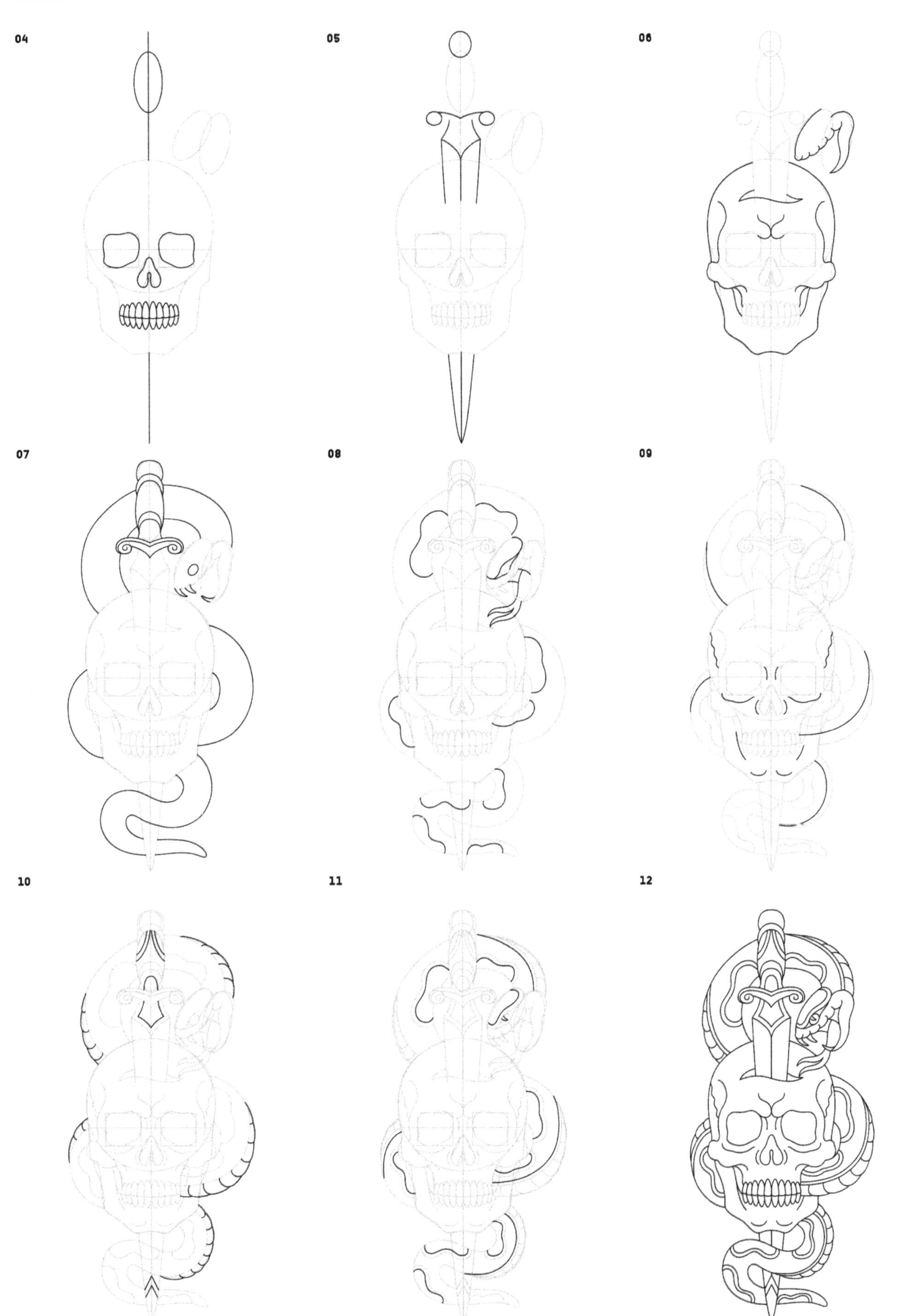

04
05
06
07
08
09
10
11
12
HOW TO DRAW TRADITIONAL TATTOOS

TIGER & DRAGON

Pro tip: Block in the legs using simple shapes

Begin defining the legs by using basic forms. Use elongated ovals for the thighs and calves, positioning them so they overlap slightly at the knees to create a natural bend. Keeping the forms simple at this stage helps you capture proportion and pose before refining the anatomy of the tiger and dragon.

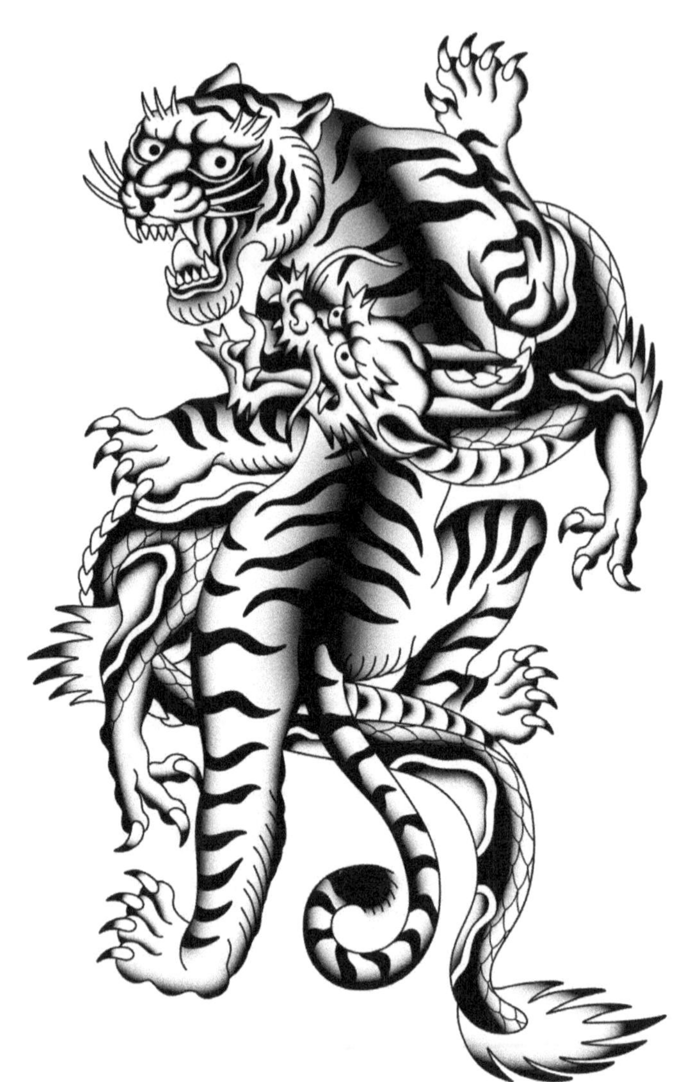

01

02

03

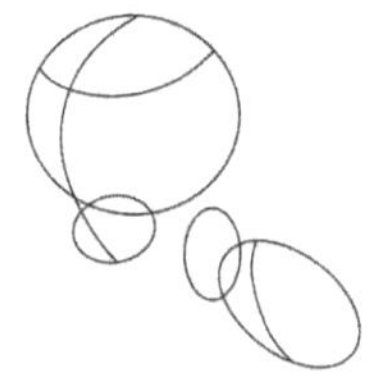

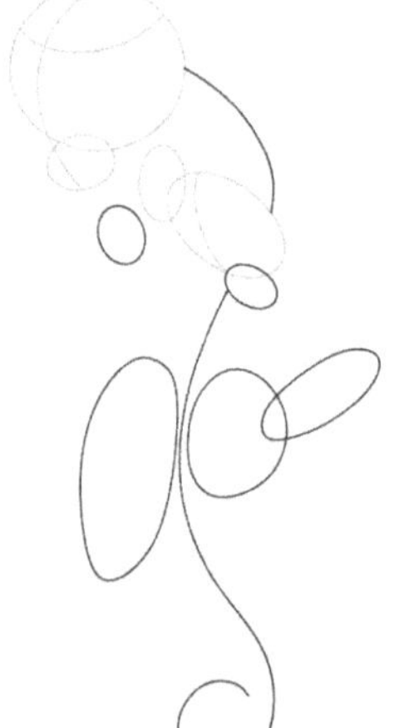

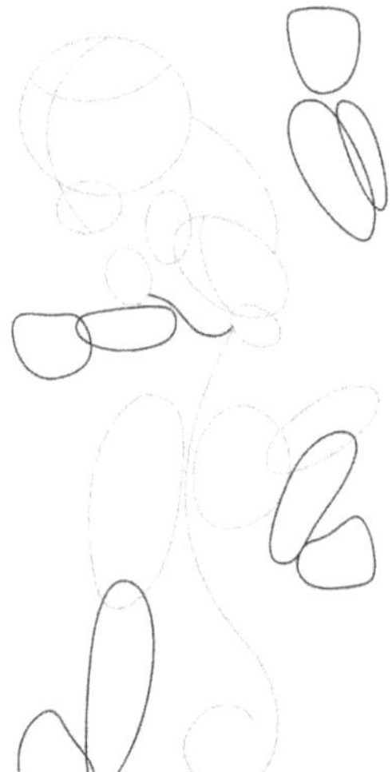

04

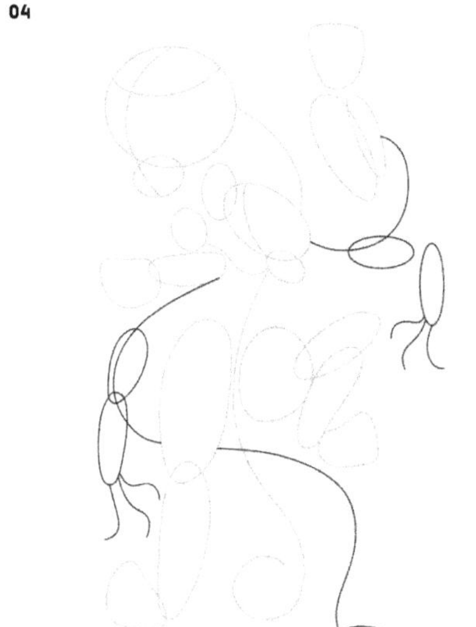

05

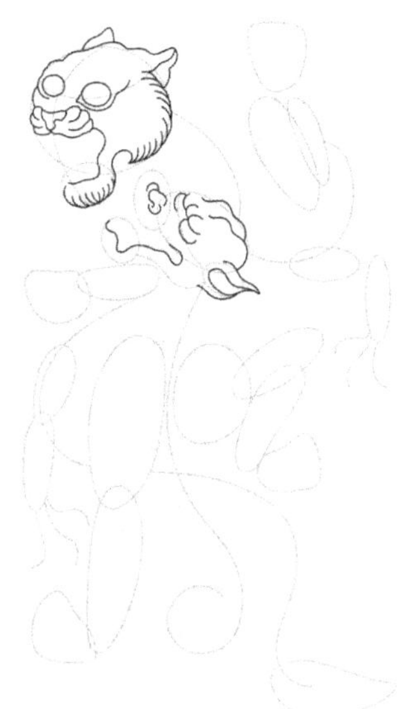

06

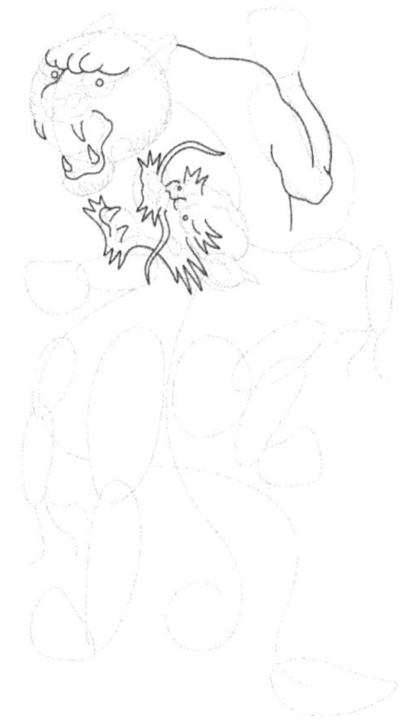

07

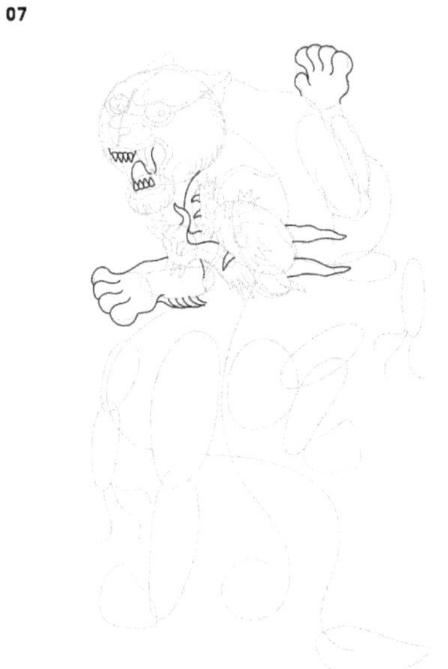

08

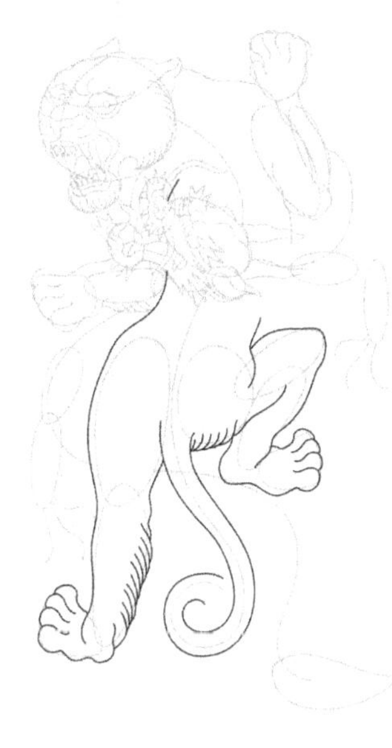

09

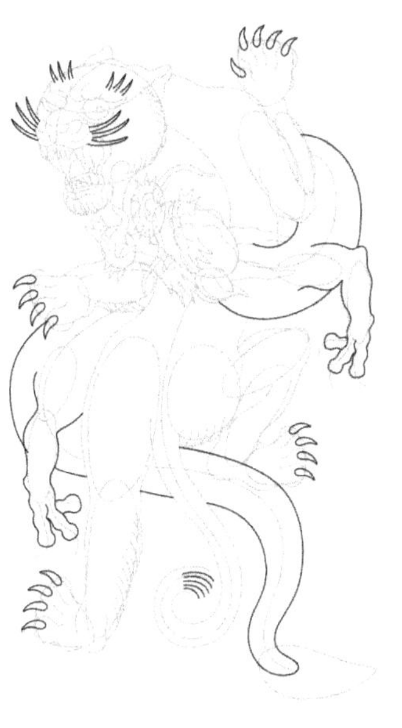

10

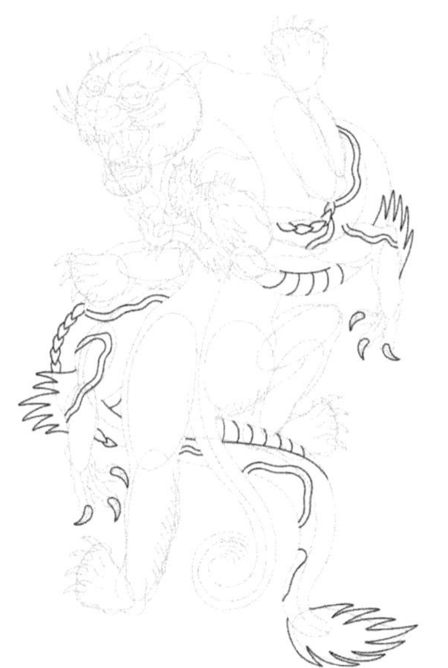

11

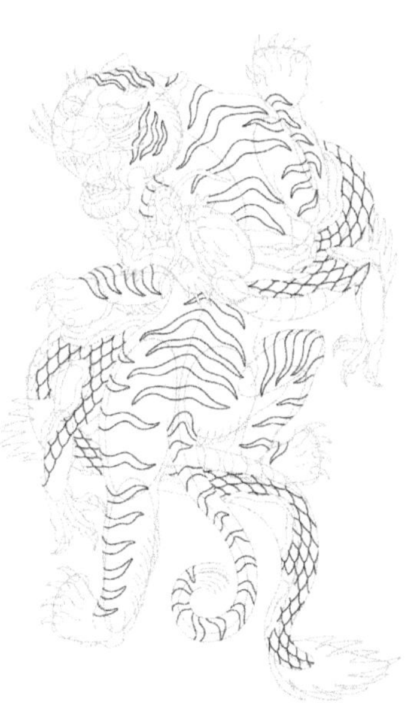

12

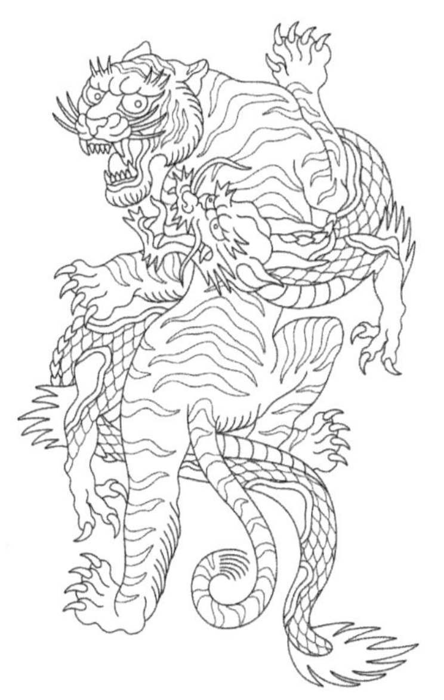

WOLF & SHEEP

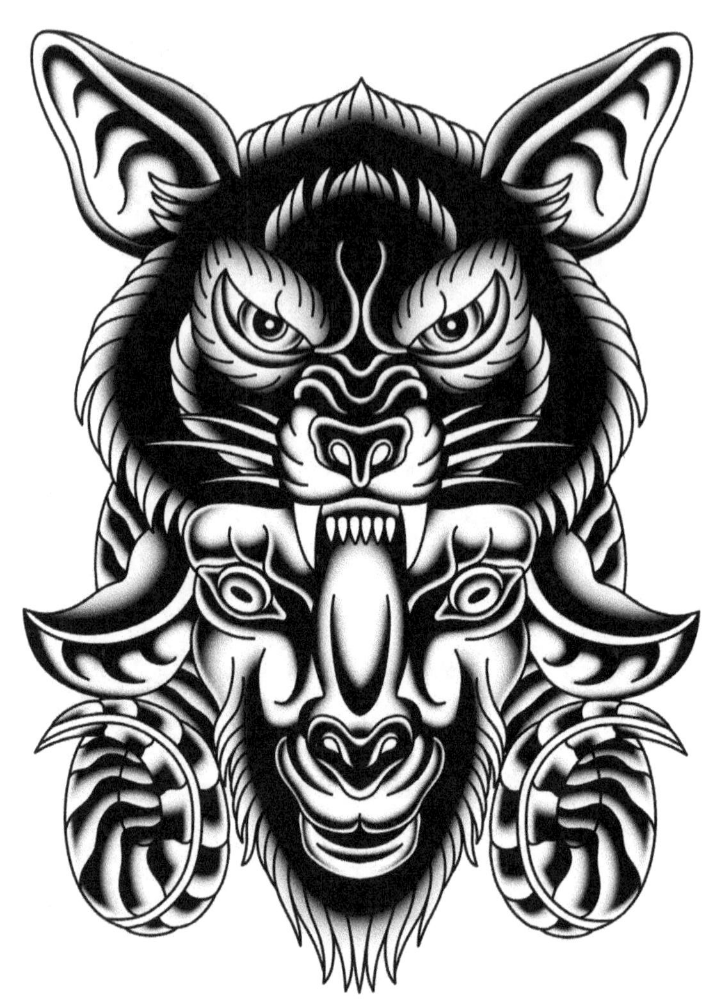

Pro tip: Size the wolf's head to overlap the sheep's head correctly

The top circle represents the wolf's head and should be about one and a half times larger than the sheep's. This allows the wolf's muzzle and jaw to fit naturally over the sheep's forehead when aligned. Keep the circles overlapping slightly to create the illusion of the wolf's head sitting convincingly on top.

01

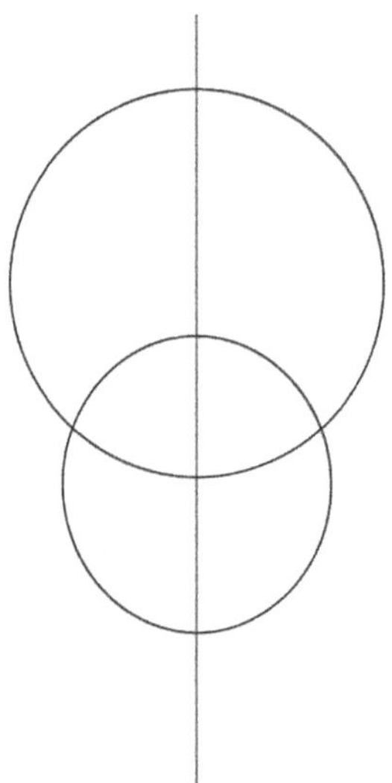

02

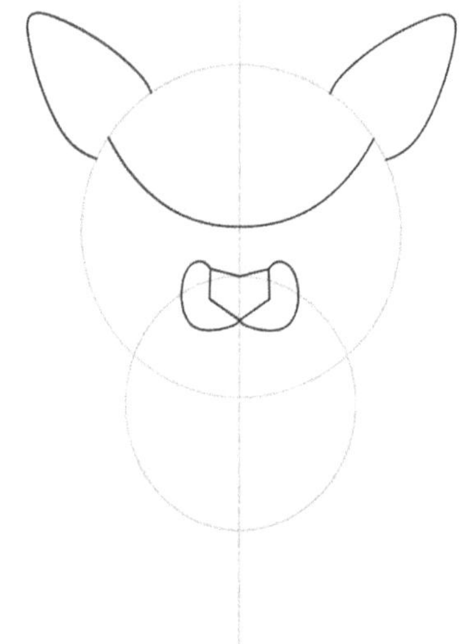

03

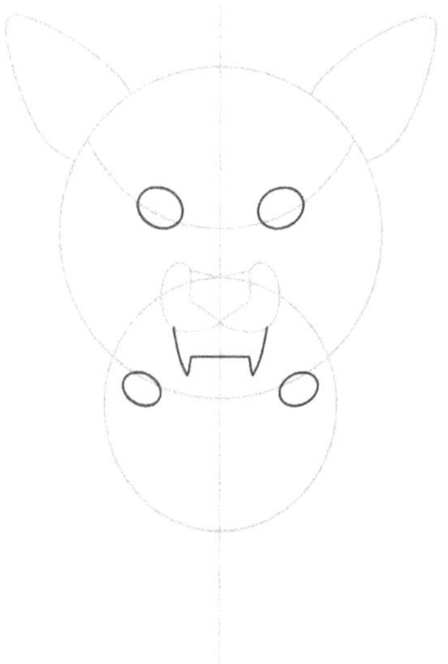

04

05

06

07

08

09

10

11

12

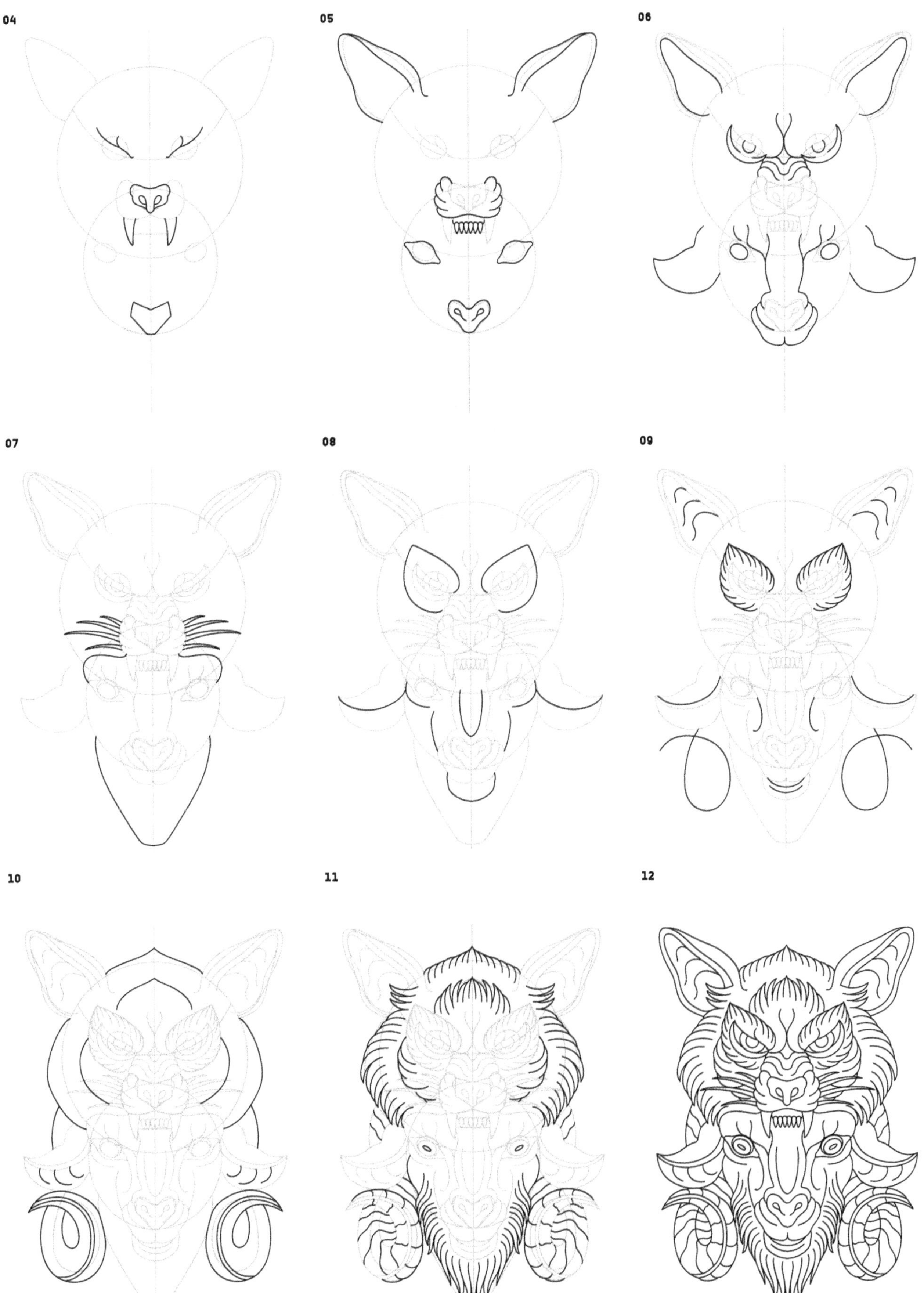

ROSE & GRIM REAPER

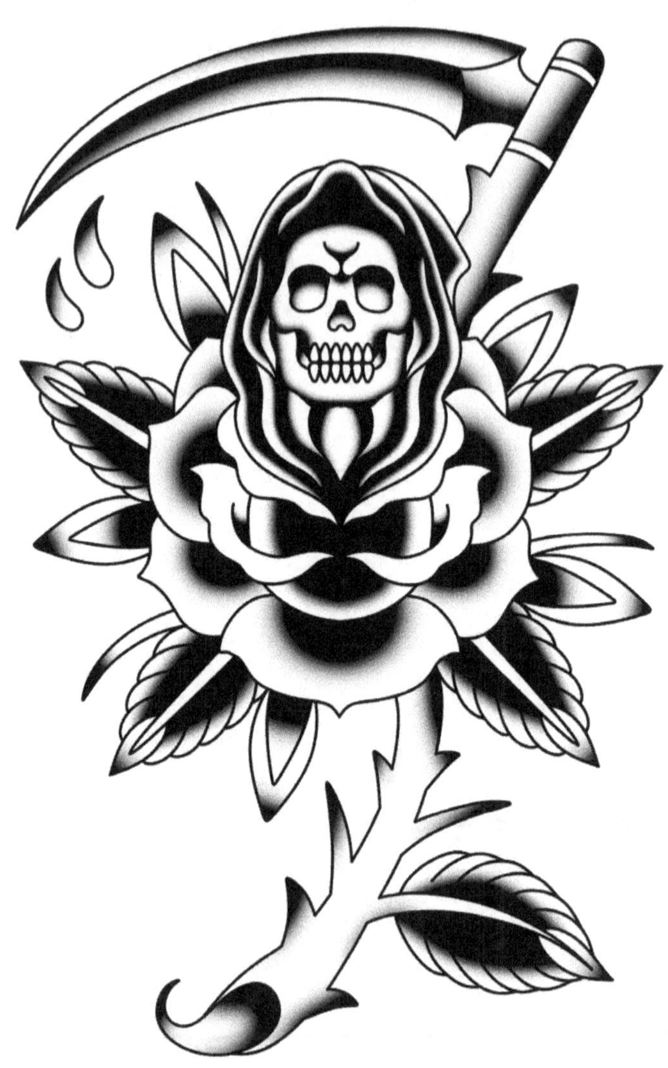

Pro tip: Use the main circle to gauge the reaper's head size and placement

Position the reaper's head so that its lower edge slightly overlaps the top edge of the main circle. The height of the oval should be roughly half the diameter of the main circle, giving a balanced proportion between the head and the underlying rose form. The vertical centre line ensures the head remains aligned with the centre of the design, helping you keep symmetry as you build the cloak and surrounding elements.

01

02

03

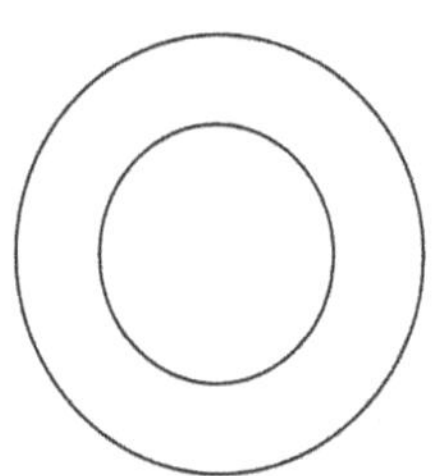

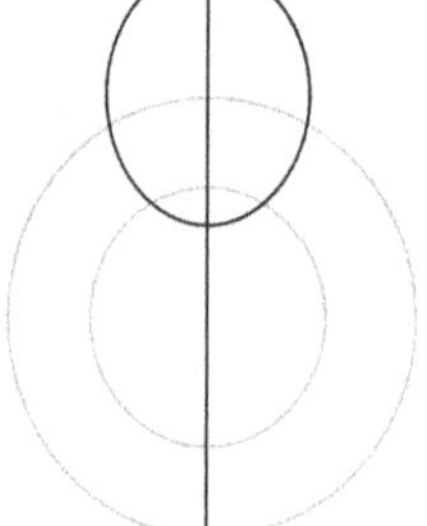

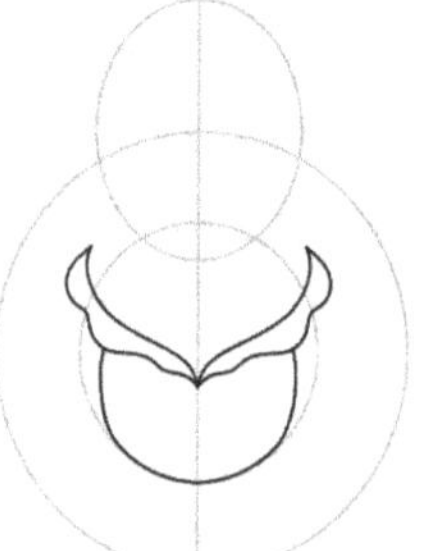

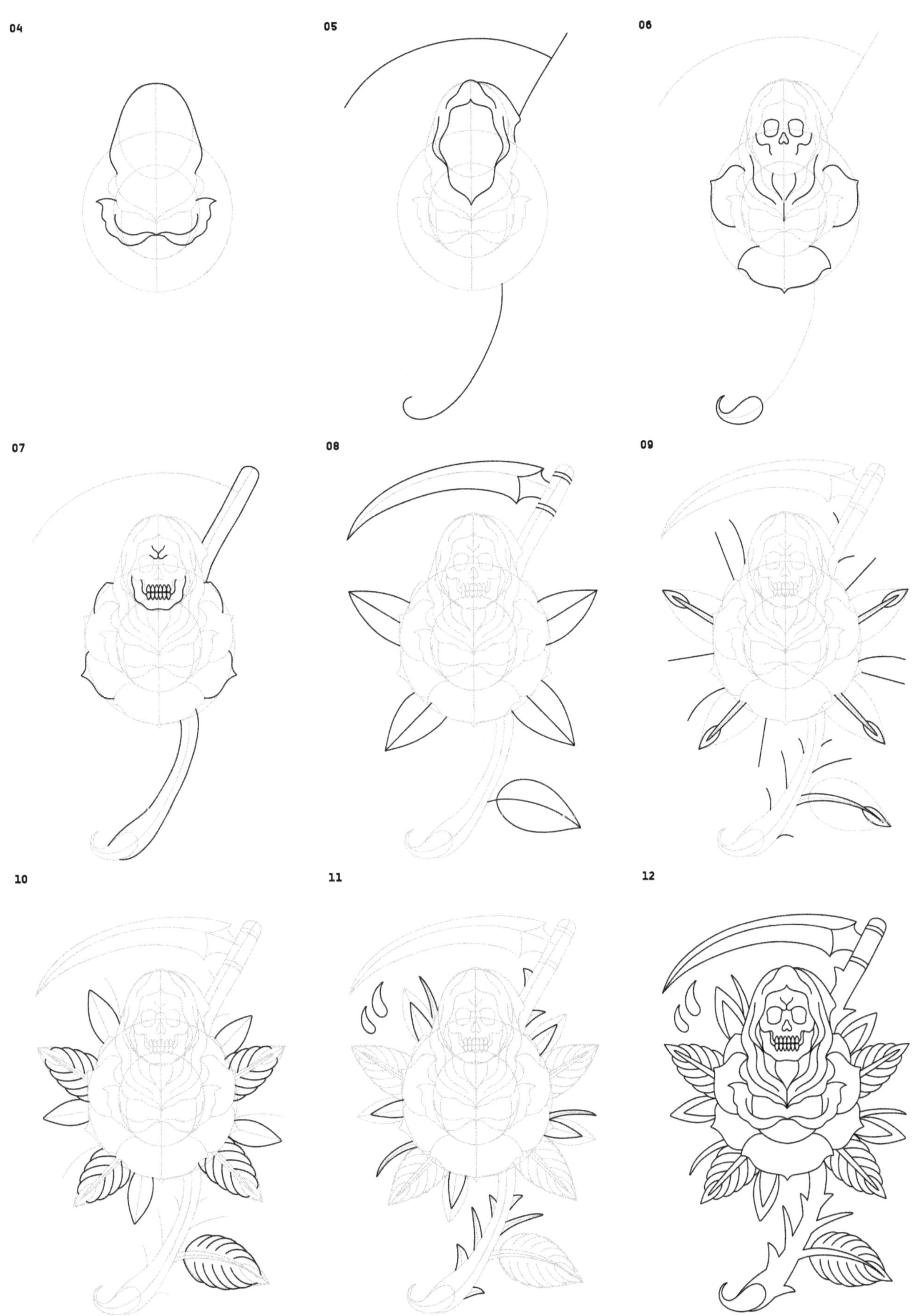

04
05
06
07
08
09
10
11
12
HOW TO DRAW TRADITIONAL TATTOOS

TIGER & SKULL

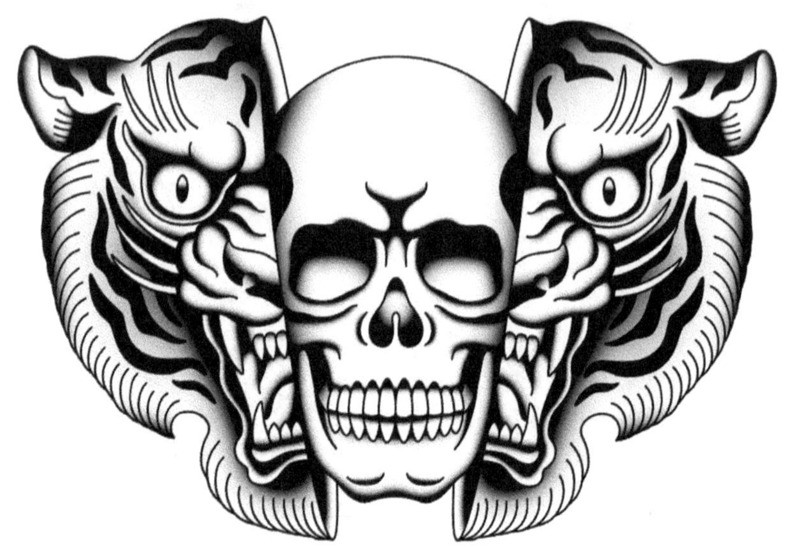

Pro tip: Use the circle to define the angle and placement of the tiger heads

Use the central circle as your guide for positioning and angling the two tiger heads. Draw the long ovals so they extend slightly further below the circle than above it to allow space for the jaw. Tilt the ovals gently inward toward the centre line to create a sense of focus and symmetry around the skull.

01

02

03

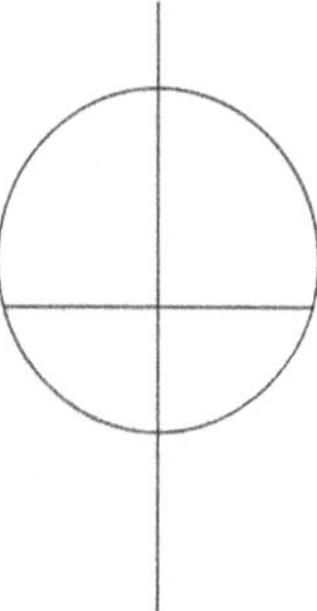

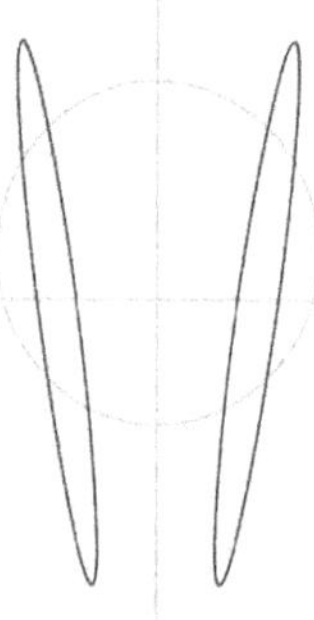

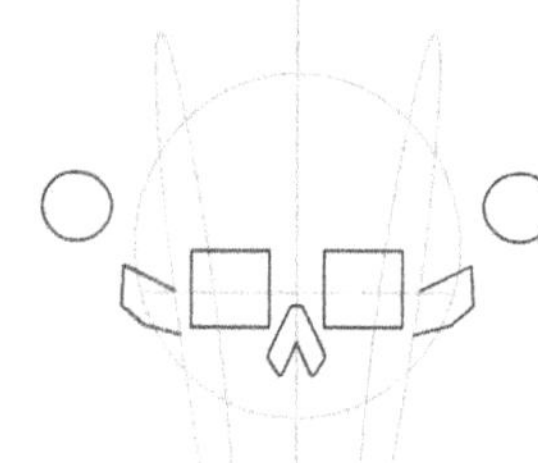

04

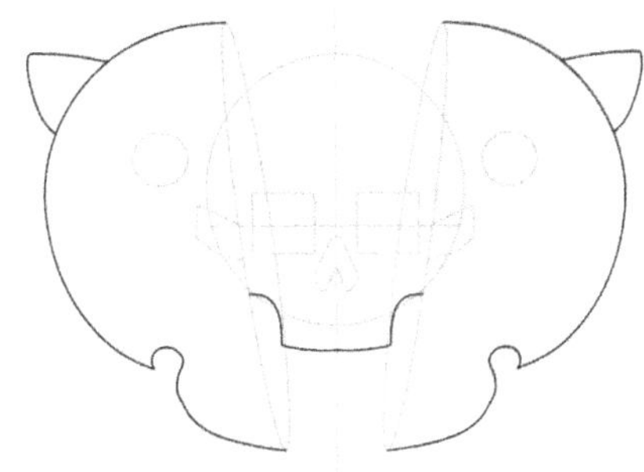

05

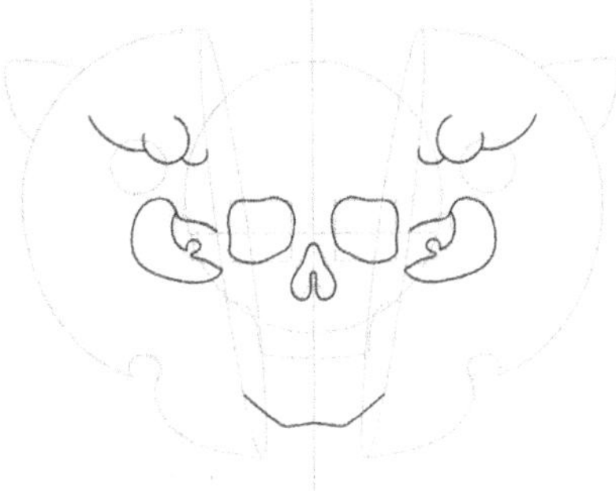

06

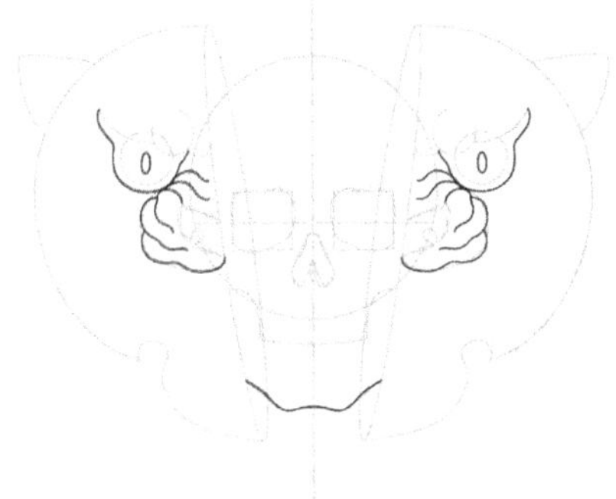

07

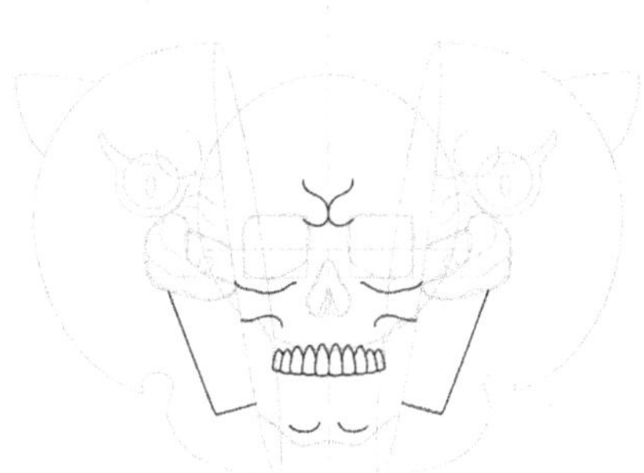

08

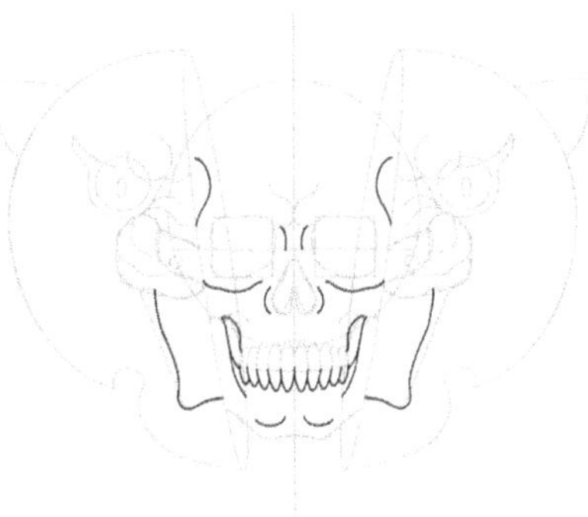

09

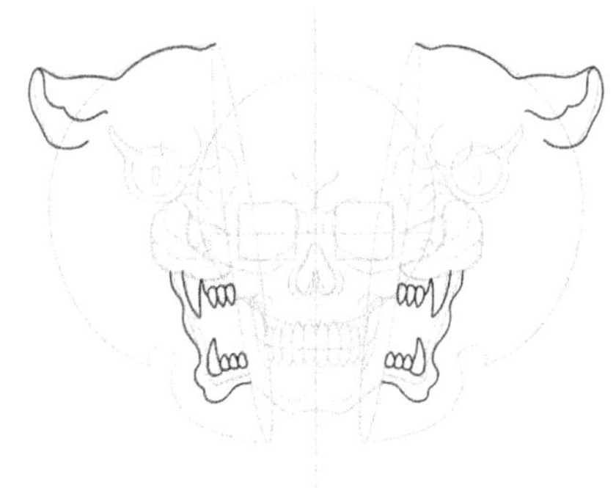

10

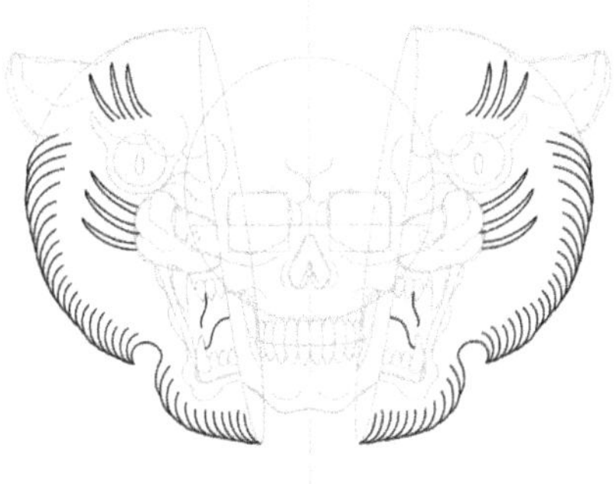

11

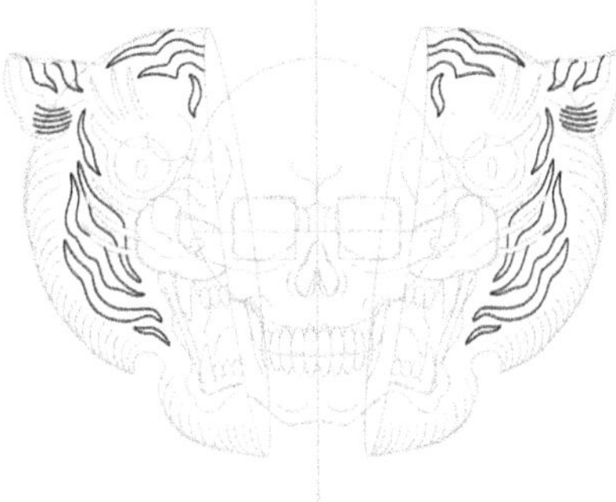

12

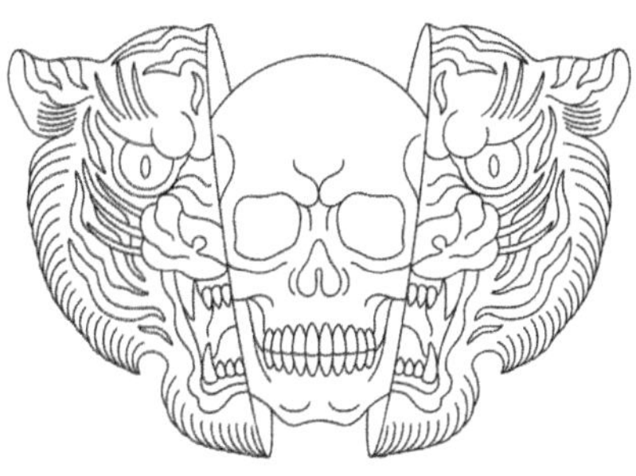

HOW TO DRAW TRADITIONAL TATTOOS

TORCH

Pro tip: Draw the flames with flow and symmetry

When drawing the fire, start by sketching long, sweeping S-curves that rise from the rim of the torch. Each flame should taper smoothly to a point and vary slightly in height to create rhythm and movement. Keep the overall shape symmetrical around the centre line, but avoid making the flames identical, small variations make the fire feel more natural.

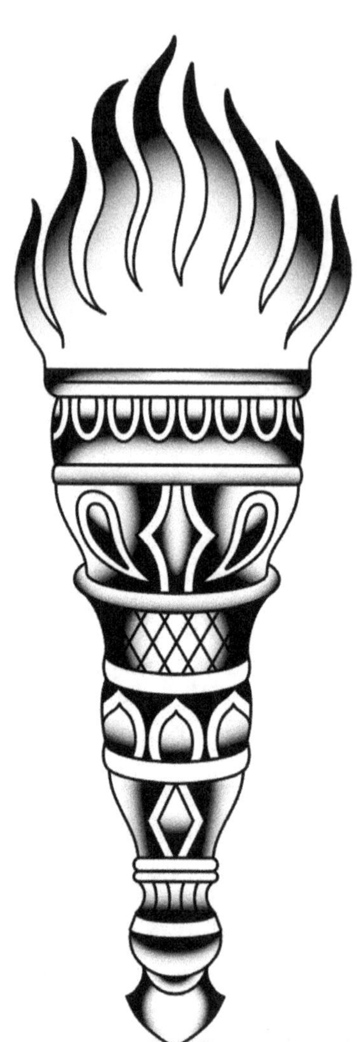

01

02

03

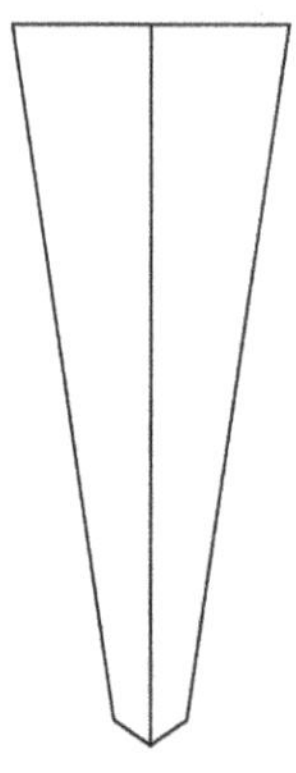

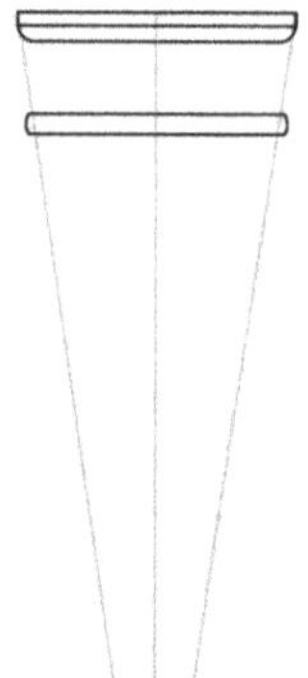

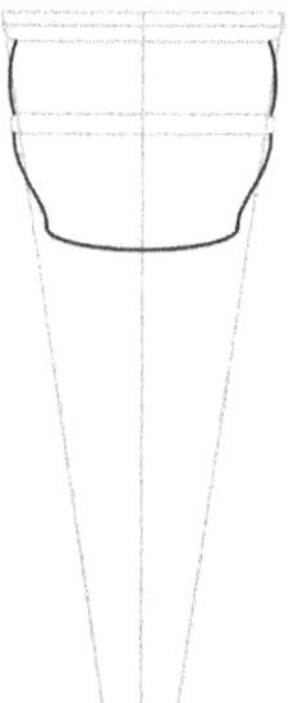

04

05

06

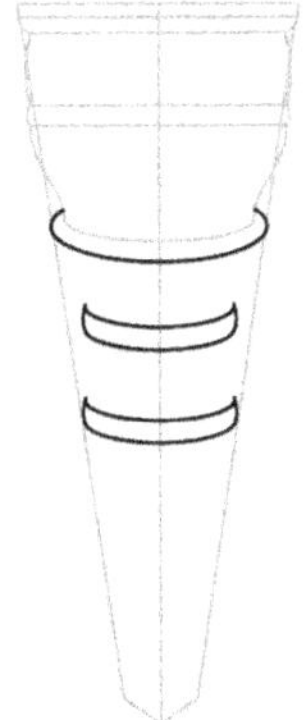

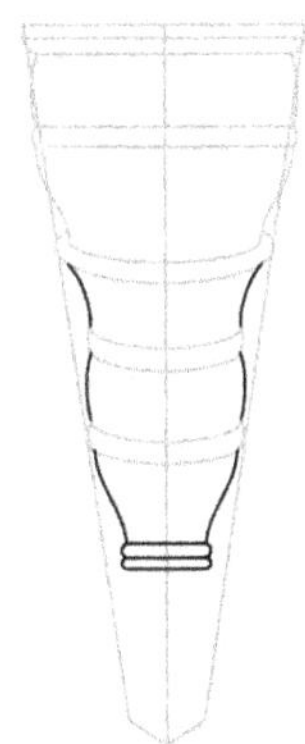

07

08

09

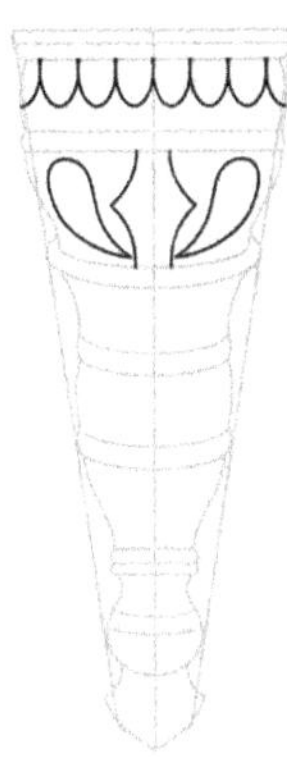

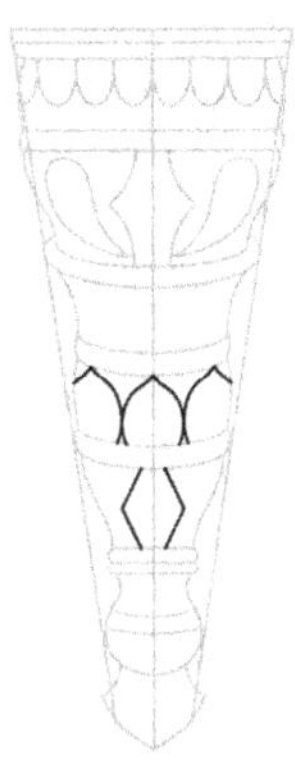

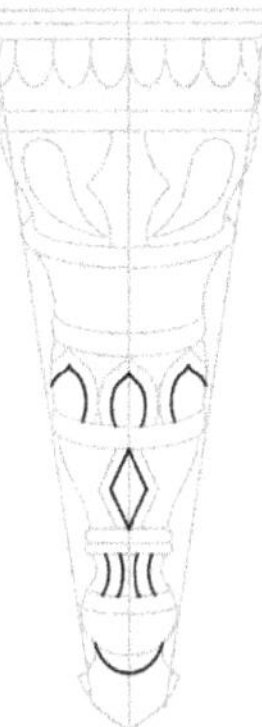

10

11

12

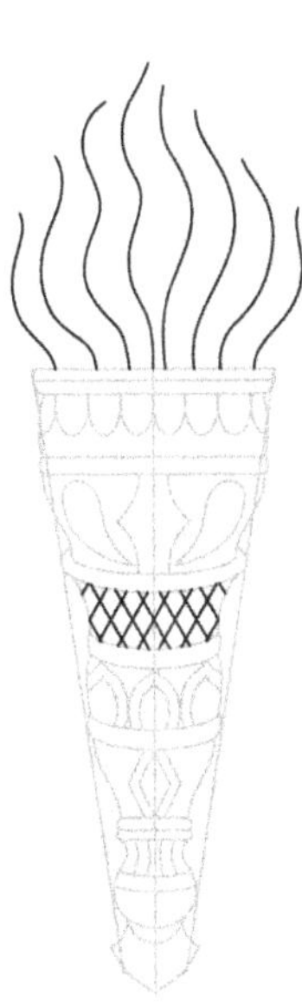

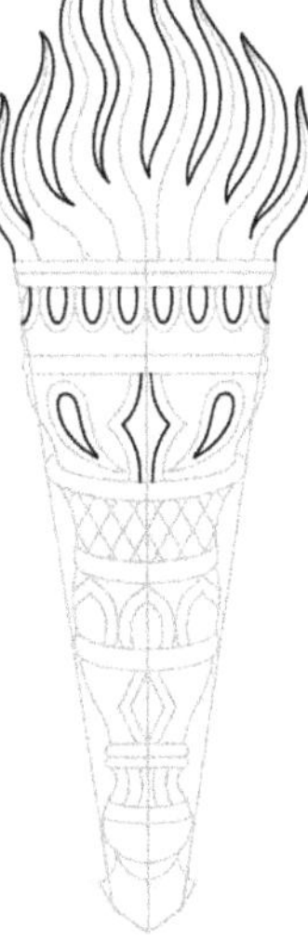

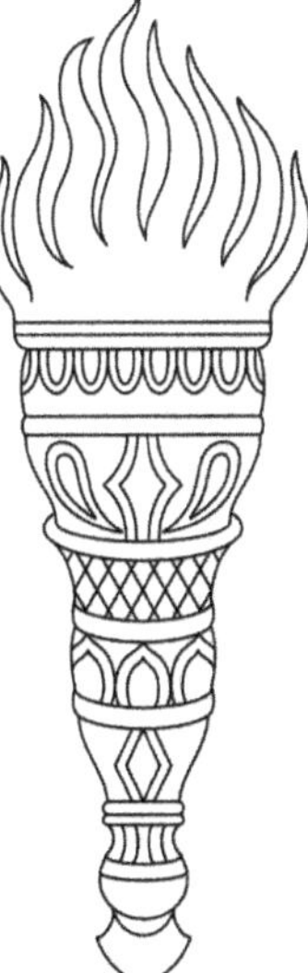

VIRGIN MARY

Pro tip: Use the head as a measuring unit for the body's height

To define the proportions of the Virgin Mary's figure, use the head as your base unit of measurement. The full body should measure roughly 6 head lengths from the base of the head to the bottom of the feet.

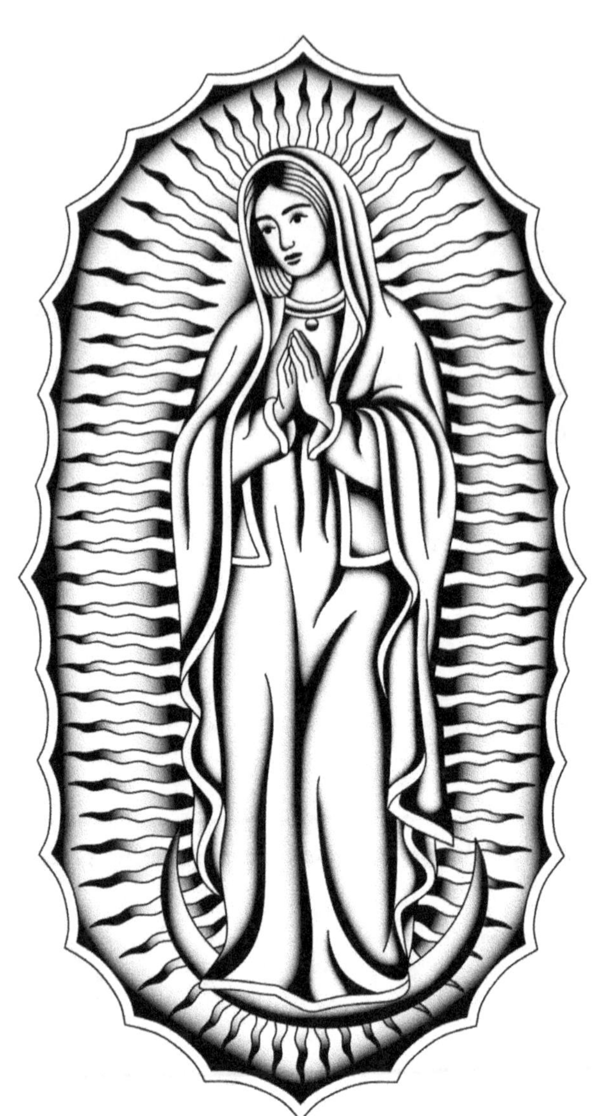

01

02

03

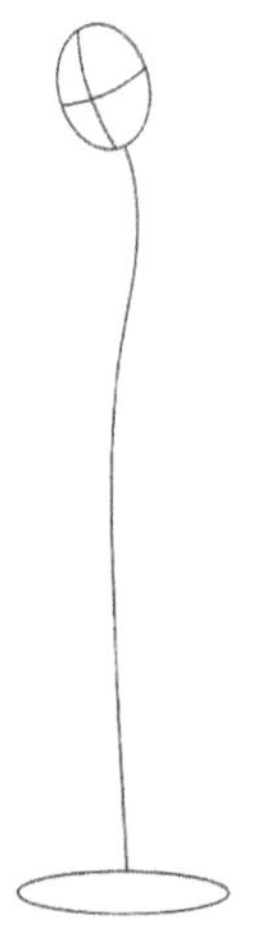

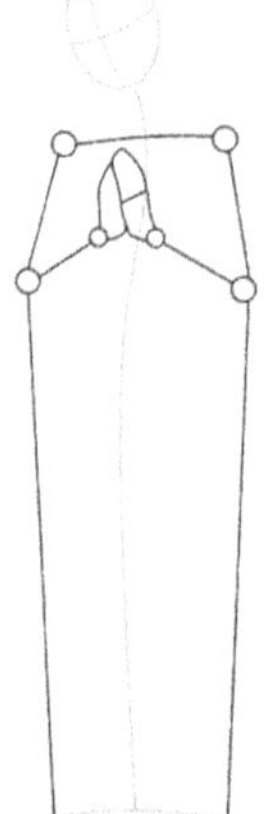

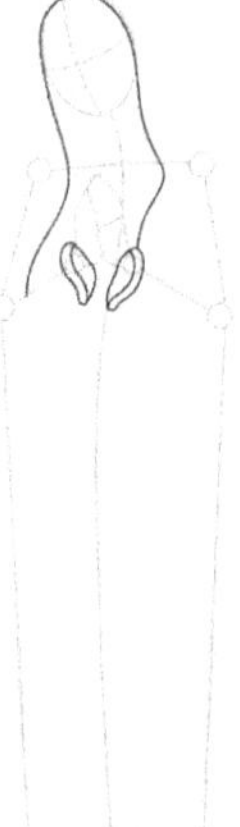

04

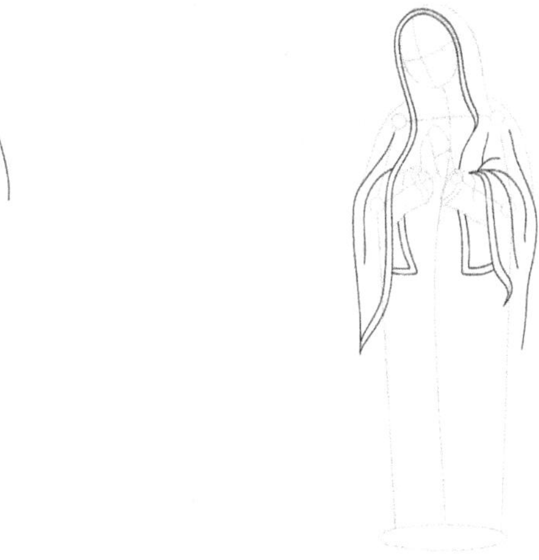

05

06

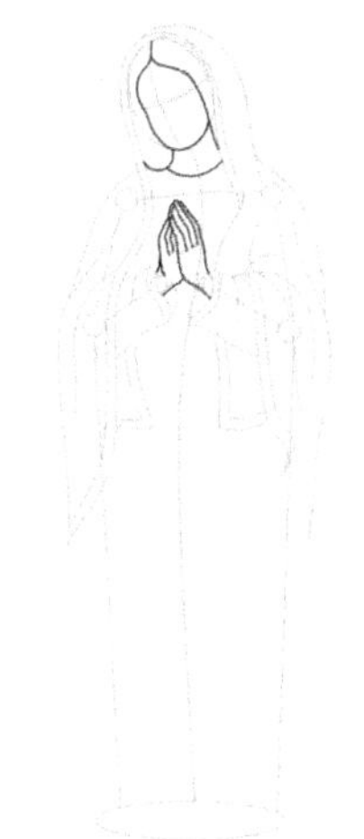

07

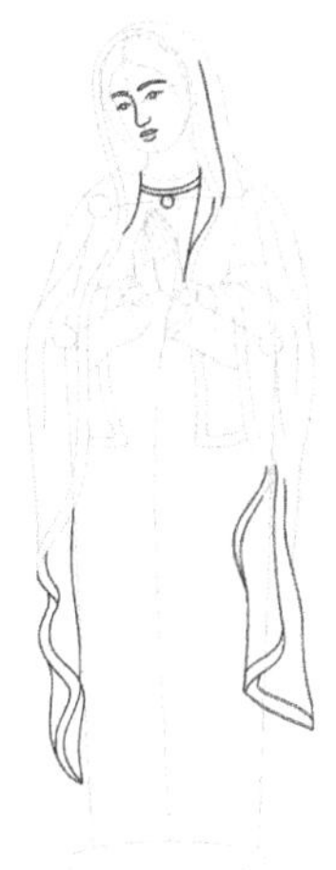

08

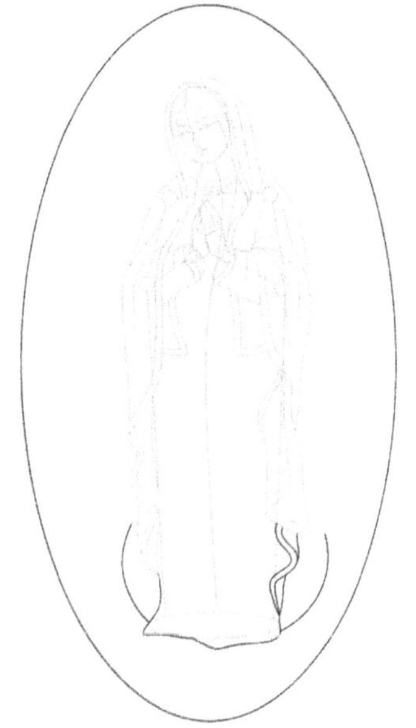

09

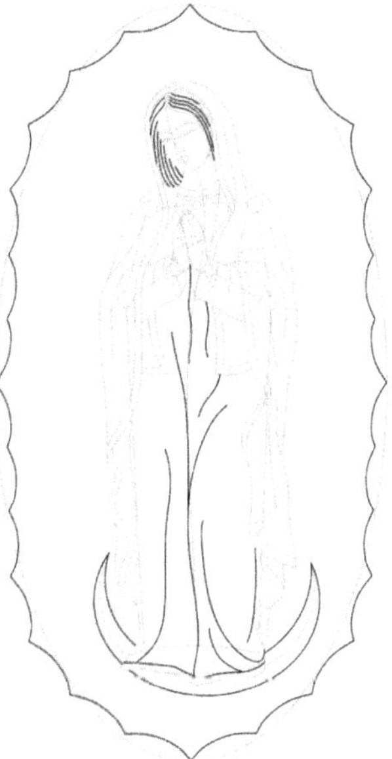

10

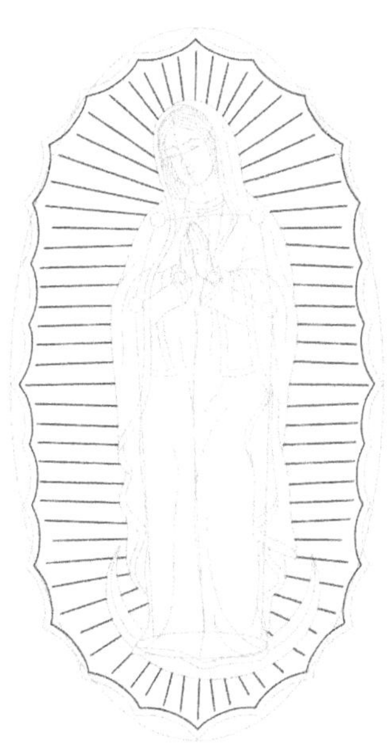

11

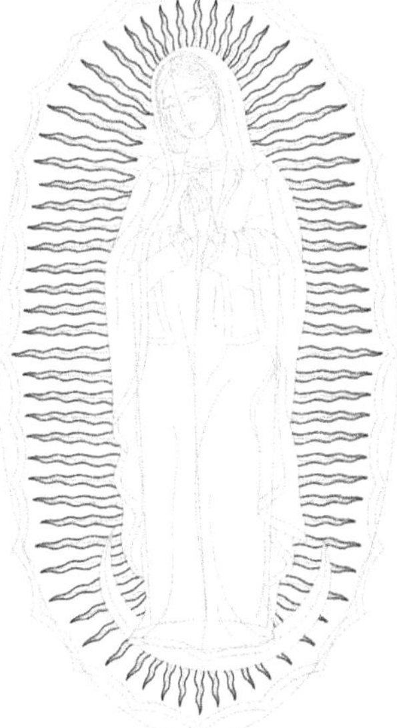

12

HOW TO DRAW TRADITIONAL TATTOOS

WOLF & TORCHES

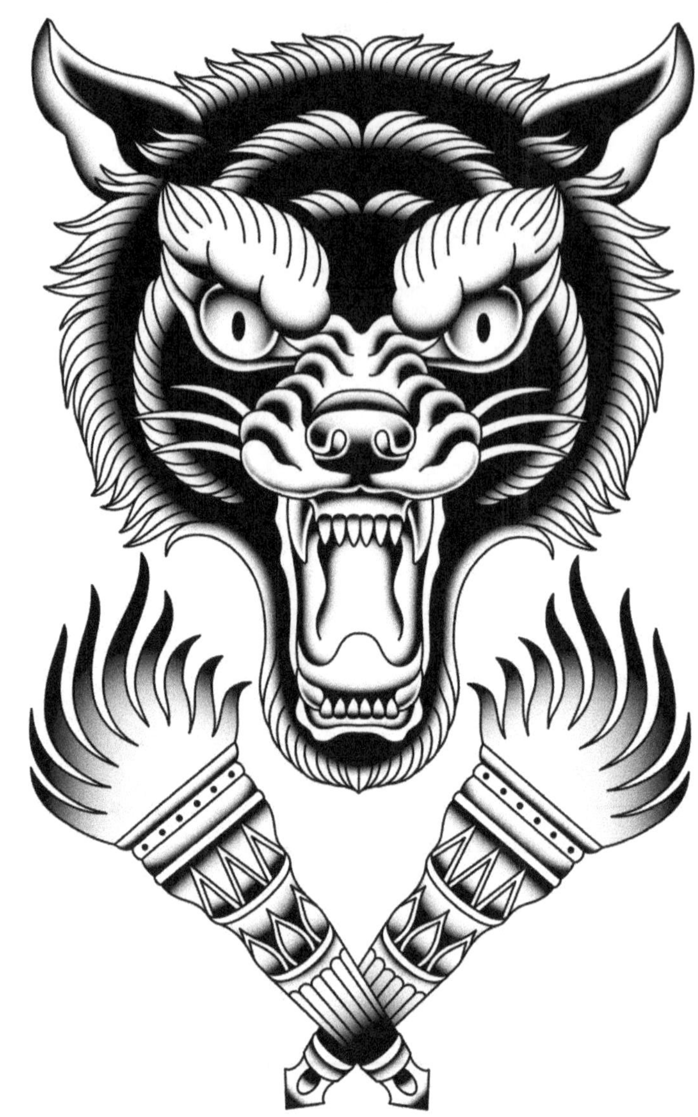

Pro tip: Size and place the jaw using the head circle

Draw a smaller circle directly beneath the head, leaving a visible gap between them. The jaw circle should be around a third of the head's size. This spacing gives the structure room for the muzzle and lower jaw to connect naturally when you refine the outline.

01

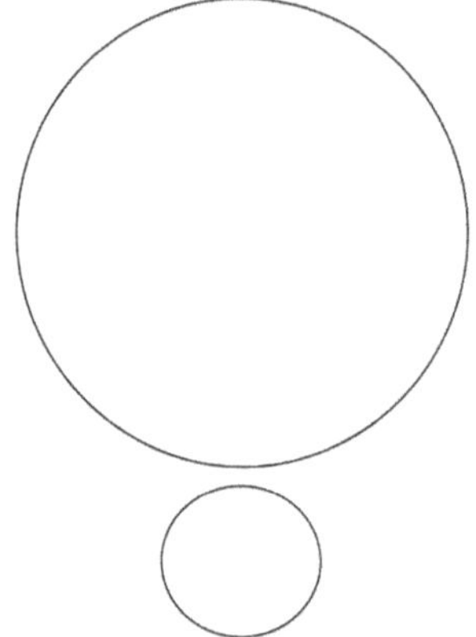

02

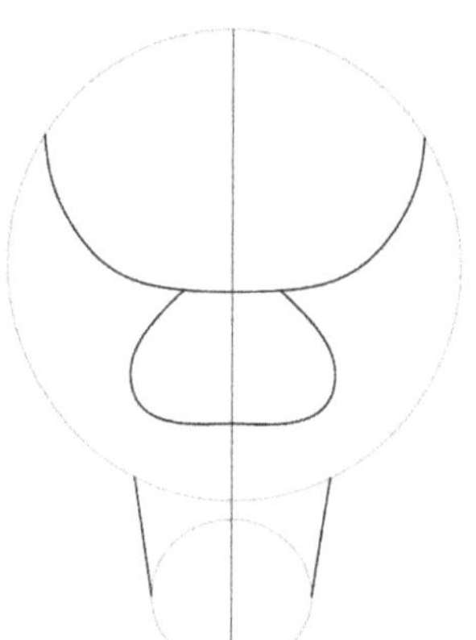

03

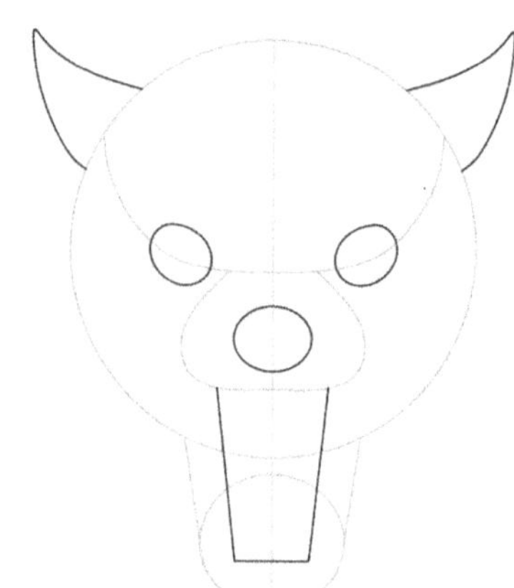

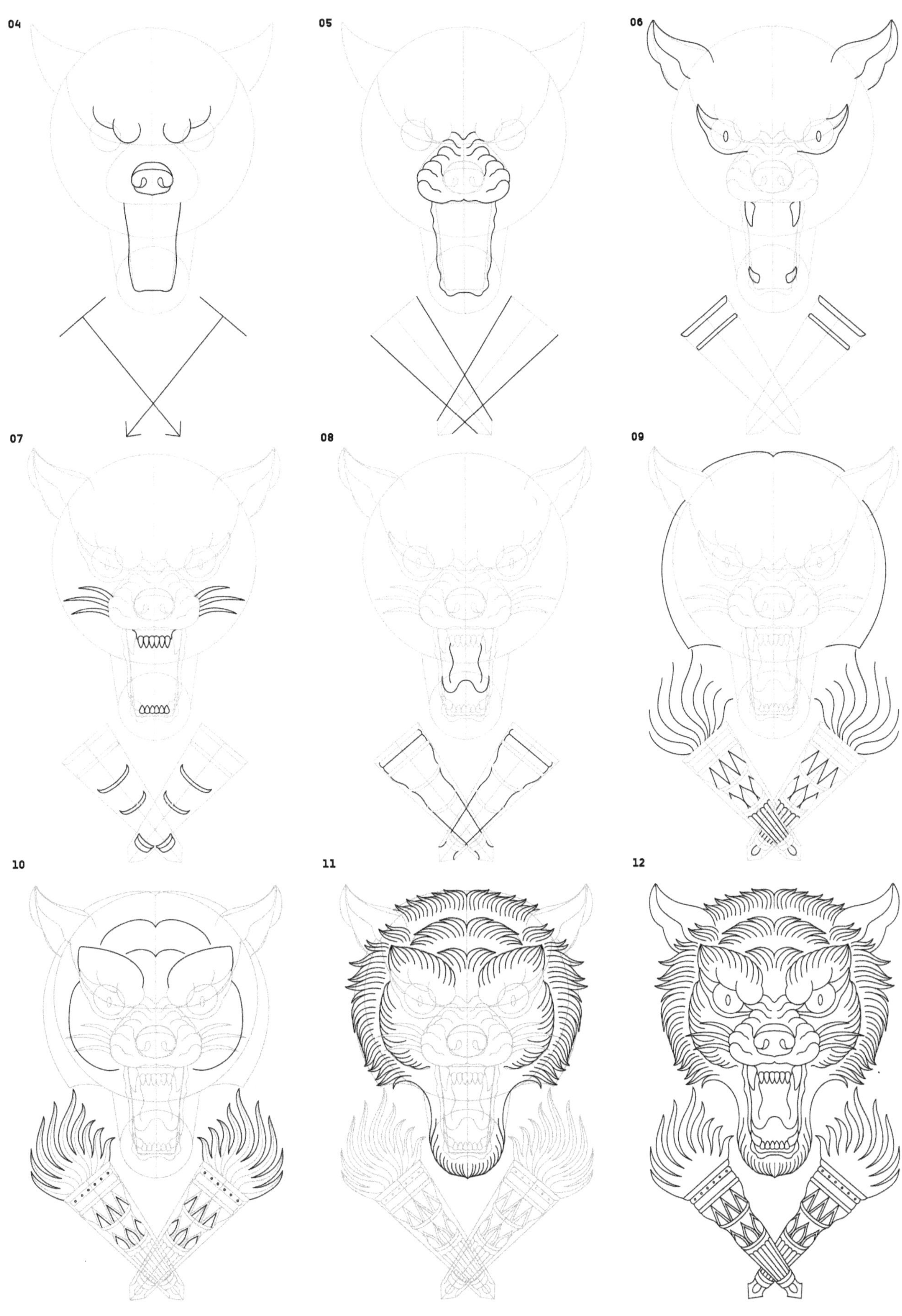

04
05
06
07
08
09
10
11
12
HOW TO DRAW TRADITIONAL TATTOOS

HOW TO DRAW
PRACTICE BOOK

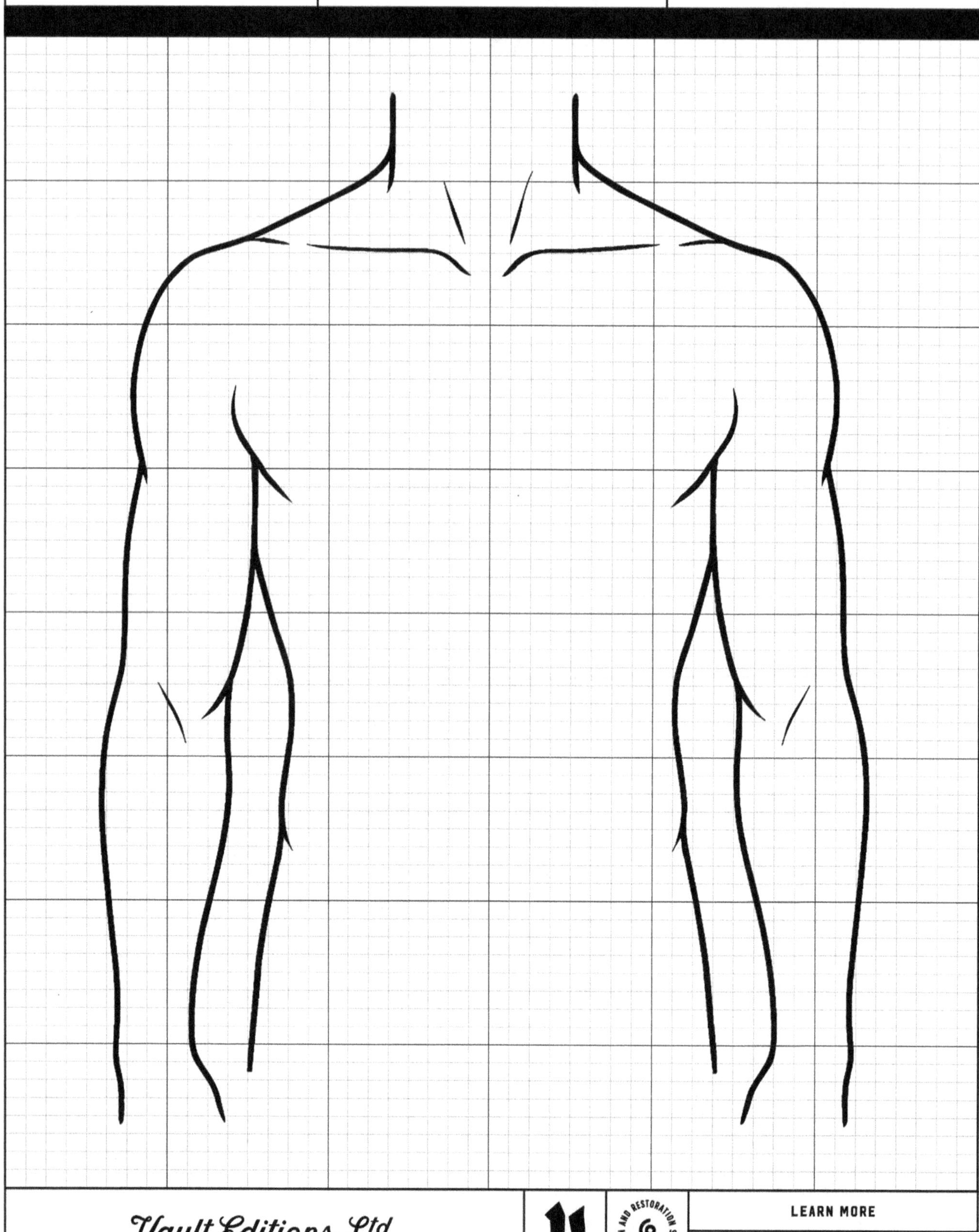

HOW TO DRAW
PRACTICE BOOK

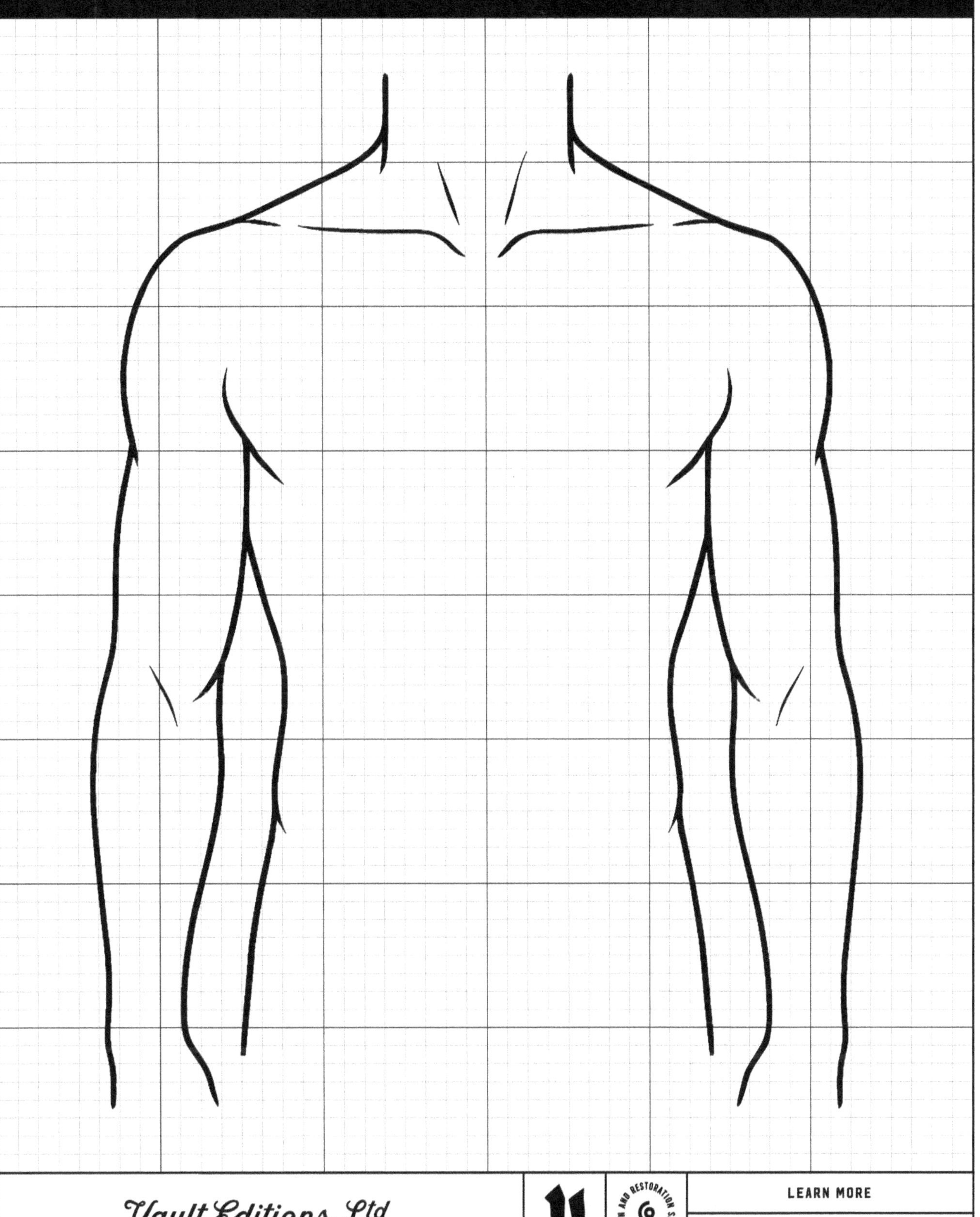

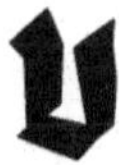
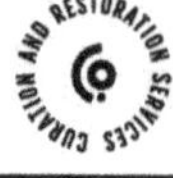
CURATION AND RESTORATION SERVICES

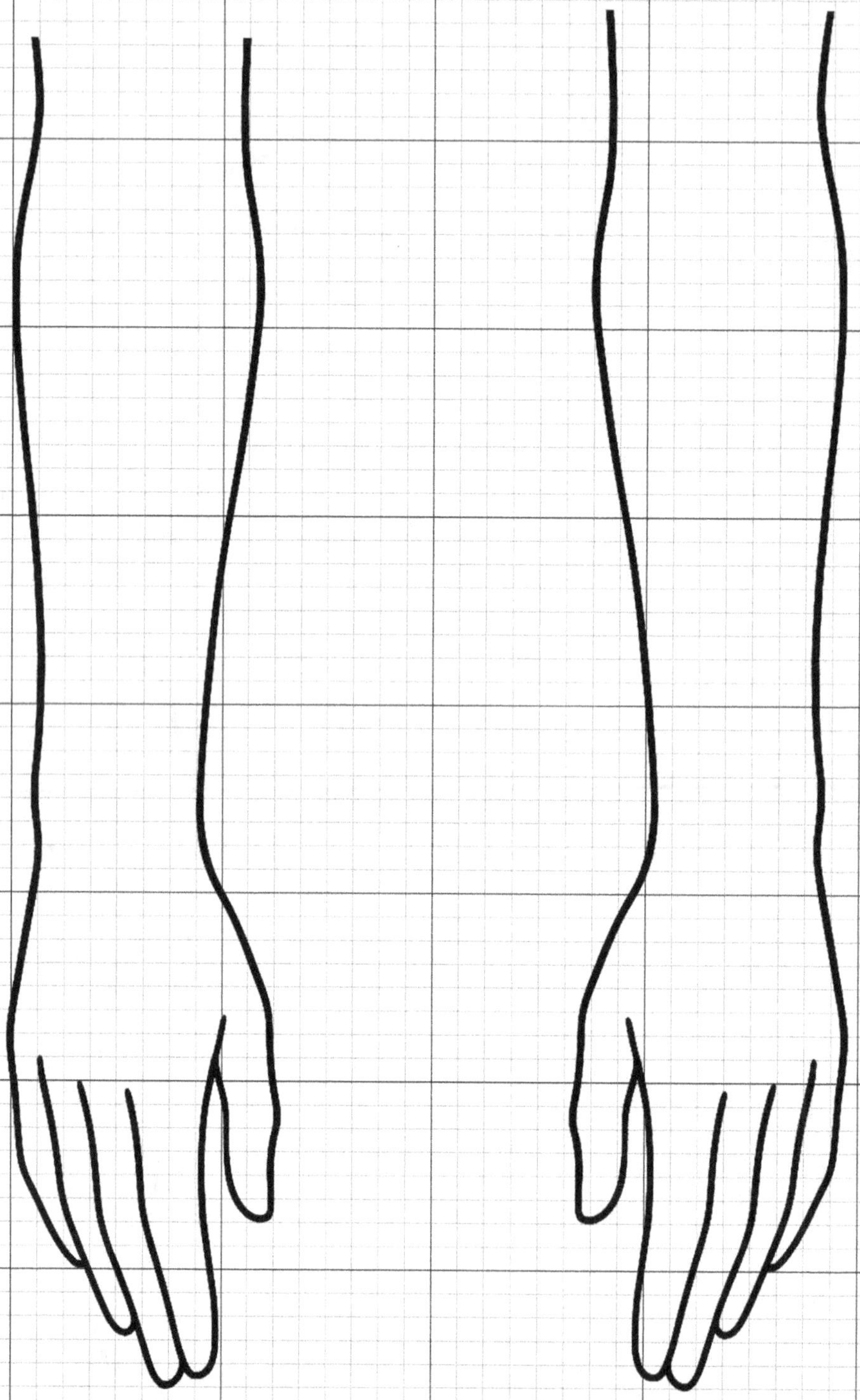

HOW TO DRAW
PRACTICE BOOK

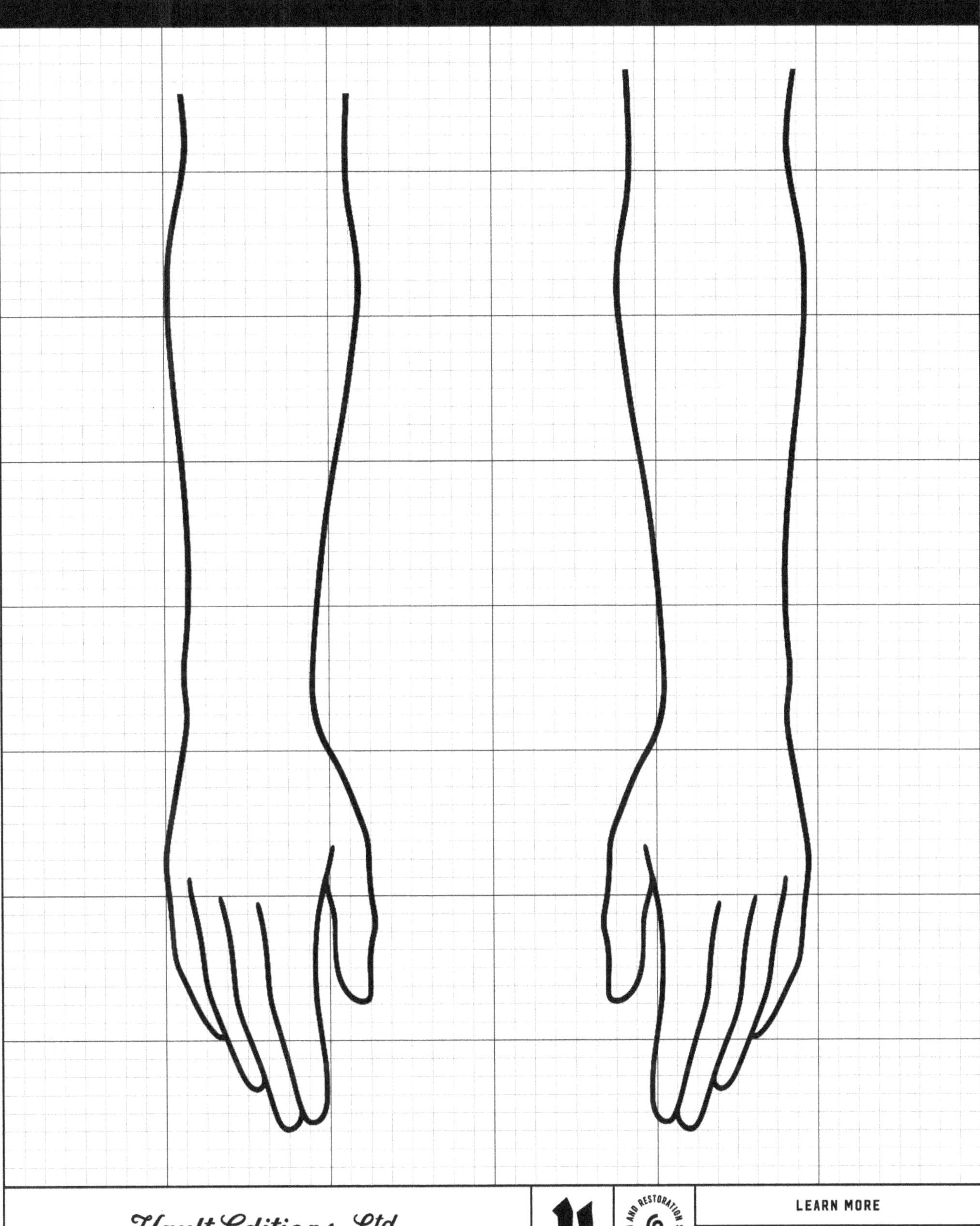

Vault Editions Ltd

LEARN MORE

VAULTEDITIONS.COM

PRACTICE
MAKES
PERFECT
TRD MRK

HOW TO DRAW
PRACTICE BOOK

PRACTICE
MAKES
PERFECT
TRD MRK

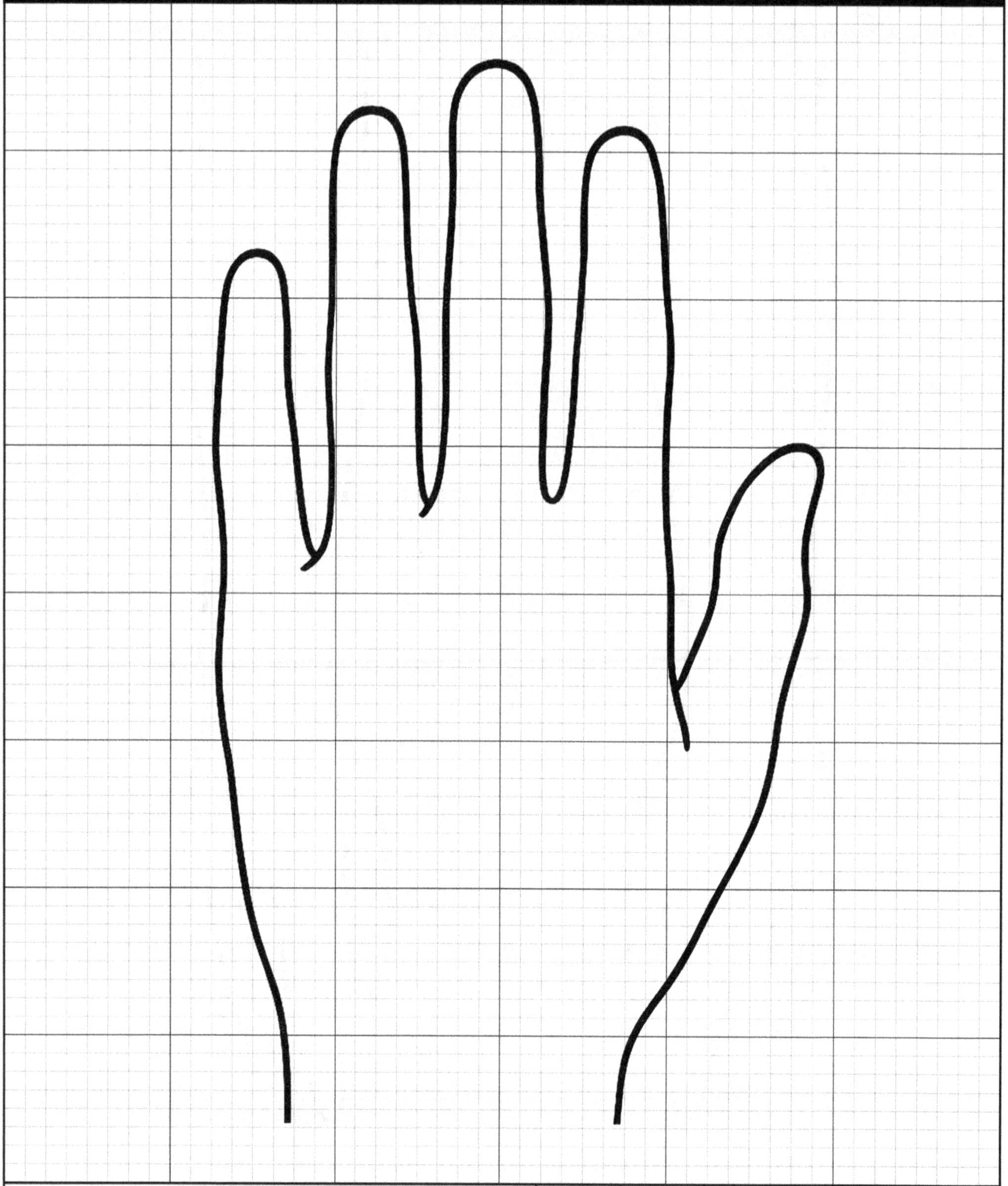

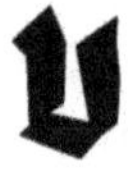
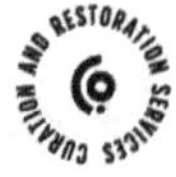

HOW TO DRAW
PRACTICE BOOK

PRACTICE
MAKES
PERFECT
T R D
M R K

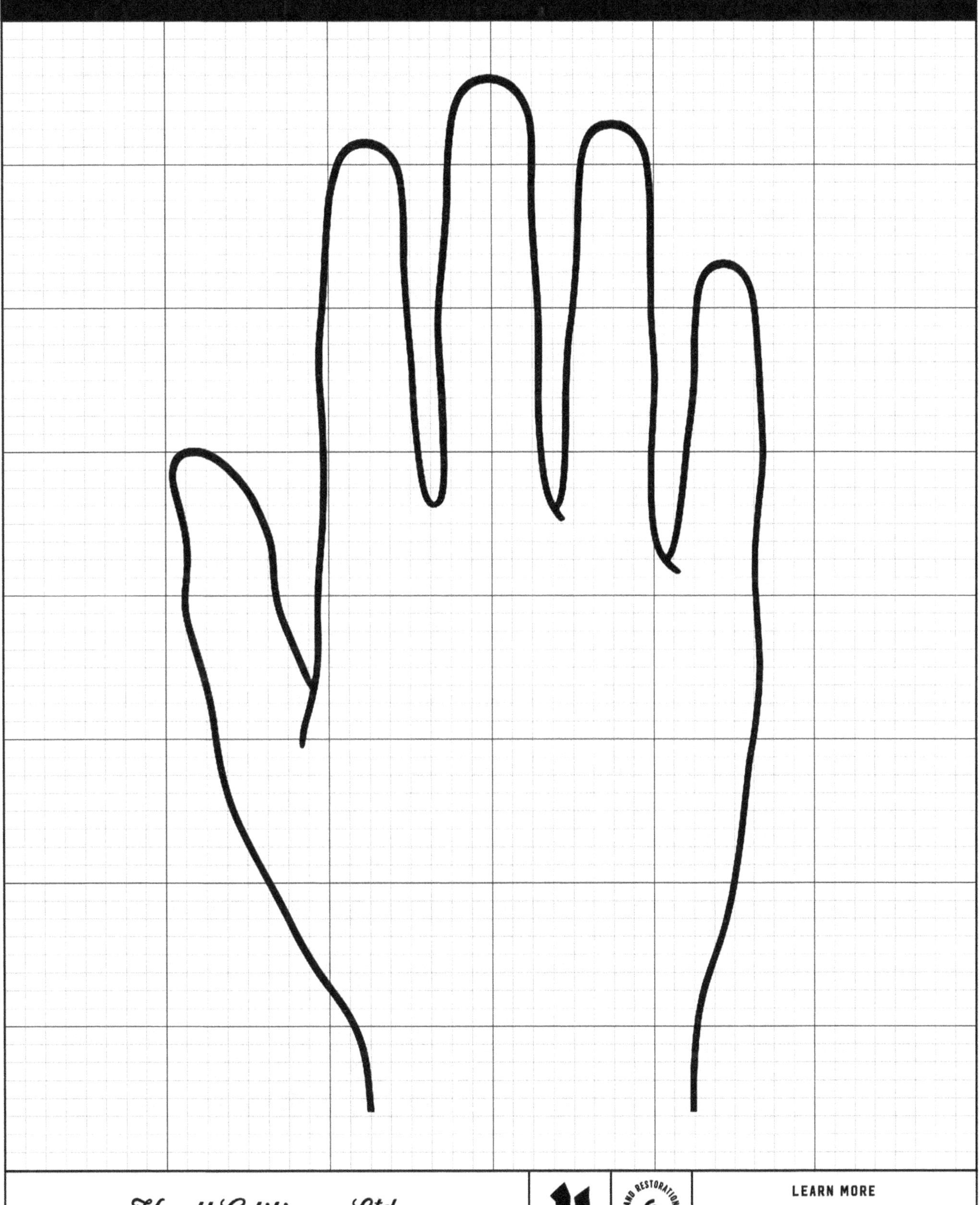

Vault Editions Ltd

LEARN MORE

VAULTEDITIONS.COM

HOW TO DRAW
PRACTICE BOOK

PRACTICE
TRD
MAKES
MRK
PERFECT

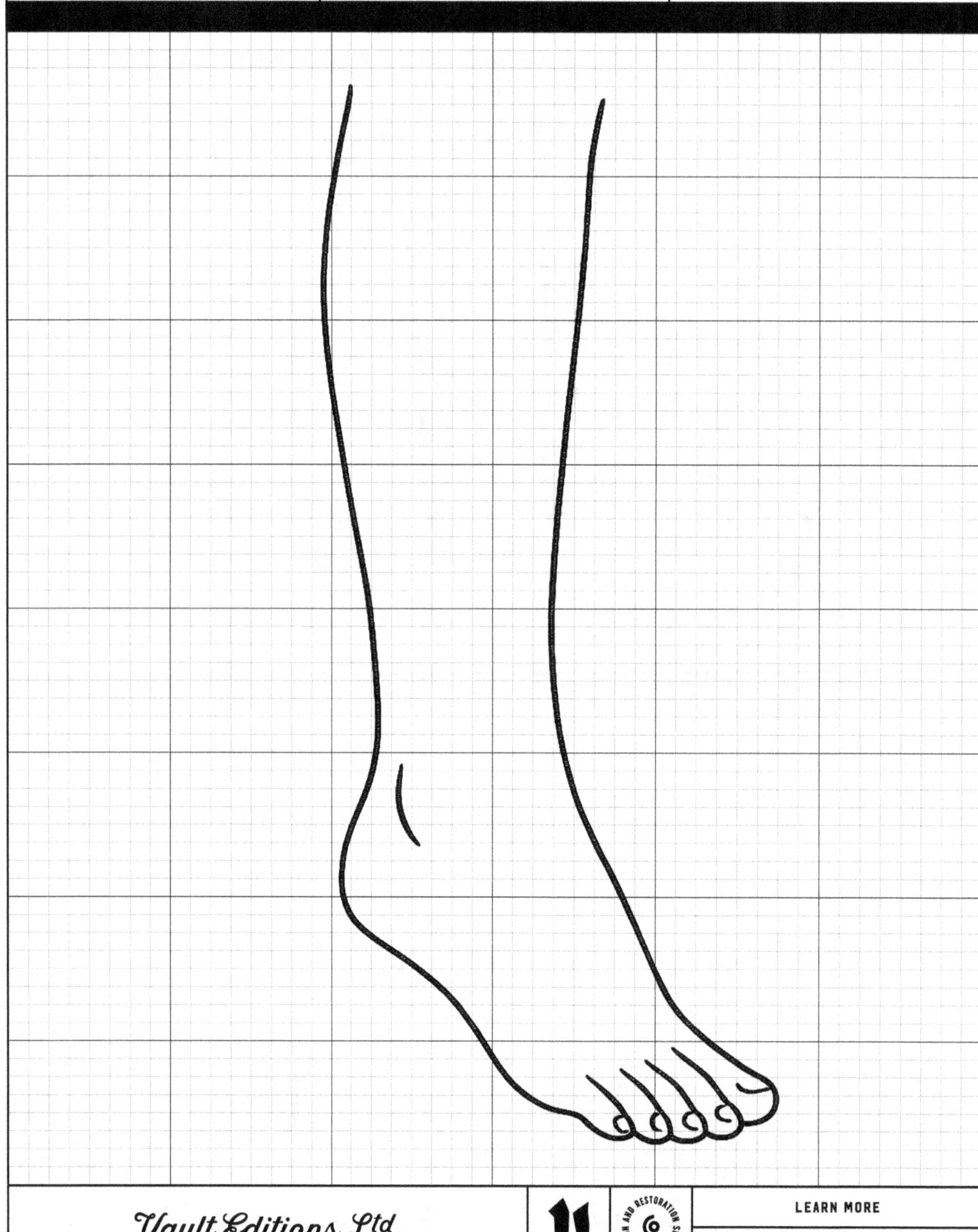

Vault Editions Ltd

LEARN MORE

VAULTEDITIONS.COM

HOW TO DRAW
PRACTICE BOOK

HOW TO DRAW
PRACTICE BOOK

PRACTICE MAKES PERFECT
T R D · M R K

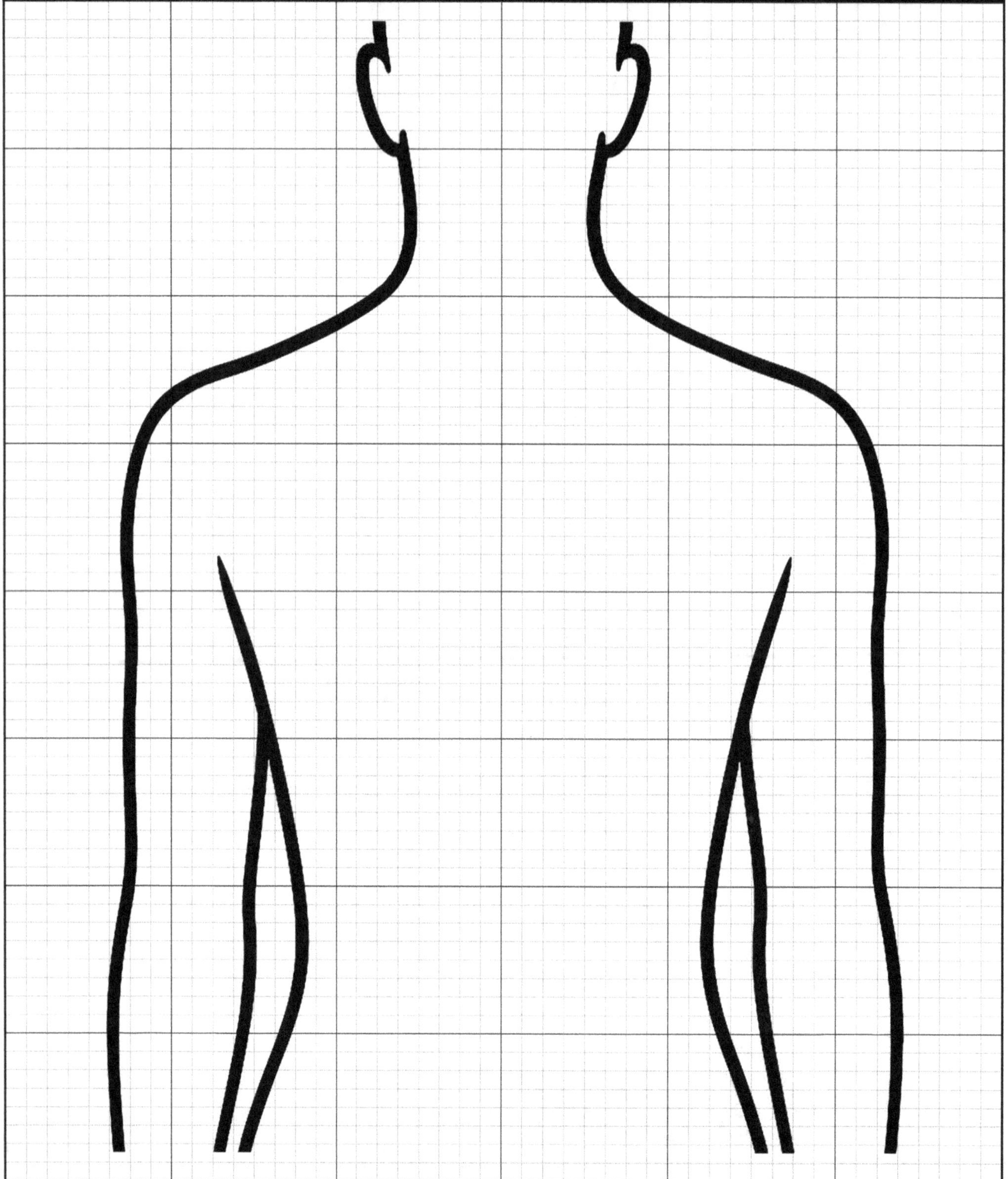

Vault Editions Ltd

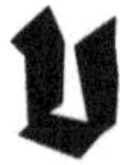
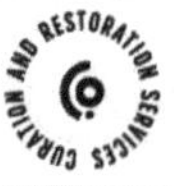

LEARN MORE
VAULTEDITIONS.COM

HOW TO DRAW
PRACTICE BOOK

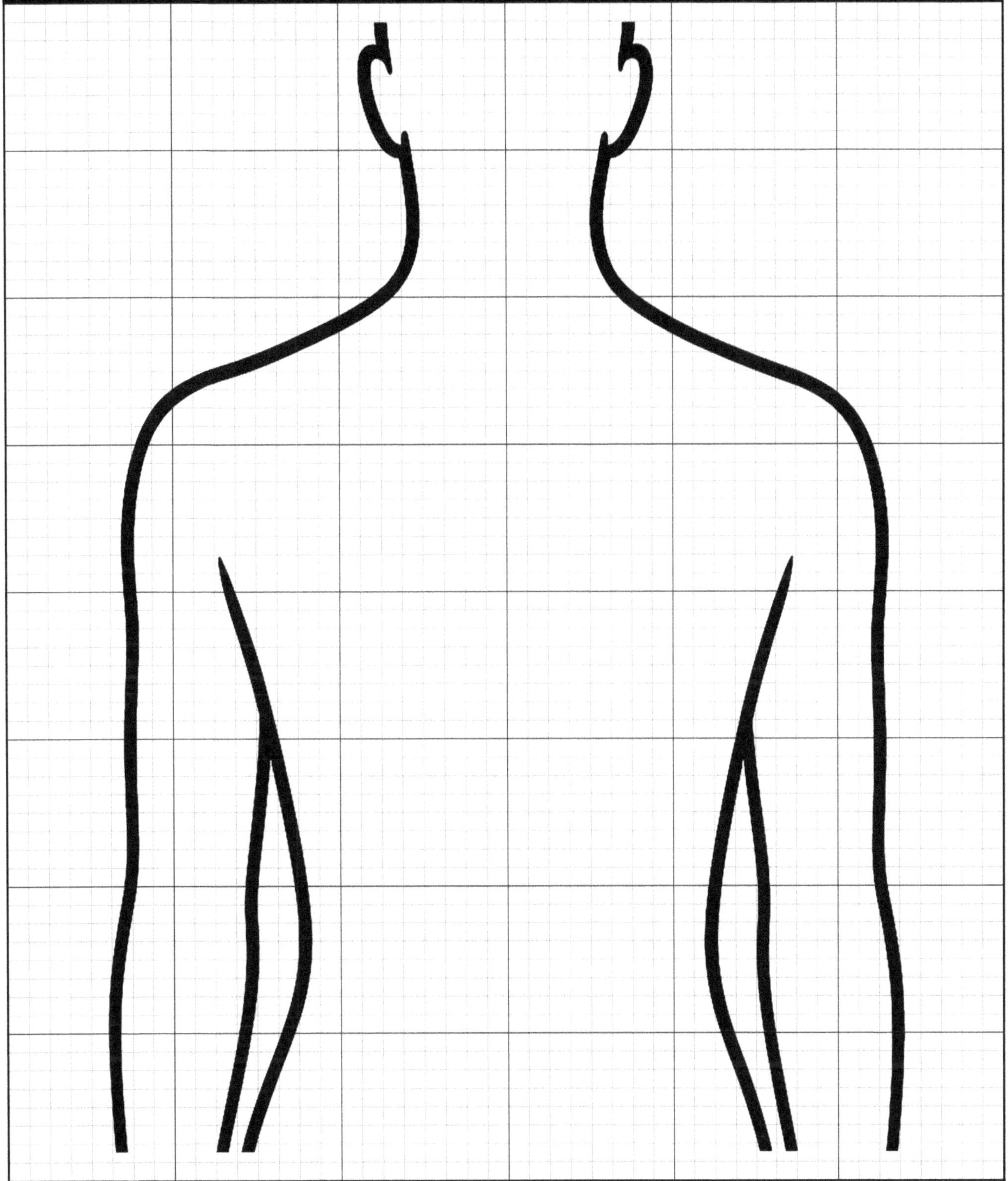

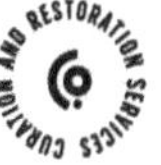

HOW TO DRAW
PRACTICE BOOK

Vault Editions Ltd

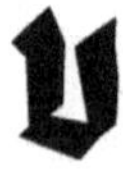

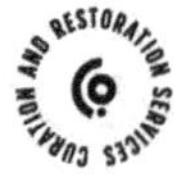

CONCLUSION

Traditional tattoo designs have stood the test of time because they speak through bold lines, clear symbols, and universal emotion. Across this book, you've explored the foundations of the style, from iconic designs like the panther, dagger, torch, and swallow, to complex compositions such as the tiger and dragon, skull and snake, and the handshake with the devil. You've learned how structure, balance, and confident line work give each design its power, and how simplicity and repetition create timeless appeal.

Traditional tattooing is a living art form. Its motifs can be reinterpreted endlessly, shaped by new stories, personal meaning, and evolving styles. As you continue to draw, remember that every design you make is part of this ongoing lineage. Study the old masters, but don't be afraid to add your own voice. Experiment with proportions, motifs, and details while staying true to the principles that define the style: bold outlines, strong silhouettes, and meaningful imagery.

Keep refining your technique, keep drawing, and keep the tradition alive through your own imagination.

ABOUT THE ARTIST

Abrom Rose, an accomplished artist with a remarkable talent for visual communication and instructional illustration, created the designs in this book. With a background in illustration and design, Abrom brings clarity, precision, and artistic sensitivity to every drawing he produces. His work is defined by confident linework, strong composition, and a deep understanding of form, qualities that make his illustrations both engaging and accessible to learners at all levels.

Abrom's approach to drawing is rooted in careful observation and a passion for traditional tattoo art, which he interprets with originality and technical skill. Whether guiding beginners or inspiring experienced artists, his ability to break down complex motifs into clear, teachable steps sets his work apart.

LEARN MORE

At Vault Editions, our mission is to provide the highest-quality reference materials for artists and designers, offering meticulously curated resources that inspire and empower creativity. If you've found value in this book, we invite you to explore more of our expertly crafted titles at vaulteditions.com, where you'll discover a world of visual inspiration and practical tools designed to elevate your creative work.

REVIEW THIS BOOK

As a family-owned and operated independent publisher, reviews are essential to the success of our business. Please leave an honest review of this book wherever you purchased it.

JOIN OUR COMMUNITY

Are you the creative and curious type? If so, you will love our community on Instagram. Every day, we share bizarre and beautiful artwork ranging from 17th and 18th-century natural history and scientific illustrations to mythical beasts, ornamental designs, anatomical drawings and more; join our community of 300K+ people today by searching @vault_editions on Instagram.

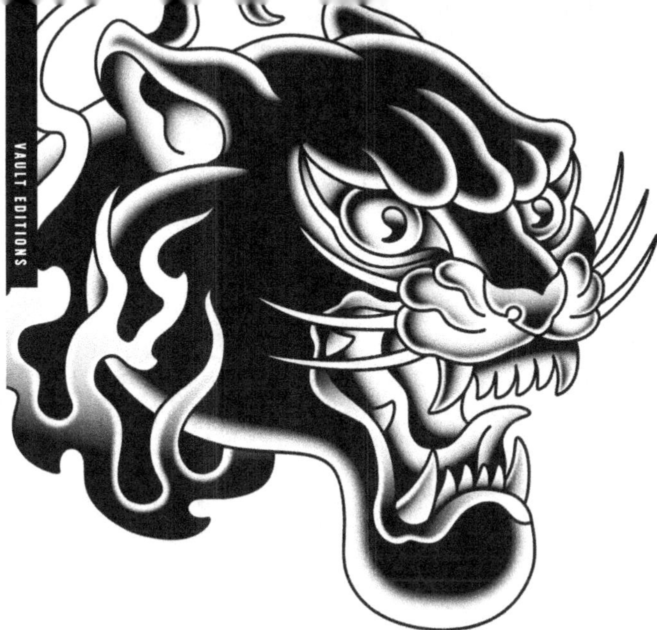

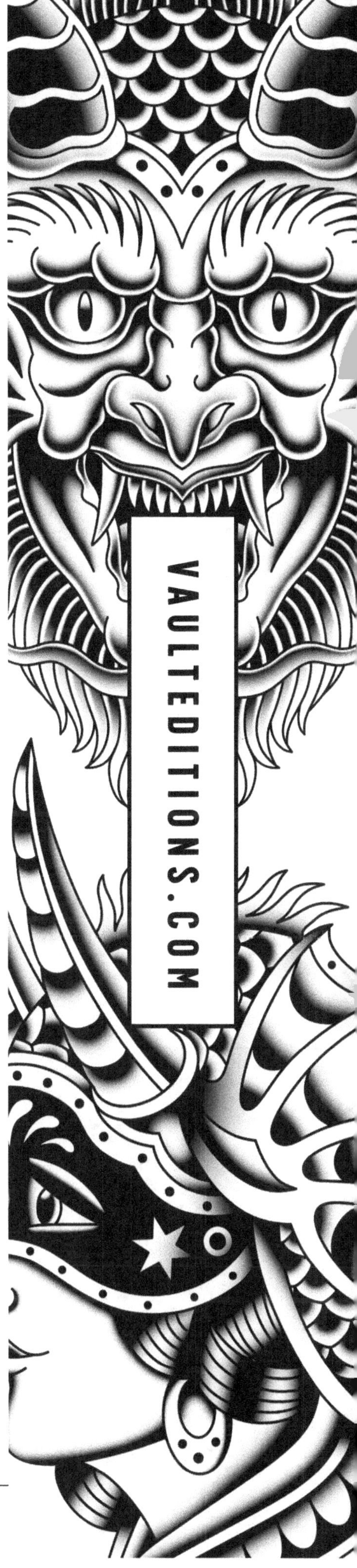

DOWNLOAD YOUR FILES

To enhance your creative journey, *How-to-Draw Traditional Tattoos* comes with a digital PDF version of the book and a specially designed set of Procreate brushes. These resources are tailored to help you refine your skills and streamline your workflow, whether working traditionally or digitally.

The digital PDF provides easy access to the book's contents on any device, so you can reference the designs anytime, anywhere. It's perfect for artists on the go, allowing you to study and practice whenever inspiration strikes.

The custom Procreate brushes are designed to support the tattoo drawing process by helping you improve your draftsmanship and build stronger technical skills. They offer precision and flexibility as you sketch, refine, and finalise your artwork, making it easier to develop clean, confident lines and consistent forms.

Download yours now and get creating!

STEP ONE

Enter the following web address on a desktop or laptop computer in your web browser.

vaulteditions.com/pages/htt

STEP TWO

Enter the following password to access the download page:

htt93861sxda

STEP THREE

Follow the prompts to access your high-resolution files.

CONTACT

For technical support, please email: info@vaulteditions.com

Copyright © 2025
Vault Editions Ltd

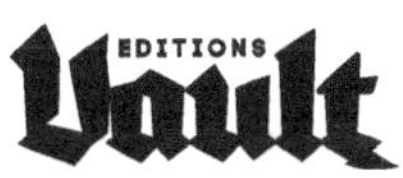

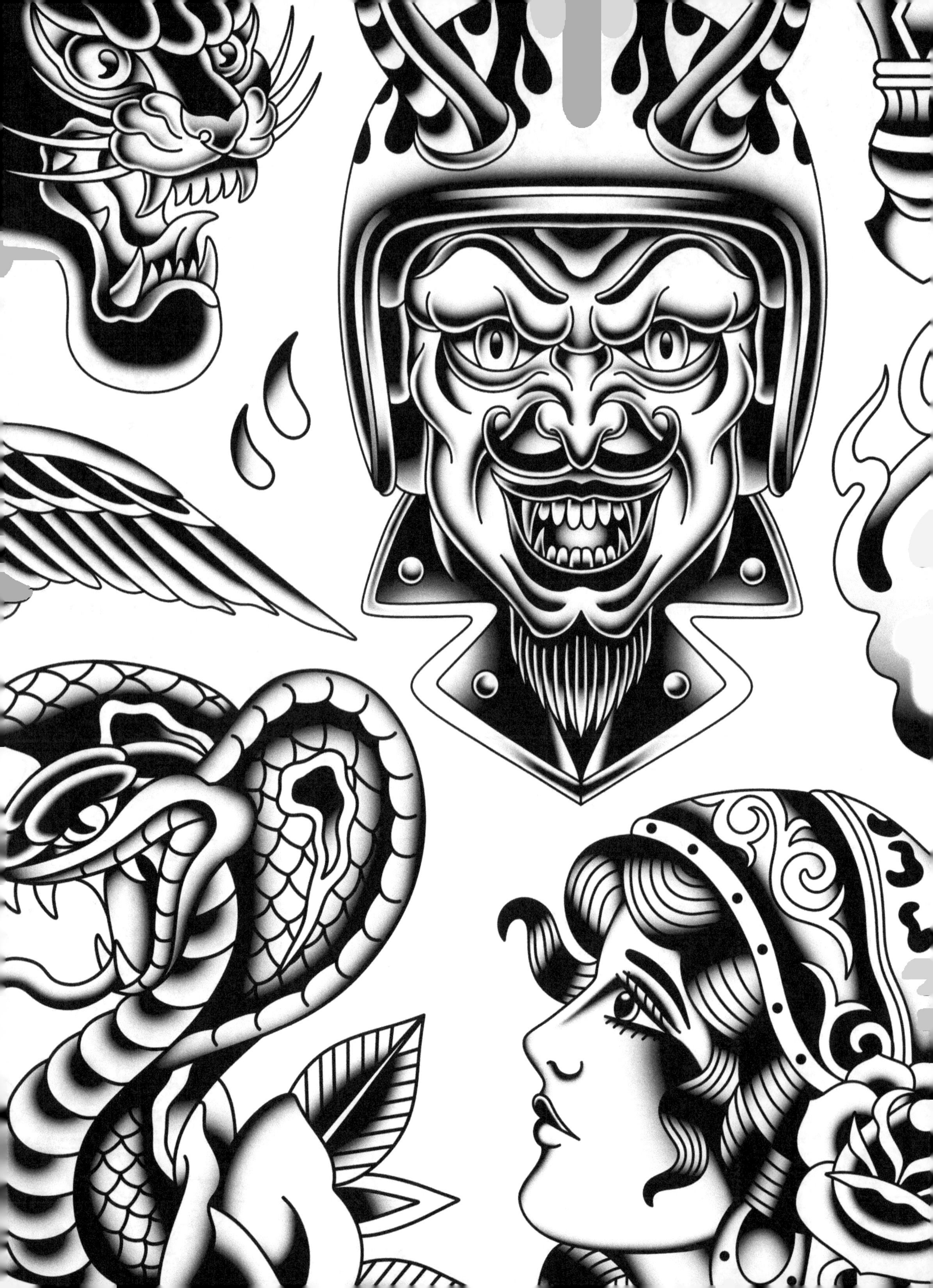

www.ingramcontent.com/pod-product-compliance
Lightning Source LLC
Chambersburg PA
CBHW080330030726
47593CB00010B/2960